CHILD AND ADOLESCENT PSYCHOLOGY FOR SOCIAL WORK
AND ALLIED PROFESSIONS

CHILD AND ADOLESCENT PSYCHOLOGY FOR SOCIAL WORK AND ALLIED PROFESSIONS

APPLIED PERSPECTIVES

GABRIELA MISCA AND PETER UNWIN

First published 2019 by
RED GLOBE PRESS

Red Globe Press in the UK is an imprint of Springer Nature Limited,
registered in England, company number 785998, of 4 Crinan Street,
London, N1 9XW.

Red Globe Press® is a registered trademark in the United States,
the United Kingdom, Europe and other countries.

ISBN 978–0–230–36843–9 paperback

This book is printed on paper suitable for recycling and made from fully
managed and sustained forest sources. Logging, pulping and manufacturing
processes are expected to conform to the environmental regulations of the
country of origin.

A catalogue record for this book is available from the British Library.

A catalog record for this book is available from the Library of Congress.

CONTENTS

LIST OF FIGURES AND TABLES

Figures

Tables

ACKNOWLEDGEMENTS

The authors would like to thank their families for their forbearance during the writing of this book.

Peter would particularly like to thank Louisa Rawstron and Alexandra Jones for their much valued assistance with the book's production.

Gabriela would also like to thank the US-UK Fulbright Commission and her American colleagues and friends for their support during her Fulbright fellowship in the USA when she completed the work for this book.

1

The relevance of child and adolescent psychology to social work

Key learning outcomes

Following the study of this chapter, learners will be able to:

- Interpret the Professional Capabilities Framework (PCF) and the Knowledge and Skills Statement (KSS) on children and families.

- Develop critical, broad awareness of the context of contemporary social work with children.

- Critically reflect on the importance of child and adolescent psychology to social work.

- Reflect on the dilemmas within inter-agency working.

- Analyse some of the key serious case reviews.

Introduction

This chapter will introduce the rationale behind this book and how it is designed to help social workers and social work students to use psychological knowledge to best inform their interactions with children and families. The need for psychological knowledge in a social work culture, where targets and budgets have dominated for some years, is all the more crucial. Practical tasks, reflective points and case studies will be used throughout the book and all are taken from real-life examples designed to bring psychological theory and knowledge alive. The hypothetical caseload of an imaginary student social worker, Helen, will be used throughout to parallel the likely challenges found with present-day social worker caseloads. It is additionally recommended that readers draw on core psychological textbooks, such as those by Nicolson (2014) and Sudbery (2009), which provide greater depth and detailed theoretical knowledge than was possible to include in this wide-ranging book, which is primarily concerned with key psychological applications across many areas of contemporary social work practice.

This chapter also sets the wider organizational and political context in which social work takes place and focuses on the importance of relationship-based practice (RBP) (Ruch, 2010) as a necessary underpinning of effective social work with children and families.

The importance of child and adolescent psychology to social work

Contemporary social work with children and young people is in turmoil, and this book will suggest that one of the reasons for this turmoil is a lack of psychological understanding about the issues behind the behaviours of children and families in today's fast-changing world. This book differs from most psychology texts in that it introduces the basics in a range of theories and models and applies them to social work practice. It aims to provide the reader – social work students and practitioners – with an overview of the fit between key psychological theories and concepts with social work practice. This book will also act as guidance for students of psychology and related disciplines who seek understanding of how to apply psychological concepts and theories in practice with children and young people, and aid their career planning and development.

The rapid development of social media in particular has brought with it a culture wherein bullying and a relentless focus on looks and body image, together with distorted views of sexualities, have presented today's children and young people with new and frightening pressures (Hamm et al., 2015). The mental health of children and young people in the UK is stated to be at an all-time low, with some 800,000 children suffering from mental health difficulties (Office of the Children's Commissioner, 2017). Could so many children really be experiencing such mental health problems due to the contemporary pressures noted above? Or are children not being allowed to deal with what might be the 'normative' pressures of a social media-dominated childhood – are we too quick to rush for psychological services or to label children as having various forms of mental illness?

Different because various forms of terminology are used when describing psychological states of mind, and this book will explore 'social and emotional well-being', which is taken largely to refer to positive mental health and wellness. According to Stirling and Emery (2016), this terminology encompasses:

[a] sense of optimism, confidence, happiness, clarity, vitality, self-worth, achievement, having a meaning and purpose, engagement, having supportive and satisfying relationships with others and understanding oneself, and responding effectively to one's own emotions.

(p. 5)

Mental health problems will be the term used in this book to refer to the emotional and social challenges faced by children and young people, and mental illness will be used to indicate that some kind of formal threshold or diagnosis has been reached (Padmore, 2016). This book will take stock of the pressures, including the rising rates of family breakup and the issues within reconstituted families, to suggest ways in which professionals, such as social workers and psychologists, might best help families and children to lead fulfilling lives.

Professional practice roles in the field of child and adolescent psychology are not easy ones for professionals, and retention rates in children's social care are poor (Bowyer & Roe, 2015). This is partly because of the nature of the abuse and violence witnessed daily by social workers, but also because of a political and managerial system that not only starts from the premise that no child will ever be harmed by a carer, but which also then shackles the ability of social workers and their educational and health colleagues from forming consistent and effective relationships with those families and children. The ever-increasing layers of audit, inspection and bureaucracy have been widely critiqued for keeping social workers from dealing with the real issues (Chararbaghi, 2007; Harris & Unwin, 2009; Tait, 2014). Social work has also been hounded by the press after a series of child tragedies, and is under increasing pressure from neoliberal government regimes, with their associated emphases on targets and performance management (Harris & Unwin, 2009; Jones, 2014). Social work is looking for a new identity and new credibility, as articulated by the Social Work Reform Board (SWRB) (DfE, 2010). Our vulnerable children and young people are looking for competence, commitment and consistency from social workers who have the time and insight to know and understand them. Social work needs to develop cultures that retain staff who can take pride and satis-faction in work which is rooted in a strong psychological understanding of how families, communities and organizations work.

Social workers are not short of guidance and advice about how to practise, and there are two main areas of practice guidance that will underpin this book: the 'bottom-up' PCF which is managed by the British Association of Social Workers (BASW, 2018) and the 'top-down' KSS (DfE, 2018). Both of these documents are found in

Appendices 1 and 2. The PCF was introduced in 2012 by the then College of Social Work (DfE, 2015b), and describes the capabilities that all social workers should aspire to develop throughout their career. Its intention is to raise standards of social work practice and encourage the lifelong learning culture propounded by reports such as the *Munro Report* (Munro, 2011) and the *Social Work Reform Board: Progress and feedback* (DfE, 2010). These capabilities have been overseen by the BASW since the abolition by the Conservative Government of the College for Social Work, a college initially set up after the death of Peter Connelly (Jones, 2014), a young boy known to social workers. An update of the PCF (BASW, 2018) added three overarching principles or 'super domains' of Purpose, Practice, and Impact to the PCF, designed to further guide social practice, as follows:

1. Purpose: Why we do what we do as social workers, our values and ethics, and how we approach our work.

2. Practice: What we do – the specific skills, knowledge, interventions and critical analytic abilities we develop to act and do social work.

3. Impact: How we make a difference – our ability to bring about change through our practice, through our leadership, through understanding our context and through our overall professionalism.

The nine domains, as slightly modified in 2018, are the interdependent ones of:

1. Professionalism

2. Values and Ethics

3. Diversity

4. Rights, Justice and Economic Well-being

5. Knowledge

6. Critical Reflection and Analysis

7. Skills and Interventions

8. Contexts and Organizations

9. Professional Leadership

All of these above domain areas have relevance to the subject matter of this book and are intrinsic to the debate and learning throughout its chapters, pitched at the level of the expectations they hold for a social worker who has just finished their professional training and is about to enter practice, this being known as the *'End of last placement/completion of qualifying course'* level (BASW, 2018).

The government had issued a more categorical *Knowledge and Skills Statement* (DfE, 2015) for children's social work which stated what social workers need to know and be able to do when children might be at risk of harm. This statement covered areas of relationship, communication, assessment and taking appropriate action, all of which will be discussed throughout the book's chapters. This statement was also updated (DfE, 2018 – see Appendix 2) when BASW and England's Chief Social Workers issued a joint statement to explain how the PCF and the KSS would complement each other:

> The KSS set out what a social worker should know, and be able to do, in specific practice settings, in specific roles and at different levels of seniority. The KSS maps on to the practice domains of the PCF (knowledge, critical reflection and analysis, interventions and skills) and should help guide every-day practice.
>
> (BASW, 2018b)

Social work with children and young people can take many forms – safeguarding children and working with disabled children and young people, young carers, young people with mental health problems, fostered children, children and young people within adoption services, refugee and sanctuary seeking children, and young people in transition to adult services. The diversity among the UK's young population is wider than ever, and even those of us living or perhaps training as social workers in largely white areas, will meet families and move to jobs in ethnically diverse areas. Misplaced ideologies and 'political correctness' stigma around working with diversity have beleaguered social work for some years, with inappropriate interpretations having been taken, which have at best led to poor outcomes and at worse led to child deaths. Laming (2003), in his report on the death of 8-year-old Victoria Climbié, a black African child, was quite clear that, while race and ethnicity were important considerations, the welfare of children overrides any cultural sensitivities. A reluctance to become involved in further investigations involving children from ethnic minorities was further exemplified with the death of Khyra Ishaq (Radford, 2010), whose mother threatened social workers with a racism complaint, as a result of which investigations were not progressed.

Qualities of social workers with children and families

Direct evidence about the desired qualities of social workers can be found in the voices of children and young people, who have spoken about transiency and lack of meaningful relationships with social workers. McLeod (2010) interviewed young people in care with a view to finding out the attributes they sought in social workers, the title of her article being '"A friend and an equal" Do young people in care seek the impossible from their social workers?'. Sustained relationships were highly valued and one young man is quoted as follows:

> My last [social worker] I had her for a lot of years and we were really great together and had a good laugh and that, but the new one I don't hardly know her.

(p. 779)

Moreover, McLeod (2010) stated that positive relationships between child and social worker were linked to better long-term outcomes for children.

Recent government-sponsored reports such as that by the SWRB (2010) and the *Munro Report* (Munro, 2011) do offer the potential of a return to the types of RBP valued by clients ('client' is the deliberate terminology preferred throughout this book as being a more individualized term than 'service user', and a term familiar to both psychologists and social workers). These above reports argued for a learning culture to be at the heart of contemporary social work, with improved development opportunities and support for social workers. The *Munro Report* (Munro, 2011) gave high praise for the Hackney Borough Council initiative *Reclaiming Social Work* (Cross et al., 2010), which apparently had the effect of a 55% drop in sickness rates and a consequent 50% drop in reliance on agency staff. The inference here is that families in that authority are better off without such a degree of reliance on agency or temporary social workers, and that what is valued are workers with the ability to develop the types of relationships that are deeper in nature, allowing the psychological working of children and families to be understood and appropriately interpreted.

Both the SWRB (DfE, 2010) and the *Munro Report* (Munro, 2011) challenged the overly bureaucratic systems that have come to characterize modernized social work; systems that have often prevented social workers from developing the types of relationships with children and young people that mean underlying psychological issues can be constructively addressed. Psychology is a profession concerned with deep understanding and respect for individuals and, championed by the

British Psychological Society (BPS, 2017), it has largely managed to avoid the performance management culture that has enveloped other professions such as social work and nursing. Psychologists also rarely suffer the negative effects of bad press whenever an individual child tragedy occurs, this situation being in direct contrast with the experiences of their social work colleagues.

Reflective point

➤ Why do you think there is a different media approach towards social workers and psychologists?

➤ Do you think that the media factor is one that makes social work more psychologically stressful than it need be?

➤ What steps could a social work organization take to change media perceptions?

Relationship-based practice in working with children and families

The *Munro Report* (Munro, 2011) also stressed that continual professional development within a learning culture which valued RBP (Ruch, 2010) represented the best way ahead for children and families. RBP is a social work approach designed to enable practitioners to work in-depth on the psychologies of families' problems, rather than in a reductionist way. Adherents of RBP would argue that the insights that flow from this approach are effective ones that help challenge power imbalances and structural oppression. RBP necessitates some degree of partnership between social workers and their clients and, although the world of performance management has largely brought about an environment in which cases are opened and closed as quickly as possible, Munro's message is clearly stated in the following extract:

> the level of increased prescription for social workers, while intending to improve the quality of practice, has created an imbalance. Complying with prescription and keeping records to demonstrate compliance has become too dominant. The centrality of forming relationships with children and families to understand and help them has become obscured.

(Munro, 2011, p. 8)

Reflective point

➤ What do you think might compromise the key ingredients to developing a relationship-based approach with a vulnerable child or young person?

➤ How might you begin to establish such a working relationship with a 15-year-old girl placed recently in a children's home because of her risk of sexual exploitation in a neighbouring town?

Wilson and colleagues (2011) state that the key ingredients of RBP are that:

➤ It recognizes that each social work encounter is unique.

➤ It understands that human behaviour is complex and multifaceted, that is, people are not simply rational beings but have affective – conscious and unconscious – dimensions that enrich but simultaneously complicate human relationships.

➤ It focuses on the inseparable nature of the internal and external worlds of individuals and the importance of integrated – psychosocial – as opposed to polarized responses to social problems.

➤ It accepts that human behaviour and the professional relationship are an integral component of any professional intervention.

➤ It places particular emphasis on 'the use of self' and the relationship as the means through which interventions are channelled.

(pp. 7–8)

The following are views from social work students known to the authors (names have been changed as they have in other narratives throughout the book) and relate to their experiences of RBP in their placements. The views range from pessimistic to optimistic about the potential for this deeper, more psychologically sensitive work with children and young people:

Andrea: RBP as a luxury

➤ During my current placement my exposure to practice has equated more with a 'processing factory' of social care as opposed to enabling practitioners to develop deeper meaningful engagement with family issues.

➤ ... workers' capacity to manage such demands is impeded, in particular, by a computerized recording system that neither promotes greater time efficiencies nor enables case narratives to be utilized and accessed for the benefit of those most in need.

➤ Practitioners remain at the beck and call of alerts driven by relentless performance indicators which in so many ways detract from the effective management of caseloads/workload and maintenance of professionalism stipulated within the PCF.

Rachel: The importance of time

➤ In giving service users, and other professionals, more time to engage with me, I have been in a position to explore and challenge concerns more comprehensively and openly as trust has been built (in most cases).

➤ This experience reflects research that has identified how service users appreciate longer, less rushed approaches to assessment/interventions. For example, by visiting one young person in care and simply sitting with her for half an hour (in relative silence) I was able to create and 'contain' a space where she subsequently felt able to share her pain, anger and distress at being away from her family.

➤ Had I just followed the procedure of a 'LAC [Looked-After Children] Visit' this late evening opportunity would almost undoubtedly never have emerged. I subsequently developed a more detailed personal and family narrative with her and explored attachment issues, thus helping her make sense of, and contextualize, current experiences.

Jane: Forming a relationship without prejudice

➤ While on placement I worked with a family who had been 'written off' by local professionals as non-compliant.

➤ Concerns had been about home hygiene and failure of the children to gain weight.

➤ On my fourth visit to the family we all went for a walk in the forest where the mother told me about her massive debts that prevented her better caring for the children. She had kept this hidden from social work and health professionals for years.

Reflective point

➤ In the above account from Jane, what do you think it was about the 'forest' setting, as opposed to the traditional home or office visit, which may have brought about a different climate of trust between Jane and her client?

The role of psychological knowledge in social work practice

This book, written some seven years after the *Munro Report* (Munro, 2011), will present new emphasis on the need for effective social workers to have a core understanding of psychological theory and application that puts the individual at the centre of their work. Psychology has a rich tradition of valuing the individual, and social work was also built on a core concern for individual therapies and interventions. Unfortunately, this individual focus has been lost to a large degree under recent decades of performance management culture, where the meeting of targets and deadlines predominates. Psychology has always kept its focus on individuals, as well as being used to help explain and predict patterns and behaviours. This book will attempt to reassert that psychology does have a central place in contemporary social work practice, even if it does not always share the political history of social work's concern with social justice and equality of opportunity. Psychological practice has not experienced the 'business culture' (Harris & Unwin, 2009) that has permeated contemporary social work and would still seem to largely operate in ways that afford primacy to individuals.

Social workers, however, can often feel distanced from psychological knowledge, associating it only with having had historical influence, being outdated, being largely clinically based and without any political relevance to their world of ethical dilemmas, budgetary constraints and conflict. Seminal psychological theorists were predominantly men – Piaget, Vygotsky, Freud, Maslow, Bandura, Erikson – and their resultant body of knowledge can be critiqued as being a male-dominated view of the world which does not acknowledge the political and systems concerns of social work. By contrast, social work is a largely female profession, originally driven by strong feminist and other anti-oppressive principles (Dominelli, 2004; Banks, 2006).

Many people enter the social work profession because they are interested in helping individuals and families whose lives are complex and often fractured. Concern and focus on the individual have traditionally been a distinct claim of excellence and differentiation for the profession of social work. However, as the world of public service has become increasing preoccupied with issues of systems conformity and compliance, so the emphasis on individualism, in regard to both the autonomy of professionals and the individual psychologies of children and young people, has become overshadowed and sometimes neglected altogether. The profile of psychology on social work training courses has lessened in recent years as the curriculum has been increasingly prescribed by government, and this book is designed partly to address such imbalance. It is the intention that this book will enthuse social workers and social work students to delve more deeply into psychological research and theory, with a view to helping make sense of the worlds of their clients. Increased knowledge about the relevance and applications of psychology should lead to greater job satisfaction and an increased knowledge base from which to work more effectively with other professionals and their systems.

Traditional psychology has always looked for patterns and causalities in its attempts to explain and predict human behaviour, and much enlightenment on the human condition has indeed come about because of the endeavours of the psychological profession. Much psychological theory, however, is based on the findings of normative populations (Brinkmann, 2016) and not always applicable to the individuals who come into daily contact with social workers. Many of the clients of social workers will have experienced dysfunctional, neglectful or abusive childhoods where developmental stages will not have neatly followed the norm and whose family and cultural contexts, say of poverty or marginalization, will present ongoing challenges to their development. The challenge of this book is to illuminate the core relevancies of accepted psychological theory and research in a way that encourages such received wisdom to be interpreted in the contemporary social work context. The voices of children and young people, so often missing from psychology and social work narratives, will be directly represented throughout this book in ways that will help make established theory and insights reflective of modern-day experiences. Some of these voices will be adapted and anonymized from children and young people encountered in the professional lives of the authors, whereas others will be taken from research reports, Inquiry findings and young people's websites.

Much learning within social work unfortunately comes from the findings of serious case reviews or public Inquiries (e.g., Laming, 2003), where a core feature is often the failure of professionals (not just social workers) to understand the psychologies and family dynamics that led to tragedy. A better understanding and confidence about challenging and interpreting behaviours may have meant that professionals would have known and understood what was going on in the lives of children such as Victoria Climbié, Peter Connelly, Khyra Ishaq and Daniel Pelka (NSPCC, 2018), and not been duped by adults' explanations or distracted by procedural matters. The circumstances surrounding the deaths of Victoria, Peter and Daniel have been widely reported in the media, and have influenced public and political perspectives on social work, in terms of both providing extra resources and further denigrating the name of the social work profession. The media and some politicians take a simplistic view of safeguarding children – remove the children from bad parents – and fail to acknowledge the complex psychological, legal and moral complexities that surround the above cases and many others concerning children and young people killed or seriously harmed by their parents or carers every year in the UK. A common factor in many child tragedies is that social workers and other professionals do not have meaningful relationships with the children on their caseloads (McLeod, 2010; Munro, 2011). Had such relationships existed, and had professionals demonstrated deep psychological understanding about their issues, then tragedies may well have been avoided.

Much recent interest in the world of safeguarding has revolved around situations whereby social workers have been unwilling to challenge cultural norms (Laming, 2003; Radford, 2010). The expectation is that social workers will look at the child first, and not at cultural considerations first. It is important to recognize that it is not only the responsibility of social workers to protect children but, that this responsibility is primarily held by their parents and carers. The responsibility is also increasingly shared across professionals, safeguarding being everybody's business. The use of the term 'safeguarding' (DfES, 2003) has taken over from the previous use of 'child protection', which in turn had derived from terminology such as 'non-accidental injury' and 'battered babies'. The term 'safeguarding' is designed to give a more preventative feel to looking after our children and to emphasize that such roles are part of all citizens' duties and responsibilities, not just the responsibility of a limited number of social workers in our communities. The term 'child protection' would generally be seen to apply where concern has been raised about whether a child is at risk of significant harm, and where a referral posing this question has been made to a statutory authority, such as children's services. A child protection case would necessarily encompass the formality of meetings, adherence to policies and possibly legal proceedings (Unwin & Hogg, 2012).

Inter-agency working

Inter-agency working is often held up as a panacea for achieving the greatest effectiveness across a range of human service professions, from safeguarding to the promotion of mental health. There is, however, no hard evidence to say that working together is always the best way forward and

much time and cost can be lost and resources wasted when professionals could have made just as good, and certainly swifter, decisions on their
own. The world of health care and social work has become increasingly
risk-averse whereby 'defensive practice', with professionals 'covering their
backs', has pervaded many professions. The sheer volume of bureaucracy
and numbers of meetings in contemporary practice have been criticized
in a number of reports (e.g., Munro, 2011) but computer work and paper-
work still proliferate and dominate. Estimates are that, for field social
workers, some four out of five days per week are spent servicing 'the system' rather than on getting to know and form effective working relationships with children and their families (Unwin & Hogg, 2012).

Reflective point

Consider the testimony below of 18-year-old Lorraine, a client of mental
health services:

> I have found that services are sparse and are geared up to be reactive rather
> than pro-active. As someone with autism and mental health needs I continu-
> ally fall between the gaps of mental health and learning disability services, with
> neither team wanting to take responsibility for my needs and provision of care.
> This leads to gaps and holes which are hugely detrimental to wellbeing and can
> lead to a crisis point developing. I have found inter agency working poor in the
> most part among social services and this has continually contributed to dips in
> my health, necessitating inpatient admissions and much higher levels of care
> than may have been necessary had there been a cohesive care pathway in the
> first place.

The quote above from Lorraine brings up another critical point about
boundaries and labelling. Some children and young people might have a
dual diagnosis like Lorraine, and find that they fall between two services.
Some services, particularly when they do not have separate facilities for
learning disabilities, are open to working with children and young people with learning disabilities, whereas others are not. Lorraine's call for a
cohesive pathway is echoed by many, and her comment about poor inter-
agency knowledge is a critical one.
  Wider reasons for the lack of consistently effective inter-agency working might start back at the level of qualifying training, most qualifying
courses across psychology, nursing, education and social work still contain only marginal involvement of students from those very professions
with whom they will be working alongside immediately upon qualification. Various logistical reasons are used to excuse this lack of initial

togetherness – timetabling, size of classrooms, demands of the individual curricula – but with the right attitude and value base, ways forward can be found. Training together would be a great way to develop a shared value base on which to establish the cohesive services Lorraine so badly needs. Funding issues are problematic also, the National Health Service budget swamping that of social care, despite the many arguments put forward at every election time or time of crisis when their interdependency is emphasized. Status, pay rates and differing statutory responsibilities of different professions are cited as other reason for interdisciplinary and inter-agency working not always being effective but, again, if one starts from the child or young person's perspective, all of this is irrelevant – they just want a joined-up service from professionals who know them and can offer appropriate and timely help and support.

Social workers protect and safeguard children by working with their entire families. Indeed, understanding child development and outcomes cannot be achieved outside of parental and family influences. A critical approach to family dynamics is what this book calls for, and throughout we will be discussing the safeguarding and developmental issues around the children and families on the hypothetical caseload of student social worker, Helen. Among others, Helen's caseload includes the Kelly family, whose children, Paul and Ria, are 12 and 11 respectively when she first meets them. The lives of Paul and Ria are subsequently depicted at several points in their childhood up until when Paul is a teenager, with other social workers working with the family in a variety of situations. Particular attention will be drawn, in the case examples and reflective points, to the role played by psychological approaches and knowledge.

Book outline

The families and individuals known to social workers have extra difficulties in coping with the above pressures on their children, and every case open to a social worker is inherently complex and dysfunctional in terms of histories of domestic violence, sexual abuse, mental health, disability, poverty, isolation, homelessness and, increasingly, cultural adaptation.

The chapters in this book address the realities of social work within this new culture of childhood although they offer no 'easy fix'. Rather, they provide insight and opportunity for reflection and application of psychological learning in ways that can help their own understanding and also help individuals and families better understand their own predicaments and challenges, hopefully pointing ways forward or ways of breaking cycles of behaviour.

After this chapter has set out the basic reasons why psychology and social work need to be intrinsically intertwined, Chapter 2 – 'Emotional development and attachment' – will introduce the topic of emotional development through childhood and adolescence. It will explore contemporary theories that explain emotional development, including neuropsychological perspectives and how children recognize emotions in others, how they learn to regulate emotions and how they think about emotions. It will also explore the role of the family in children's emotional development, as well as incorporating a cross-cultural perspective on emotional development. Key links to the relevance for social work practice will be drawn throughout, such as identifying delays in children's emotional development (e.g., disabled children), and potential links with inadequate parenting (e.g., child abuse and neglect). This chapter will review attachment theory in light of recent research findings from longitudinal research studies on attachment, from infancy through adulthood, and will be considered also from cross-cultural perspectives. Attachment will be considered from both children's and carers' perspectives, in the context of both family and family substitute care settings, such as foster care.

Chapter 3 – 'Cognitive development' – will explore some of the key theories in child and adolescent cognitive development, including the recent developments on social cognition or 'theory of mind' and a child's understanding of the 'social world'. The theoretical perspectives will be explored in relation to their application for social work practice – including memory and life-story work with children, and looked-after children and their educational outcomes. Also, psychological perspectives on disabled children will be considered in the context of 'normative' child development, and alternative perspectives on disability explored as well as the challenges for parents and carers with learning disabilities.

Chapter 4 – 'Social development: From childhood to adolescence' – will review contemporary theories on adolescence and social development, and their relevance for social work practice with young people. Major themes in adolescent development will be explored such as identity formation (including ethnic and gender identity), peer and romantic relationships, the pressures of contemporary media and social networking. The particular relevance of these theories for working with adolescents living in substitute forms of parental care, such as foster care, will be explored by use of case studies. The issues will also be examined from a cross-cultural perspective wherever possible. Reflections from young people will directly give the 'voice of the child' to this chapter. There is a focus on the topic of aggression and violence in peer relationships, specifically regarding bullying/cyberbullying and dating violence, recent phenomena where research findings are very relevant to social work. Themes emerging from the recent awareness of radicalization of young people and child sexual exploitation (CSE), including the systematic sexual abuse of vulnerable young people by organized groups, will also be discussed highlighting cultural, identity and self-esteem factors.

Chapter 5 – 'Parenting' – will examine current psychological perspectives on parenting, and the role of family in supporting child and adolescent development. The significant implications for social work practice with children growing up in adverse family environments, and those separated from their parents and/or growing up in substitute care, will be considered. Different parenting styles will be discussed, and case studies from foster care, including the Kelly family, will be used to illuminate issues for social work. The recent body of research and theoretical knowledge on same-gender parenting will be reviewed, and its relevance discussed for social work practice.

In Chapter 6 – 'Safeguarding children and young people' – a range of perspectives and research findings on the impact of child abuse and neglect on subsequent development and recovery from early experiences of child maltreatment will be explored. Evidence-based interventions with children who have suffered abuse and neglect will be considered from cross-cultural perspectives. Links to best safeguarding practice and foster care will be made throughout the chapter and, again, testimony from young people who have survived abuse and neglect will directly inform this chapter.

Chapter 7 – 'Understanding child and adolescent mental health' – will examine the relevance of knowledge of child and adolescent psychopathology for social work practice in the arena of Child and Adolescent Mental Health (CAMHS). It will provide an overview of assessment and diagnosis of children's and adolescents' difficulties; consider contemporary practice and ethical considerations in psychotherapy with children and adolescents; and examine the realities of multidisciplinary working in CAMHS settings. The mental health of children and young people will be presented as a mainstream, rather than only a specialist, area of practice, with the stance being taken that all social workers should have a deep understanding of psychopathology surrounding children and young people.

In Chapter 8 – 'Conclusions' – we review the main themes explored and their relevance for social work and psychological practice with children and young people. This final chapter will bring together reflections on the bodies of research considered, and will reiterate the skills and values necessary for best practice with children and young people, bringing together key knowledge from the disciplines of social work and psychology. The need for all professional staff to develop relationship-based ways of working with children, young people and their families will be emphasized, and the importance of tackling structural pressures on young people's mental well-being, such as poverty and the all-pervasiveness of social media, will be re-emphasized.

Each chapter will be relevant to elements of the PCF (BASW, 2018) and also to parts of the KSS (DfE, 2015b) for approved child and family practitioners. As stated above, the PCF is a complicated model, which has the intention of framing social work as a profession where development continues throughout a career lifetime. The capabilities specifically cited in the chapters are those at the *End of last placement / Completion of Qualifying Course* level. Additionally, once qualified, social workers have to practice to the Standards of Proficiency (SoPs) as laid down by the Health and Care Professions Council (HCPC, 2017), which is the regulatory body for qualified social workers, whose role is essentially to assure the public that social work practice is safe and competent. The contention of this book is that a core understanding of the psychological drivers and influences on both human and organizational behaviour is a prerequisite in order to be that safe, competent and fulfilled social worker.

Summary

This chapter has introduced the importance of psychological knowledge underpinning best practice with children and families. The context of managerialism and performance management were portrayed as having dominated social work at the expense of investment in the types of RBP that enables deep psychological understanding, insights and authentic knowledge about a child or family's situation. Such psychological insights were seen as crucial if decisions are to be meaningful, rather than just meaning that the boxes can be ticked and performance targets met.

The content of the rest of the book was then outlined, emphasizing the continuous use of case studies, reflective points and tasks, many of which reflect the caseload of a hypothetical student social worker, Helen.

Further resources

Barefoot Social Worker website, www.radical.org.uk/barefoot/ (Accessed: 27 January 2018)

A radical and passionate take on the problems facing social work.

Barnardo's website, www.barnardos.org.uk/ (Accessed: 27 January 2018)

Well-respected children's charity who have carried out much innovative work with children, families and communities.

British Association of Social Workers website, www.basw.co.uk/
resource/?id=1137 (Accessed: 27 January 2018)

This site has all the details on the PCF, its levels and domains as well as rich and contemporary information across all areas of social work.

Health and Care Professionals Council (2017). *Standards of Proficiency: Social Workers in England*, www.hpc-uk.org/assets/documents/10003B08Standardsof proficiency-SocialworkersinEngland.pdf (Accessed: 14 September 2018)

This website includes details of disciplinary hearings which give detailed insight into the challenges within contemporary practice.

Munro Review of Child Protection: A child-centred system, www.gov.uk/
government/publications/munro-review-of-child-protection-final-report-a-child-centred-system (Accessed: 27 January 2018)

Munro's final report which recommended proposals for reform in order to meet the needs of children and families, and to support social workers.

NSPCC Website www.nspcc.org.uk/services-and-resources/research-and-resources/search-library/ (Accessed: 27 January 2018)

For further examples of serious case reviews see the NSPCC website repository. This site can be searched by inputting the name of the child or local authority.

Signs of Safety website, www.signsofsafety.net/signs-of-safety/ (Accessed: 27 January 2018)

This website utilizes the perspective of the everyday practice of social workers to address the strengths-based approach to safeguarding children and young people.

Social Work Action Network website, www.socialworkfuture.org/ (Accessed: 29 January 2018)

This website takes a more political view of the pressing issues in social work and offers a variety of alternative discourses.

2

Emotional development and attachment

Key learning outcomes

Following the study of this chapter, learners will be able to:

➤ Describe theoretical perspectives on attachment theory.

➤ Relate theories of emotional development and attachment to the children and young people with whom they work.

➤ Develop perspectives on the relative influences of nature and nurture on emotional development.

➤ Explore the role of culture in the emotional development of children and young people.

➤ Use research evidence and the findings from serious case reviews to critically evaluate the contemporary roles and skills expected of social workers in terms of their understanding of child development.

Introduction

This chapter will introduce the topic of emotional development and attachment through childhood and adolescence, a critical area of knowledge for social workers which will be returned to in Chapter 5 of this book, where parenting issues are discussed. Attachment theory will be explored in depth as a framework for understanding emotional development. This highly influential theory in social work practice with children and families will be reviewed in light of recent research findings from longitudinal research studies on attachment, from infancy through adulthood and from cross-cultural perspectives. The emotional upheavals that characterize the lives of many children and young people in contact with social workers are such that the standard milestones of development may be attained at different rates and levels.

In many of the arenas in which contemporary social work takes place, psychologists and other therapists may be very effective at diagnosing and intervening in individual children's lives. However, the structures and systems which set the context of individual difficulties are perhaps the root cause of much unhappiness in today's children and young people. Some of these difficulties may well be caused by poor or neglectful parenting but what influence does the removal of support services, benefit cuts, inappropriate housing, zero-hours contracts and unemployment have on the emotional welfare of families? Traditionally, psychologists have not addressed such wider issues and, in recent years, social work has also lost much of its campaigning edge. However, the British Association of Social Workers (BASW) has recently rekindled its quest for social justice and there are green shoots in the fields of psychology, where the movement *Psychologists against Austerity* (2018) and publications such as *The Power Threat Meaning Framework: Overview* (Johnstone et al., 2018) are beginning to address the structural inequalities which lie behind psychological distress.

The hypothetical caseload of an imaginary student social worker, Helen, is introduced in the case study 'The Kelly Family', and will be used throughout the book to illuminate the likely challenges found across present-day social worker caseloads. One of the most challenging cases on Helen's caseload is the Kelly family, whose two children, Paul and Ria, variously experience periods in local authority foster care. These two children have encountered real difficulties in respect of their emotional and cognitive development; their experiences of parenting; their adolescent years; their formation of relationships; and the issues of psychopathology, abuse and neglect that surround them. Their lives will not all be negative, but will portray elements of both success and failure as social workers attempt to work with the Kelly family in respect of the issues and losses that are at the heart of this book.

Case study: The Kelly family

Aim: To explore theoretical issues from psychology and social work that informs best practice with children and families.

Helen is a social work student embarking on her first social work placement with Children's Social Care in the metropolitan borough of Smoggley, a declining industrial, multicultural area of the north-west of England.

Paul and Ria's parents, Mohammed Ishbal and Mary Kelly, have had a volatile relationship in the 14 years that they have been together, as a result of which Paul, 12, and his 11-year-old sister, Ria, have had several episodes of foster care. Ria is currently

▶

◄

in a separate foster home to Paul as it was considered in the best interests of their development that they be separated. Both parents are unemployed and drink heavily when they have money but are usually remorseful when sober. Both met when Mary was 16 years old and working in a local factory, since closed down. Home conditions are adequate and the parents have a three-bedroomed housing association property. Some concern has been expressed by neighbours to the local social work team that when the couple are drinking heavily, there are often other adults in the house, several of whom seem regularly to stay overnight. When the children were babies, two visits were made to the home by social workers warning Mary and Mohammed that the children must always be cared for by suitable babysitters. Allegations had been made that the children were often left with different male and female adults, and sometimes with primary school age children from the neighbourhood.

Mary Kelly is of Irish descent and one of seven children. Her parents (who divorced when Mary was 12 after a domestically violent marriage) and siblings disowned her when she took up with Mohammed, saying that races and religion should never mix. Her mother did, however, have contact with the children and cared for Paul several times as an infant when Mary went in and out of rehab. Mohammed has two successful businessmen brothers who are busy with their own lives and families. His parents, who came to England from Pakistan for work in the 1950s, are both deceased. Mary describes herself as a lapsed Catholic and Mohammed describes himself as a lapsed Muslim.

Helen's initial task is to read Paul's extensive online case file and to prepare for her supervision by making links between Paul's case and theoretical perspectives from the fields of psychology and social work that might inform her approach during her day placement.

The following is an excerpt from the previous day's entry on Paul's file:

Phone call from Paul's foster carers, Mrs and Mr Walton, requesting emergency respite placement for Paul following another violent outburst last night. Paul was out with 'friends' without prior agreement and came home after midnight. When challenged, Paul kicked in the sitting room door and smashed the sideboard, swearing and shouting at Mr and Mrs Walton 'Don't tell me what to do, you are not my parents'. Mrs Walton suspects that he has been drinking. This is the third episode of violent outburst towards his foster carers over the past month and Mr and Mrs Walton are getting worried and anxious about this turn in Paul's behaviour.

Actions: Emergency respite placement has been arranged for Paul: Meeting to be arranged with Mr. and Mrs. Walton to discuss placement needs and continuity issues.

Task

➤ What theoretical perspectives from the fields of psychology and social work might Helen bring to bear on the above scenario?

➤ How might this knowledge provide insight into the heightened emotions that are present?

The dynamics of the Kelly family are not untypical of families known to social workers. The children and young people in these families often have additional complexities, which make an already difficult time even more difficult. People like to hark back to 'the good old days' when children could play out all day, when mums and dads stayed together, when life was less materialistic, and when families and neighbourhoods looked after their own. Quite when this time was is perhaps rather more difficult to specify – was it the 1950s or the 1960s when racism, domestic violence, sexual discrimination and abuse of children by the establishment was the (unspoken) norm? All generations tend to look back on theirs having been a better childhood, but there is no doubt that the pressures of being a young person in today's society brings with it a whole new set of psychological and emotional challenges presented by the all-pervasive social media, celebrity culture and the internet. Partly due to a fear of allowing children to play out unsupervised by adults, our children spend more and more time on computers, in cyberspace and in the development of a network of virtual friends. The pressures and dangers that come with widespread use of the internet are considerable and range from distorted views of body image and sexuality to online sexual exploitation. Cyberbullying has led to an increasing number of suicides among young people (Hamm et al., 2015), and a contemporary preoccupation with material and educational success, rather than happiness in childhood, has dominated our school culture. Some schools have invested in social workers and counselling staff on site, but many either see the emotional and psychological support of their children as somebody else's business, or simply do not have the resources for such provision.

The case study of the Kelly family is further developed below to enable reflection on issues of attachment, nature, nurture and emotional well-being. By the end of the chapter you will know more about a range of theoretical perspectives and psychological approaches to emotional well-being and behaviours that arise as a consequence of emotional distress:

Case study: The Kelly family – continued

Following the phone call from Paul's foster carers, Mr. and Mrs. Walton, requesting emergency respite placement for Paul following another violent outburst last night, Helen, the student social worker, is undertaking a home visit, accompanied by her supervising social worker.

Mrs Walton seemed distressed by the episode, but she reminisced:

> *We have fostered Paul on several occasions since he was 3 … we cannot forget the 3-year-old angelic boy arriving to our house clutching a toy rabbit in his hands and his smiley, friendly face. He always settled in so quickly and felt like our son. We did*

▶

◀

explain to him when he was 8 or 9 that we are not his parents but that we are taking care of him until a 'forever family' will be found for him, except one never has, and he has returned home quite a few times, only for things to break down again. And I remember when we had visitors, him going to every adult and asking 'Are you my forever mummy and daddy?' It was heart-breaking … but we knew we had to stay with him on his journey until the right family will be found for him to be adopted.

Paul's case file notes mention that he was on the then at-risk register since birth, due to his mother's substance misuse issues. His mother also spent several episodes in hospital at the time when Paul was 8 months old, due to her substance addiction issues. During her spells in hospital, Paul was cared for by his maternal grandmother and returned to his mother when she was well enough to return home. However, at the age of 3 his maternal grandmother died and consequently his mother's mental health deteriorated significantly, leading to her being sectioned [under the Mental Health Act 1983]. Then Paul was taken into care and placed in the foster placement with Mr and Mrs Walton.

Task

➤ In light of the information given about Paul's early years, what theoretical perspective might be helpful in understanding his current behaviour?

➤ For example, how might attachment theory help in understanding the effect of Paul's early experiences on his current behaviour?

➤ What losses will Paul have suffered in his life and how might these have affected his behaviours?

Theoretical perspectives on emotional development

Emotions colour every aspect of our lives, so perhaps it is not surprising that emotional development underlies many other aspects of development such as cognitive and social development. Understanding and handling their own emotional world and the emotional world of their services users is an important knowledge and skill that social workers need to develop (Howe, 2008). We begin developing the ability to understand and talk about emotions – both our own emotions and others – from an early age, for example, 2 and 3-year-olds talk about the emotions of their doll or of fictional characters. These abilities develop through childhood and adolescence, for example, adolescents are capable of realizing the gap between the inner feeling and the expression of these feelings in different contexts. Adults are capable of reflecting on and managing their own emotions as well as other's emotions, and such aptitude for 'emotional intelligence' (Goleman, 1995) is essential for social work professionals (Howe, 2008).

Further reading

Howe, D. (2008) *The Emotionally Intelligent Social Worker*. Basingstoke: Palgrave Macmillan.

This is a unique book written by an accomplished social work scholar, applying the concept of emotional intelligence from management and business to social work.

Nature and nurture in emotional development

Emotional development is a complex interplay between biological and genetic determinants (nature) and environmental influences (nurture), mainly represented by the array of relationships with parents or main carers in early life as well as relationships with others throughout our life course. Temperamental characteristics play an important moderator role in emotional development. Temperament has been initially viewed as a predisposition, with a biological basis and inherent in the child, to respond emotionally in different ways to different situations/stimuli in the environment. Early temperament researchers such as Thomas and Chess (1977) have proposed the concept of 'goodness of fit' to illustrate the interlinked nature of such emotional predispositions and the environment. Recent evidence from behaviour genetic studies supports the idea of considerable heritability in temperament (Sanson et al., 2011). However, interactions with parents or other caregivers and peers also make important contributions to our emotional development.

Many of the children and young people known to social workers will come from chaotic and dysfunctional backgrounds where domestic violence, substance misuse or having a parent with a learning disability might mean that a child is not going to receive a consistent or guaranteed response to its needs. Children are resilient for the most part, and there are many examples known to professionals whereby children brought up in the most abject conditions have gone on to thrive and enjoy fulfilling lives and relationships, as evidenced in the testimony below:

Voice of the child: Les

Les (who is now an adult, 23 years old), recounts his early experiences at home:

> All I can really remember is hearing shouting all the time and hearing doors slam at night. I lost my sight because my mum was not bothered about my eye condition and never took me to appointments. I remember being taken into care and

mum saying that I should spit and swear and smash the place up so I could come back home. I did all the things mum said and ruined my foster placements. As I got older, however, I realized that my family did not have my best interests at heart and I rejected them, choosing what I now know to have been the nurture of a great foster home over the nature I had been given. I know where I come from but I reject that identity and want to forge my own path in life.

While the basic emotions have a strong biological determination, our ways of experiencing and displaying emotions are highly influenced by the way we think about emotions. Such 'emotion schemas' (similar to cognitive schemes – see Chapter 3) are developed through infancy and childhood as the child learns to both interpret and regulate emotions through interactions with significant others, such as their carers, and are highly influenced by the culture of reference.

Further reading

Oatley, K., Keltner, D. & Jenkins, J. M. (2013) *Understanding Emotions*, 3rd edn. Hoboken, NJ: Wiley.

This is a very useful, accessible and engaging text, including the latest research findings and developments to assist in your journey of understanding emotions and emotional development.

Reflective point

Daniel Pelka, as referred to in Chapter 1, was a 4-year-old Polish boy killed by his carers in Coventry after a long period of physical and emotional cruelty and neglect. The Serious Case Review pertaining to Daniel's death is available on the NSPCC website (NSPCC, 2018), a most useful resource which collates nationwide reports that might otherwise be deleted at local Safeguarding Board level, after differing periods of time.

Having read Daniel Pelka's Serious Case Review, reflect on the following questions and discuss them in pairs or small groups:

➤ Try to imagine the emotional atmosphere in the Pelka household and why Daniel presented at school as a quiet child.

➤ Why might his sister not have spoken to school staff about the reality of home life?

➤ Why might Daniel's mother not have shown protective behaviours and emotional warmth to Daniel?

A major developmental milestone during the first year of life is that of forming stable and positive attachment relationships, and this in turn increases the effectiveness of parenting and socialization in later life. The rest of this chapter will explore why and how attachment develops and how the quality of the early attachment relationships influences later development.

Emotional development and attachment

Our emotional development is largely determined by the early attachment relationship that we form with the main carer in our lives. Research evidence supports the idea that a stable and positive attachment relationship in early life is important for later emotional development and functioning (Morris et al., 2017). However, there have been various extrapolations of this relationship between early attachments and later development, and this chapter will explore the (re)formulated predictions of attachment theory as a much-used framework in social work practice.

The lives of children known to social work teams are often very fragmented and lacking in stable friendships and relationships. The importance of emotional well-being for children is increasingly recognized, friendships early on in a child's life helping build resilience and well-adjusted adults (e.g., Foley & Leverett, 2008). Friendships are particularly important for young children because they allow them to learn to be resilient and develop skills in relationships, such as cooperation. There is an obvious difficulty for children who have fragmented family backgrounds, particularly those in the care system who are often not in a single place for long enough to allow themselves to make attachments with too many people (Sinclair et al., 2005). This lack of attachment is then associated with a range of other problems – for example, emotional problems, poor cooperative play and a tendency for conflict, poor sociability, and poor school adjustment. For children who come into the care system with the accumulated needs of a lifetime of distress, uncertainty, inconsistency and confusion, the primary aim of all significant adults should be to provide them with positive experiences and opportunities. Social workers hold key historical knowledge about the children with whom they work and need to use this knowledge in ways that help a child make sense of their world and promote emotional well-being and resilience.

Bowlby's (1980) theory of attachment (discussed in more detail later in the chapter) has great influence in contemporary social work practice, and at its core is the belief that babies have an innate drive to develop a closeness to a protective adult in order to feel safe. Babies born into chaotic, dysfunctional families where substance abuse and domestic violence may be present are unlikely to experience consistent and close caring regimes. Bowlby's contention is that the patterns set in these early months and years are the ones that stay with that child as they develop into adulthood. The effects of poor attachment are now believed to be temporary and reversible under the right circumstances (Cairns, 2004), which is a positive message for foster carers, social workers and other professionals who have the challenge of finding ways to work with children and young people that are consistent and do not mirror previous patterns of rejection.

The evidence suggests that babies can and do form more than one attachment relationship (Cairns, 2004). For example, a child can be attached securely to mother, father and a regular caregiver. It is possible, however, for a child to be secure with mother and insecure with father, insecure with mother and secure with father, secure with both parents or insecure with both parents. What is clear is that a secure attachment with at least one caregiver seems to buffer a child from the poor development we might otherwise see following insecure attachment with others. This buffering effect can be an essential element for the development of a child in foster care who was unable to form a secure attachment relationship with their birth mother or father who may have abused or neglected them.

All children need a secure primary attachment as the base from which other relationships are able to develop, and the child is then able to sustain the first attachment while forming another, which is particularly important for children in the care system who are likely to see several changes of placement given the way the system works. The key message is that social workers, teachers and foster carers coming new to a child's life must take the necessary professional steps to understand a child's history and preferred attachment style in order to minimize disruption to any progress gained towards emotional resilience and maturity. Children who receive this type of truly individualized attention and consistency are likely to develop positive self-images and present in a friendly and trusting manner to their peers which is likely to be reciprocated. Many children who have experienced continued attachment problems tend to project a fearful and rejecting manner to others that is likely to perpetuate the cycles of rejection and negativity so often characteristic of children and young people brought up in the care system, many of whom have difficulty in sustaining relationships in adulthood (Bradford et al., 2016).

Reflective point

> ➤ What might be the arguments for and against adopting children as early on in their lives as is possible?

> ➤ Why are children adopted after the age of 1 year more likely to experience problems in their adoptive family than children adopted at earlier ages?

Theoretical perspectives on attachment: Attachment theory

Attachment theory is a highly influential theory in social work practice, specifically in the area of practice with children and families. Its popularity with social work can be traced back to its roots: original ideas of attachment theory spoke of maternal deprivation and proposed explanations of behaviour based on our early experiences and quality of relationship and/or separation from our primary carers: the mothers (see Bowlby, 1980). At the centre of social work practice with children and families is the endeavour to support children being cared for within their (birth) families, although many of the children that social workers are working, or will work, with are unable to live with their birth parents. What these children have in common is that they have had their primary attachment bonds interrupted. It is therefore intuitive to make the link between these early experiences of separation and loss and their later adjustment. Recent government policy (Unwin & Misca, 2013) has promoted adoption as the preferred choice for children at risk as compared to previous practices and policies that have given parents several attempts at rehabilitation. The belief in the critical need for stable early attachment is a key underpinning theory behind this policy change.

John Bowlby is the originator of attachment theory and its core tenet that the early attachment of infants to their caregiver is the outcome of an evolutionary mechanism designed not only to guarantee the survival of the dependent and vulnerable infant but also to provide enduring psychological connectedness between human beings (Bowlby, 1980). Attachment theory puts the emphasis on the role of early experiences in shaping the expectations and beliefs a child constructs concerning the trustworthiness and responsiveness of significant others. According to the theory, a person who is cared for in a consistent and responsive manner forms the expectation that others will be both available and supportive when needed (Ainsworth, 1979). Such expectations, or internal working models (IWMs), not only influence the way through which people regulate their emotions but also they can determine to a great extent an individual's social development and interpersonal relationships in later life. In Bowlby's view, these working models of relationships become slowly stable and unconscious over time. As individuals use these models as the basis for their interpersonal behaviours, expectations and interpretations, so they become resistant to change (Bowlby, 1980).

Reflective point

Can you think of anybody in your social circle who has talked to you about their early childhood and how the degree of their attachment to a key carer has affected the nature of their relationships in adulthood? They may not use the term 'attachment' but they may talk in terms of coldness or closeness to parents or carers.

For example:

➢ If their father was distant emotionally, or a very affectionate man, do they seem to have chosen a similar type of partner?

➢ Have others cognitively taken the decision to seek close adult relationships with people who have quite different traits to their childhood carers?

➢ If their mother was undemonstrative are they also undemonstrative with their children?

Voice of the child: Kerry, ex-foster child

I remember being left at home by my mum and having to wander the street in my nappy aged about 3, asking anybody I met for something to eat. My mum would turn up at a neighbour's or a foster home at any old time. Sometimes she hugged me and cried a lot; other times when she came to collect me she didn't say one word.

Reflective points

➢ What type of attachment style do you imagine Kerry had as she grew up?

➢ What effect might this early experience have had on Kerry's relationships in her adult life?

Bowlby subsequently hypothesized that IWMs may be malleable and open to some degree of modification in the context of negative interpersonal or attachment-related experiences throughout the lifespan (Ainsworth & Bowlby, 1991). Indeed, research has reported that a number of variables such as stressful life events, family risk and depression are good indicators of change from security to insecurity or disorganization (Moss et al., 2005).

In contrast, factors such as relationship satisfaction, greater emotional openness and fewer negative life events (Vondra et al., 1999) have been found to be associated with change towards attachment security. These latter findings perhaps particularly fit with the values of the social work profession which believe in people's potential for change (BASW, 2012).

What is attachment and how is it developed?

Attachment is conceptualized as a dyadic and reciprocal relationship where infants elicit proximity seeking behaviours to gain a response with the ultimate aim of ensuring survival (Bolen, 2000). Originally individuals were thought of as being biologically programmed to form an emotional bond with their primary caregiver to ensure survival and proximity. One of the predictions is that failure to initiate a bond with the primary caregiver or the formation of insecure attachment within the first two years of life severely inhibits cognitive, social and physical development (Atwool, 2006).

Attachment is thought to develop typically around 8 months when proximity seeking behaviours emerge (Bretherton, 1992). Bowlby (1980) suggested that these early experiences are internalized and individuals develop an IWM which promotes stability of attachment behaviours and development across the life course, although some research posits that life experiences increase the likelihood of IWM malleability (Atwool, 2006). The works of Ainsworth and Bowlby (1991) revolutionized our understanding of how separation, privation and deprivation influence development (Bretherton, 1992).

How is the quality of attachment relationship measured?

The standard method employed in studies for assessing attachment type in infancy is the Strange Situation Procedure developed by Ainsworth and Bell (1970). On the basis of reunion behaviours in the Strange Situation Procedure, infants are classified as securely or insecurely attached, the latter being divided into three subgroups: avoidant, ambivalent or disorganized attachment styles.

Secure children use the caregiver as a safe base from which they can explore the environment, seek direct comfort from their caregiver and are easily soothed upon reunion. Avoidant children reduce their attachment distress and seem to be more interested in exploration. Ambivalent-resistant children display increased attachment needs and are difficult to soothe when distressed. Lastly, disorganized children do not demonstrate a particular strategy for protection and exhibit illogical behaviour such as freezing upon reunion and hand flapping.

Reflective point

> ➤ Imagine the situation of Lisa, a 3-year-old whose parents were heavy users of heroin and alcohol. She never knew if her mummy or daddy would be up in the morning and able to give her breakfast and her daily regime was very chaotic.

> ➤ What type of attachment might characterize this situation? How might knowledge of attachment theory help a foster carer/social worker to approach ways of caring for Lisa if she came into foster care due to neglect?

The Strange Situation Procedure (Ainsworth & Bell, 1970) has been used to provide empirical support for attachment theory. The 20-minute controlled laboratory procedure records attachment behaviours of infants when their mother leaves the room and is temporarily replaced by a stranger before her return. In a continuity perspective, Ainsworth and Bell's (1970) results contribute to understanding the effects of early attachment on behaviour across the life course. Secure attachments reflect positive self-worth, avoidance reflects feelings of unworthiness, and resistant infants seek attention whereas insecurely attached infants demonstrate higher behavioural dysfunctions (Bretherton, 1992).

Four attachment styles were identified above including secure, insecure-avoidant, insecure-resistant and insecure-disorganized, which are thought to reflect an individual's IWMs (Atwool, 2006).

1. Securely attached infants displayed explorative behaviour, stranger avoidance and distress in the caregiver's absence although upon return they are able to settle quickly. The infant shows clear signs of specific attachment towards the carer. Secure children use the caregiver as a safe base from which they can explore the environment, seek direct comfort from their caregiver and they are easily soothed upon reunion.

2. Insecure-avoidant attachment manifests by infants displaying no distress in the caregiver's absence, equal comfort towards the stranger with little interest upon the caregiver's return.

3. Insecure-resistant infants were ambivalent and dependable, intensely distressed in the caregiver's absence, stranger avoidant and later

showed resistance towards the caregiver. Ambivalent-resistant children display increased attachment needs and are difficult to soothe when distressed.

4. Insecure-disorganised attachment reflects a combination of avoidance and resistant behaviours. Disorganized children do not demonstrate a particular strategy for protection and exhibit illogical behaviour such as freezing upon reunion.

It is important to clarify that that there are variations of attachment patterns classifications and the example given above (adapted from Atwool, 2006) is not the only one (for a regularly updated handbook on attachment theory and research, see Cassidy & Shaver, 2016). The value of the attachment classification rests on the predictions that research has made about later development, and these attachment styles should not be seen as personal traits. Social workers and other professionals should be careful to always see the whole child and not only see labels relating to a child's specific attachment style.

Reflective point

➤ What might be the drawbacks to a child being 'labelled' as having a particular type of attachment style?

Some of the 'atypical' attachment patterns have been identified, particularly among high-risk groups such as abused, neglected or maltreated infants (Shapiro & Levendosky, 1999). For example, the disorganized/disoriented attachment pattern (Barnett et al., 1999) had prevalence among social risk samples, particularly maltreated children. Being fearful of the attachment figure, or having an attachment figure that is frightened, is thought to be a common experience of children who develop this type of attachment and who appear to lack a consistent behavioural strategy. The avoidant/ambivalent attachment pattern (Crittenden, 1999), characterized by combinations of moderate to high avoidance and moderate to high resistance, is prevalent among children from economically disadvantaged backgrounds, including children who were abused and/or neglected, and who would have been classified as insecurely attached. A further category, the disinhibited/diffuse attachment behaviour, has been found to characterize children who show apparently affectionate, 'indiscriminately friendly' behaviour to strangers whom they approach when in distress. This form of attachment behaviour has been reported as strongly associated with institutional upbringing (O'Connor et al., 2000).

Voice of the child: Kerry, ex-foster child

My mum regularly brought me home a new 'Dad' when I was at primary school. Sometimes they were nice, sometimes they were harsh to me and some used to punch my mum. None of them seem to have lasted very long and mum always seemed to love them more than me, but I remember a nice one called Dave who had a motorbike and bought me loads of sweets. He never hit mum.

Reflective point

➢ Kerry reports having to compete for her mum's attention while in her early years. What effect might this experience have on her view of adult relationships/parenting?

Exercise: Critical thinking on attachment theory

Helen, student social worker, is undertaking an assessment of James, a 10-month-old boy, thought to be at risk due to his mother's substance abuse and mental health issues. Helen noticed that when his mother, Mary, left the room, James noticed her leaving but did not seem to be affected at all, and continued to play unperturbed. When Mary returned, James again ignored her.

➢ In the light of attachment theory, how might Helen interpret James' behaviour?

➢ What concerns might be present regarding James' emotional development?

➢ Might there be alternative explanations for James' behaviour?

Attachment and influences on attachments across the lifespan

Traditionally used to describe affectional bonds between infants and their primary caregivers (Bowlby, 1951), the term attachment has been broadened to include other developmental periods, such as adolescence (Brown & Wright, 2001) and adulthood (Bartholomew & Horowitz, 1991). While infant attachment primarily ensures proximity and survival (Atwool, 2006), attachment in childhood facilitates the development of language acquisition, social skills and a sense of self. In adolescence, attachment assists with the regulation of emotions and development of identity and peer relationships, and in adulthood, supports the emergence of intimacy, cohabitation and marriage during adulthood.

One area of great interest for practice is what the determinants of an infant's attachment style are. In light of research evidence, there is agreement that while the attachment is a universal system, the style of attachment that each individual develops derives originally from parenting. For example, research undertaken at the National Institute of Child Health and Human Development (NICHD, 2002) reported maternal sensitivity as a robust predictor of child attachment styles, as attachment styles were consistent from 15 months to 36 months. Less responsive mothering, combined with longer hours in day care, was indicative of insecure-ambivalent childhood attachment (NICHD, 2002), suggesting that early separation has a continuous effect on attachment behaviours, consistent with Bowlby's (1980) conceptualization of IWMs.

Most research focuses on attachment continuity from infancy onwards, as there is the assumption that attachment behaviours typically develop around the age of 8 months (Bowlby, 1980). However, it can be argued that factors during pregnancy and immediately after birth can affect attachment formation in infants. For example, O'Connor and colleagues (2002) reported a significant relationship between maternal prenatal alcohol exposure and childhood insecure attachment among 42 single mothers from high poverty backgrounds. The findings provide insight into the long-term effects of alcohol and substance abuse, and the implications on child development and attachment. However, this research is limited to small selective samples. Future research should consider the implications of pre-birth experiences on attachment style in more depth to facilitate the understanding of attachment across the life course.

An important point to note is that attachment should be viewed as a two-way relationship: in as much as caregiver factors influence attachment formation and attachment style, so do factors related to the infant (Misca & Smith, 2014). For example, an infant's temperament will affect the type of attachment formed (Harris, 2000). Another category of factors would be medical factors related to the infant – such as the infant's health (e.g., the demands of colicky babies can lead to difficulties in the formation of secure attachment bonds, and the separation of premature babies from caregivers can similarly pose difficulties).

A long-held belief is that early emotional and physical deprivation can have adverse effects on subsequent development, including hindering the ability to form meaningful relationships with attachment figures (Stein, 2006). Support for this idea comes from studies of inter-country adopted children who are rescued from institutional care such as orphanages

(Misca, 2014a, 2014b). For example, attachment security scores were significantly lower and indiscriminately friendly behaviour was prevalent among children adopted into Canada from Romanian orphanages in comparison to the control group (Chisholm et al., 1995), indicating that the lack of an attachment figure in the first two years is detrimental to later emotional and social development, supporting original ideas of attachment theory (Bowlby, 1980). Chisholm (1998) conducted a three-year naturalistic follow-up, suggesting that even severely deprived children were able to form an attachment in their adoptive homes, although the quality of these relationships was variable, suggesting some prominent lasting effects.

However, recent research with children 'rescued' from early deprivation through adoption and fostering suggests that there is great variability in individual responses, depending on the length of exposure to the poor rearing environment and disputing the assumption of attachment continuity. For example, institutionally reared Romanian children who were placed in family foster care before the age of 24 months were more likely to form a secure attachment and less likely to develop insecure-disorganized attachments (Smyke et al., 2010). Such research reinforces the idea that a positive caregiving environment can reverse, to an extent, the consequences of deprivation (Smyke et al., 2010), thus pointing to the remarkable resilience in human development.

Reflective point

> How might attachment theory help an adoption social worker in supporting adopted children and their adoptive families post-adoption?

> What would be an appropriate range of strategies to suggest to a new adoptive parent whose 2-year-old adopted daughter appears to be disorganized-attached?

> How might a social worker best advise the adoptive parents on this issue?

Influences of early attachments through the lifespan

Among the most enduring questions in attachment theory and research is whether the attachment patterns formed in infancy remain stable across the life course, and whether parents 'transmit' their attachment styles to their children (Misca, 2009). A meta-analysis of the existing longitudinal data (Fraley, 2002) indicated that attachment security is only moderately stable across the first 19 years of life.

Childhood

There is evidence in support of the assumption of attachment continuity and of infant attachment style having an influence on development from infancy to childhood. For example, it has been shown that infant attachment styles predict school success and dyadic attachments in teacher–child and parent–child relations within childhood (Bergin & Bergin, 2009). Higher grades were associated with secure attachment, socialization, lower attention deficit hyperactivity disorder (ADHD), lower delinquency and high emotional availability, whereas insecurely attached infants projected low academic aspirations and achievements and lack of friendships in childhood (Easterbrooks et al., 2012). Behavioural concerns were most prevalent among boys from risky social backgrounds (Pasco-Fearon & Belsky, 2011), suggesting that the environment may disrupt attachment continuity and development.

Longitudinal research suggests that continuous insecure attachment inhibits social development in childhood as insecure classified infants transitioned into childhood with atypical behaviour, as opposed to securely classified infants who showed typical child development (Goldberg et al., 2003). In a different study, observations based on the Strange Situation Procedure at 1 year and laboratory tests during childhood revealed that maternal sensitivity influences friendship quality in childhood (Mcelwain & Volling, 2004).

Recent research evidence supports the idea that early attachment patterns formed are susceptible to chance, usually when there are changes in a child's relationships with significant adults in their environment. For example, a recent study investigating attachment patterns among a group of foster children at 2 years and again at 3 years of age (Jacobsen et al., 2014) found that the majority of foster children who were securely attached at the age of 2 remained so at age 3. These results are indicative of the protective nature of early secure attachments. Importantly, however, the study also showed that among children classified as disorganized at age 2, significantly less remained so at the age of 3. The study brings evidence of positive 'plasticity' in attachment patterns in early childhood, suggesting that young foster children are able to form secure attachments when placed with stable and foster carers.

Another important question in attachment theory and research concerns the continuity or change across generations, that is, to what extend are attachment patterns 'transmitted' from parents/caregivers to their infants/children? A recent study, using data from an ongoing 37-year longitudinal study of the development of children born into poverty (Minnesota Longitudinal Study of Risk and Adaptation, or MLSRA; Sroufe et al., 2005), indicated that infants are more likely to form disorganized attachment relationships if their mothers had histories of attachment disorganization. Specifically, in this research study approximately half of mothers who had themselves formed disorganized attachments in their infancies had children who formed a disorganized infant–caregiver attachment relationship. This findings provide some evidence that poor early attachment relationships may be transmitted across generations, from main caregiver(s) to infant(s), indicating that early interventions to support positive attachment and parenting are required.

Reflective points

> From an attachment theory perspective, what are the challenges for primary school age children in foster care, in terms of forming new relationship with their caregivers?

> What sort of support would help children in foster care, and their foster carers, overcome some of these challenges?

> What additional risks might exist for a foster child who was willing to go to any new stranger?

Adolescence

Adolescence brings with it particular challenges for social work, many social work systems such as safeguarding being geared towards younger children. In times of resource constraints and ever tightening prioritization of need, adolescents and their problems may get less than equal treatment. All teenagers experience rapid hormonal changes in puberty, have increased sexual drives, identify most strongly with their peers and yearn for independence (Collins & Laursen, 2004). Heightened sensitivities and emotions accompany the neurobiological changes of adolescence, often resulting in challenging forms of behaviour, whether aggressive or defiant.

Where families and social networks are supportive then the associated risk-taking in adolescence involving substances, intimate relationships and rebellion can be balanced by increased maturity and achievement. However, for adolescents with fragmented backgrounds the risks of the adolescent years may well outweigh the positives. Spending time with gangs of peers might be a healthy and positive lifestyle choice for teenagers with stable backgrounds, but for adolescents with fractured backgrounds who might be living in poverty with little hope of a better life, such drivers for peer acceptance and esteem might lead to involvement in criminal activity such as drug dealing and violence.

Case study

Helen, student social worker, is working with Ronnie, a 13-year-old young person who is beginning to display aggressive behaviours in his foster home and to 'push the boundaries'. Ronnie has confided in Helen that he was hoping to join a drug dealing gang in order to get the 'respect' that he does not get at home or in school.

- How might Helen use an understanding of teenage psychology to help keep Ronnie safe from harm?

Romantic relationships

Romantic 'relationships' are likely to mean different things to different adolescents, depending on their nurture and experiences. For example, a teenage girl who has grown up in a household characterized by sexual abuse or domestic violence is likely to have a distorted view of adult relationships and 'normative' behaviours. Without the guiding hands of parents or friends, such teenagers might all too easily fall prey to peers or adults wishing to sexually exploit them, whether physically or online. These risks can sometimes be compounded by professionals, such as social workers or psychologists, who see risky behaviours as 'lifestyle choices'. For example, some professionals in the Rotherham CSE Inquiry (Jay, 2014) were noted as viewing the exploited young women as knowing what they were getting into, and therefore deserving of the consequences. The fact that comprehensive therapeutic support was not swiftly and uniformly offered to the Rotherham victims indicates the low priority such young people are sometimes afforded. The reality for many adolescents is that they experience neglect and abuse, and they are vulnerable in different ways to babies and younger children. For example, Brandon and colleagues (2012) found that neglect and rejection of 11- to 15-year-olds featured more significantly in the serious case reviews they studied than was the case for any other age group.

New risks to adolescents appear with every generation, recent generations having seen the advent of the internet with its associated benefits and dangers. Online bullying, sexual exploitation and within-relationship violence have become real problems for young people today, and the all-pervasiveness of sexualized images have distorted young people's views of healthy relationships. This culture is causing significant rises in mental ill-health (Jobe-Shields et al., 2016) and associated behaviours such as self-harming and binge drinking (NICE, 2017a). Other very recent risks to vulnerable people have emerged, encouraged by social media, in respect of terrorism. The Jihadist movement has encouraged adolescent boys and girls to leave their homes in the UK to fight for the Muslim cause in the Middle East (Stanley & Guru, 2015), to such an extent that guidance, the *Prevent Strategy* (HM Government, 2011), was issued to schools and colleges. This controversial guidance, which could be interpreted as further encouraging prejudice against ethnic minorities, highlighted the signs of young people who may be at-risk. Today's young people also live with a real fear of terrorist explosions occurring in cities and at special events, on a scale never experienced by previous generations of young people.

Reflective point

> What psychological influences might lead a trio of Muslim teenage girls to leave stable homes and schools to join a Jihadist movement in Syria?

Attachment continuity

Supporting the assumption of attachment continuity, secure attachment in infancy and childhood are correlated with stable romantic relationships in adolescence (Dykas et al., 2006). However, negative life events and dramatic transitions in adolescence predict discontinuity of attachment (Aikins et al., 2009).

Weinfield and colleagues (2004) argued that attachment style changes with life's transitions, but no particular life event is associated with discontinuity or continuity of attachment. However, significantly more insecure attachments were prevalent among divorced families than unified families – 89% and 35% respectively (Hamilton, 2000) – indicating that parental divorce and negative life events are significant contributors of discontinuity in attachment (Lewis et al., 2000). This supports the idea that IWMs are malleable under certain environmental conditions (Atwool, 2006). Lewis and colleagues (2000) conducted a longitudinal analysis among 84 white middle-class participants, measuring attachment in infancy using the Strange Situation Procedure during infancy, childhood recollections at 13 years and the Adult Attachment Interview (AAI) in young adulthood. This study reported discontinuity between infant attachment styles and adolescent maladjustment.

Attachment and culture

Bowlby's ideas of the importance of early care in the onset of attachment and the long-lasting impact of early experience are challenged by evidence from cross-cultural studies (Rothbaum et al., 2000), which reveal that attachment relationships with single attachment figures are not the most salient factors in socialization and social adjustment in all communities or cultures (Waters & Cummings, 2000). Moreover, the secure attachment style that has been identified as prevalent in two-thirds of the Western samples is not the prevalent style of attachment in other cultures. For example, what a Western mother may see as clingy attachment behaviour (associated with insecurely attached children), a Japanese mother is more likely to see as a behaviour signifying inter-dependence between herself and the child. Fish (2004) reported that only half of Appalachian, USA, infants in their study were classified as securely attached during the Strange Situation Procedure; however, at 4 years this slightly increased, thus challenging Western research that report attachment continuity from infancy to childhood (Mcelwain & Volling, 2004).

The important message to take from these above findings is that, although the attachment relationship is universal, parents' attachment beliefs, values and practices differ significantly around the world. Ulti-mately, a professional must achieve an accurate understanding of how a family or a parenting style is influencing child development and see a child holistically, rather than as a behavioural label. Serious case reviews such as that of Victoria Climbié (Laming, 2003) and Khyra Ishaq (Rad-ford, 2010) have all demonstrated how tragic consequences can occur when professionals do not challenge the parenting practices of other cultures, sometimes for fear of being labelled as racist. To show interest and ask questions about a different culture is both to show respect and to enable better communication/safeguarding.

Reflective point: Attachment and culture

In a multicultural society such as Britain, a cross-cultural understanding of attachment is essential for practitioners working with children and their families.

- ➢ How can a cultural understanding of attachment influence how we assess parent–child interaction and child development?

- ➢ As a social worker in a multicultural city, how might you go about developing a knowledge base about the different attachment styles and expectancies of diverse cultures?

- ➢ How deeply might a social worker have to understand the emotional norms in a different culture before they can practise in an effective manner?

Interconnectedness of developmental dimensions: Emotional development and disabled children

In this section, we will explore the interconnectedness of developmental dimensions, reflecting in particular on links to cognitive development, which is more fully discussed in Chapter 3.

The emotional health of children with learning disabilities is an area that has been given comparatively little attention by social workers, limitations in cognitive functioning perhaps leading to a belief that such children do not experience the same levels of emotions as children and young people without cognitive impairment. An alternative view would be that children with learning disabilities experience greater emotional problems, because of an inability to articulate, and because of the social environment that can display discriminatory attitudes. Emerson and Hatton (2007), in a UK review of statistical data study, found that that 36% of children and young people with learning disabilities had mental health problems, in comparison to a figure of 8% in other children. Poor social environments were identified by Emerson and Hatton (2007) as contributory factors leading to higher incidence of emotional disorders, conduct disorders and hyperactivity among all children, particularly when a learning disability was also present.

Reflective point

> - How do emotions influence the process of children's learning?

> - How might this be different for children with learning disabilities whose cognitive abilities are limited?

> - In what ways might teenage girls with mild learning disabilities be more at risk from cyberbullying or online grooming than their peers without learning disabilities?

Children with learning disabilities are also less likely to be resilient in the face of a number of risk factors which will impact their emotional health, such as neglect and bullying, and may respond with challenging or self-harming behaviours. Schneider and colleagues (1996) studied the prevalence of self-harming behaviours in people with learning disability, self-harm being seen as often providing a physical and emotional outlet. Self-harming behaviours were evidenced as mainly beginning before the age of 5, and were noted as becoming more frequent and severe over time, especially without any effective interventions.

Case study

Helen, student social worker, has been working with Sherylle, a 14-year-old foster child of mixed race who has mild learning disabilities and a history of self-harm. She has been in several foster homes during her life and is currently with Jo and Martha Hunt, a couple in their 60s. Sherylle has come from a background of neglect, her mother having been unable to satisfactorily care for Sherylle as she has become older and more assertive. Jo and Martha are not very competent on computers or aware of cyber risks.

Task

> What interventions might Helen advise if Sherylle was repeatedly posting sexualized images of herself on social media? Sherylle self-harms whenever her foster carers take away her mobile phone or internet access.

Paclawskyj and Yoo (2004) reviewed the use of behaviourist interventions (e.g., social skills training/reinforcement and desensitization) with adults who have learning disabilities, and mental health problems, and found some encouraging evidence. The use of cognitive approaches across a range of mental health problems from depression to anger management have also proven effective (Lindsay et al., 2004; McCabe et al., 2006). The social environment, however, and the management of social risk, is the underpinning key to success when working with the emotional issues concerning children and young people with learning disabilities. In the case study of Sherylle above it might be seen that the environment – for example, access to a mobile phone and awareness training for the foster carers – are practical challenges to be addressed before any psychological interventions are likely to be effective.

Summary

Emotional development in children and young people is a complex area, long disputed by a range of different theorists and practitioners. Many child development 'truths' are based on mainstream populations, usually from the Western world. The challenge for social workers is even more complex in that their populations of children and young people have often come from chaotic or abusive backgrounds, where emotional responses and survival strategies may be quite different from other populations. Additionally, most social workers now work with children and young people from a wide diversity of backgrounds, and have the additional complexities of cultural norms, expectations and practices to also take into consideration for effective child-centred practice.

It behoves all social workers to be knowledgeable about the issues detailed in this chapter, and to base their assessments and plans on this established body of knowledge. Most critically, however, social workers must interpret and customize this knowledge in the context of seeing every child and young person as a unique individual, part of whose temperamental uniqueness is shaped by attachment and culture.

Further resources

Attachment Aware Schools training programme, www.bathspa.ac.uk/education/research/attachment-aware-schools/ (Accessed: 23 January 2018)

'Attachment aware' schools and communities in which all children and young people experience the nurturing environments they need to grow and achieve.

Kids Matter website, www.kidsmatter.edu.au/mental-health-matters/social-and-emotional-learning/social-development (Accessed: 23 January 2018)

An Australian website which covers a range of developmental issues including mental health.

NSPCC (2018) *National Case Review Repository*, https://learning.nspcc.org.uk/case-reviews/national-case-review-repository/ (Accessed: 14 September 2018)

This site enables searches to be made if you have the name of the subject child or local authority where a Serious Case Review was conducted.

Psychologists against Austerity (2018), www.psychchange.org/psychologists-against-austerity.html (Accessed: 23 January 2018)

This site represents the views of psychologists for social change. It highlights the effect of inequalities on well-being and mental health.

3

Cognitive development

Key learning outcomes

Following the study of this chapter, learners will be able to:

➤ Describe theoretical perspectives in understanding cognitive development.

➤ Explain notions of cognitive adaptation, cognitive schemata, zone of proximal development and scaffolding.

➤ Apply concepts of cognitive adaptation, cognitive schemata, zone of proximal development and scaffolding into areas of direct work with children.

➤ Critically explore the role of culture in cognitive development.

➤ Use research evidence to critically evaluate theoretical perspectives on cognitive development, and their application in working with children in applied settings.

Introduction

This chapter will explore some of the key theoretical perspectives in cognitive development, including the recent developments on theory of mind and children's understanding of the social world. These theoretical perspectives will be explored in relation to their application for practice.

Social work holds to values of inclusivity and openness, and these values extend to a consideration at all times as to whether clients really understand what is happening in their lives and the assessments and plans social workers make around them. Formal settings such as reviews, case conferences and courts are intimidating for people not used to their protocols and familiarities, and involvement can often be tokenistic. The use of jargon, failure to address questions in terms that a client can understand

and a failure to explain systems and time frames around decision-making can be very confusing. Where parents and carers have learning disabilities, these issues become particularly pertinent, and are perhaps one of the reasons why a disproportionate number of children whose parents have learning disabilities are in the care system (Tarleton et al., 2006).

Cognitive ability is also a core consideration for social workers in respect of children in care, whose educational attainment and likelihood of attending higher education fall very significantly behind the achievements of other children. In 2008, only 14% of children in care achieved 5 A*–C grade GCSEs compared with the national average of 65% for all children, these figures linking directly with future employment possibilities (DCFS, 2009). This is not because of their cognitive potential, but the lack of opportunity for their cognitive abilities to flourish due to emotional upheavals in their lives, the changes of placements and, historically, the lack of attention paid by professional staff across a range of disciplines to the educational attainment of children in care. These issues of learning disabilities and children in care will be returned to throughout the chapter.

Theoretical perspectives in understanding cognitive development

Cognitive development refers to the changes in how humans think and learn through their development from infancy to adulthood. It is important to clarify that the difference in cognitive development between infants and children and adults is not only quantitative – in the sense that children know less – but also qualitative as there are significant differences in how children think about and understand their experiences. Various theories and research have put forward ideas of how our cognitive abilities develop over the lifespan, particularly from infancy/childhood through to adulthood, where the most important leaps occur in cognitive development. In this section we will focus on two influential perspectives: Piaget's (1964) theory of cognitive development and Vygotsky's (1978) socio-cultural theory, highlighting their strengths, limitations and applications in contributing to our understanding of cognitive development.

Piaget's stage theory of cognitive development

One of the most popular and influential theories of cognitive development is that of the Swiss scientist, Jean Piaget. Piaget's theories have been popular since the beginning of the twentieth century and became particularly popular in the 1960s as an alternative to the theories around behaviourism which were predominant at the time. Unlike behaviourism, which viewed development as a process provided by the environment and events experienced by the child, Piaget proposed that children make active sense of their experiences and construct their own knowledge – hence his theory being also referred to as constructivism.

According to the theory of constructionism, children make active sense of their world and experiences and construct their own knowledge, doing so through various processes based on the concept of schema. Schema is a unit of knowledge that is used to understand a situation. Piaget proposes that we are born with a set of schemas, such as reflexes. When a new experience fits into an existing schema this is simply incorporated through a process of assimilation. For example, one of the innate reflexes is sucking and the newborn will apply this schema to any new object that s/he comes in contact with. However, when a new experience does not make sense and cannot be assimilated through existing schemas, this creates confusion, a state of disequilibrium. In order to achieve a state of equilibrium or adaptation to the environment, the infants and children must thus adopt a new approach through the process of accommodation. For example, when children name all animals 'cats' they assimilate, but when corrected and learn that some animals are named 'dogs', they accommodate their schemas to the new type of stimulus. Assimilation and accommodation work in tandem to support children's organization of their knowledge into increasingly complex structures.

The main concepts are:

> Schema, referring to a cognitive framework that places concepts, objects and experiences into categories or groups.

> Assimilation, the process of fitting new experiences into existing mental schemas.

> Disequilibrium, referring to a state of confusion in which schemas do not fit experiences.

> Equilibration, representing an attempt to resolve disequilibrium and return to a comfortable cognitive state.

> Accommodation, the process of changing the mental schema so it fits with new experiences.

Piaget conceptualized cognitive development as a succession of qualitatively different stages, earlier stages being the building blocks of later development. Not all children will reach these stages at exactly the same ages but they have to pass the stages in the same order and no stage can be skipped. The cognitive development is seen as occurring across three major periods and the major feature of each period is summarized in Table 3.1.

Table 3.1 Summary of Piaget's stages of cognitive development

Stage	Age range	Main features of cognitive development
Sensorimotor	Birth–2 years	*Circular reaction*: the infant uses repetition of a reflexive action that results in a pleasurable experience *Object permanence*: the infant understands that an object still exists even when s/he cannot see it
Pre-operational	2–7 years	*Symbolic representation*: the child acquires the ability to use symbols and words *Childhood 'egocentrism'*: children's inability to consider other points of view *'Magical' thinking*: children create causal links where none exist
Concrete operations	7–12 years	*Reversibility*: children acquire the ability to reverse mental operations, such as conservation tasks
Formal operations	12 years onwards	*Abstract mental operations and hypothetico-deductive reasoning*: adolescents acquire the ability to form hypotheses and to reason logically about these hypotheses (*'if... then....'*) *Post formal and dialectical thinking*: (young) adults have the ability to analyse and bring together contradictory thoughts and emotions

Further reading

Beilin, H. (1992) Piaget's enduring contribution to developmental psychology. *Developmental Psychology*, 28(2), 191–204. doi: 10.1037/0012-1649.28.2.191.
Flavell, J. H. (1996) Piaget's legacy. *Psychological Science*, 7(4), 200–203.
These articles explore the context in which Piaget developed his theory, and the contributions of his theory to the study of children.

Applications of Piaget's cognitive theory

Piaget was not directly interested in applying his theory to educational practice. However, the educational implications of Piaget's theory have been constantly highlighted, for example using Piaget's concepts to design a developmentally based curriculum for the primary grades (Black & Ammon, 1992). The tenets of Piaget's theory have various implications for working with children and adolescents in a variety of settings.

For example, the concept of object permanence and the timescale for infants achieving this is of particular relevance in understanding attachment formation (discussed in Chapter 2). In order for the infant to be able to establish an attachment to his/her caregiver, the infant needs to have an understanding that an object (or person in this case) exists even when s/he cannot see it. This is an example of interdependence of various domains of development: cognitive and emotional in this case.

Practical learning: How to test for object permanence formation?

For example, before achieving object permanence, infants do not seem upset when parents leave the room ('out of sight, out of mind'), but then become suddenly very upset when seeing a parent leave (as they suddenly know the parent still exists even when not in view). You can test this out in a naturalistic way with infants between birth and 2 years of age.

Another example of object permanence is the inability to achieve reversibility at the pre-operational stage, meaning that the child cannot mentally reverse or undo an action. The irreversibility applies to relationships as well – for example, the child will correctly identify that s/he has a brother, but will be unable to realize that his/her sibling has a brother or sister. This may present a significant challenge when discussing or explaining family relationships to children who are at the pre-operational stage.

'Magical thinking' which refers to children at the pre-operational stage creating causal links where they do not exist could also explain why children at this stage may blame themselves for parents' divorce or parental violence – as they will infer a causal link between their own behaviour and that of parents. Such beliefs may prove to be persistent and may create cognitive distortions that could prevail for a long time.

Exercise: Applying theory into practice

Helen, student social worker, is working with Mike, a 5-year-old boy who has lived with his foster carers, Mr and Mrs Storme, since he was 3 months old. Mike is now in the process of being adopted.

➤ In light of your knowledge of Mike's cognitive development at his age, how might Helen best explain adoption to him and how could she help prepare him for the adoption?

Another feature at the pre-operational stage is the child's egocentrism, meaning the inability of the child to consider others' points of view. However, Elkind (1967) argued that there is a re-emergence of egocentrism in late adolescence – at the point of entrance to college or of a new life situation/transition – when adolescents believe that they are the centre of others' attention ('imaginary audience') and that their experience is in some way unique and has only ever happened to them ('personal fable'). These can be instrumental in the emergence of distorted self-image and eating disorders in adolescence.

Reflective point

➤ How could Helen, student social worker, use concepts of 'adolescent egocentrism' and 'imaginary audience' to help her understanding of the occurrence of eating disorders (anorexia and bulimia) in a 14-year-old fostered girl who came into care after a history of familial sexual abuse?

Further reading

Elkind, D. (1967) Egocentrism in adolescence. *Child Development*, 38(4), 1025. doi: 10.2307/1127100.
Schwartz, P., Maynard, A. & Uzelac, S. (2008) Adolescent egocentrism: A contemporary view. *Adolescence*, 43(171), 441–448.

Evaluation of Piaget's theory

Piaget's theory has had a great impact on subsequent research in the field of cognitive development, with many studies attempting to replicate or reformulate the theory. Its uniqueness is in approaching cognitive development as a series of qualitative stages focusing on how infants and children discover, understand and construct the reality. Piaget's contribution to the understanding of cognition was to move beyond simple mechanisms of learning or individual differences in intelligence.

There are, of course, several caveats when applying Piaget's theory of cognitive development to practice. While the age stages outlined by the theory can be useful tools in helping practitioners understand how children view the world differently at different stages and thus how best to support them in these journeys of discovery, it is imperative that the stages are seen as guides which are not as set in stone and for individual differences to be taken into account. This is particularly relevant in working with children whose backgrounds of disability or abuse may prevent them achieving the stages predicted by the theory. Evidence from cross-cultural studies highlights one of the main limitations of Piaget's theory the lack of accounting for the cultural context of cognitive development, raising important questions about the universality of the stages across cultures (Robinson, 2007).

Exercise: Piaget's theory and culture

Undertake a brief literature search, and use contemporary research evidence, to summarize the arguments regarding the cultural limitations of Piaget's theory, such as:

➢ Are the stages of cognitive development universal?

➢ How does Piaget's theory account for the cultural context of development?

Vygotsky's socio-cultural theory

As highlighted above, one of the limitations of Piaget's theory was the lack of consideration given to the social and cultural context of cognitive development. By contrast, Vygotsky's theory (1978) focuses on the social and cultural processes where learning takes place as a main determinant of cognitive development.

Cognitive development is seen as the result of children's interaction with 'experts' – members of their own culture: parents, teachers, older/more experienced children/peers or siblings. Such interactions most benefit the development of more complex abilities such as language and complex problem solving. When children and their 'expert' partner solve problems together, the child will develop beyond his/her current capabilities; this is called 'zone of proximal development', which is seen crucially as the child's potential for development through social experience. While in Piaget's theory the infant child was seen as a 'lone scientist' discovering the world, Vygotsky's approach emphasizes the collective and social dimension of development through support from more experienced members of the culture.

Zone of proximal development and scaffolding

The concept of zone of proximal development enables us to understand how cognitive development arises from interactions with more experienced partners. However in order to be effective, the zone of proximate development needs to provide stimulation within the immediate developmental proximity. If the gap is too wide, the stimulation fails to support development. The role of the more experienced partner is to break down complex tasks, model and encourage and support the learner.

Another important concept proposed by the socio-cultural theory is that of scaffolding. In scaffolding, the amount and type of support is adjusted to the child's needs. For example, the amount of support is gradually decreasing, enabling the child to ultimately perform the task on his own.

Reflective point: Emotional scaffolding

Scaffolding is what the adult (or more skilled partner) does to move the child through the zone of proximal development to independent performance. The concept of scaffolding can be applied across a variety of contexts and content areas. For example, it has been suggested that children who are not provided with the words and concepts to recognize and understand their feelings ('emotional scaffolding') find it difficult to regulate their emotions, leading to a range of emotional and behavioural issues (Howe & Fearnley, 1999).

➢ How would you help a 5-year-old child, recently accommodated in a foster home due to parental neglect, to recognize and understand their feelings of sadness and loss using scaffolding techniques?

➢ How would this differ from using scaffolding to help a 15-year-old to recognize and understand their feelings of sadness and loss after the death of a parent they had helped care for over a period of three years?

Further reading

Howe, D. & Fearnley, S. (1999) Disorders of attachment and attachment therapy. *Adoption & Fostering*, 23(2), 19–30. doi: 10.1177/030857599902300205.
Howe, D. & Fearnley, S. (2003) Disorders of attachment in adopted and fostered children: Recognition and treatment. *Clinical Child Psychology and Psychiatry*, 8(3), 369–387. doi: 10.1177/1359104503008003007.

Applications

The immediate potential for application of the socio-cultural theory of cognitive development is in the educational field where principles of collective and inclusive education are widespread.

Further reading

Wood, D. & Middleton, D. (1975) A study of assisted problem solving. *British Journal of Psychology*, 66(2), 181–191. doi: 10.1111/j.2044-8295.1975. tb01454.x.
Wood, D., Wood. H. & Middleton, D. (1978) An experimental evaluation of four face-to face teaching strategies. *International Journal of Behavioural Development*, 1(2), 131–147. doi: 10.1177/016502547800100203.

Another important corollary of the theory regarding the role of culture is in cognitive development. Research evidence supports the ideas that children learn highly complex cognitive skills that would not normally be attained by children at their age, but which are important in their culture. The research example below provides such a compelling example.

Carraher and colleagues (1985, 1988) studied children aged between 9 and 15 years who were selling goods on the streets in Brazilian cities. These young vendors were performing complex mathematical problems (i.e., selling in bulk, accounting for daily changes in pricing due to inflation, and the lack of a pricing scheme that could be memorized), even in the absence of formal, school education. The researchers compared the young vendors' performance in two types of tasks: firstly on a familiar commercial transaction between a vendor and a customer, and secondly a similar mathematical problem presented as in school (using pen and paper). The findings highlighted significant differences between the young people's performances in the two tasks: on the familiar commercial transaction, the children were correct 98% of the time, whereas when the same problem was presented in the form of a school exercise, only 37% were able to provide the correct answer. This research provides a compelling example of the importance of the context for cognitive development.

Reflective point

The research studies below highlight the fact that in practice children's abilities may be underestimated because the appropriate context to test their cognitive skills is not provided.

➢ Critically reflect on how children and young people who fail in school might have their abilities underestimated. How could such situations be prevented?

➢ How could Vygotsky's ideas about the role of culture in development be used to understand children's development in a multicultural society such as ours?

Further reading

Carraher, T. N., Carraher, D. W. & Schliemann, A. D. (1985) Mathematics in the streets and in schools. *British Journal of Developmental Psychology*, 3(1), 21–29. doi: 10.1111/j.2044-835X.1985.tb00951.x.
Carraher, T. N., Schliemann, A. D. & Carraher, D. W. (1988) Mathematical concepts in everyday life. *New Directions for Child and Adolescent Development*, 1988(41), 71–87. doi: 10.1002/cd.23219884106.

The development of social cognition and 'theory of mind'

Vygotsky's ideas about the role of cultural and social factors in cognitive development have raised keen interest in studying how children learn from others and how children come to understand the thinking of other people. The field of study concerned with how children understand mental states is known as 'theory of mind' (often abbreviated as ToM).

A number of Piagetian concepts have been used as precursors in the study field of social cognition. For example the concept of object permanence is thought to be crucial in the development of differentiation of self from others. It has been argued that it is only in their second year of life that infants recognize themselves in the mirror (Amsterdam, 1972), which coincides with the achievement of object permanence as proposed by Piaget. Moreover the concept of child as being 'egocentric', unable to understand others' points of view, links in with the development of social cognition through to complex social understanding and reasoning which culminates in understanding other people's views and role taking.

Reflective point

➢ In light of the arguments presented in the articles listed in the 'Further reading' section below, reflect on the cross-cultural validity of the children's mirror recognition test.

Further reading

Amsterdam, B. (1972) Mirror image reactions before age two. *Developmental Psychobiology*, 5(4), 297–305. doi: 10.1002/dev.420050403.
Broesch, T., Callaghan, T., Henrich, J., Murphy, C. & Rochat, P. (2011) Cultural variations in children's mirror self-recognition. *Journal of Cross-Cultural Psychology*, 42(6), 1018–1029. doi: 10.1177/0022022110381114.

Theory of mind

Initial formulations of theory of mind (also known as ToM) explored how and when children understand the thinking of other people (Rosnay & Hughes, 2006). This has been investigated with a variety of experiments or 'false-belief tasks' (Wimmer & Perner, 1983). One of the most common and widely used is the 'Sally–Anne' task developed by Baron-Cohen and colleagues (1985, p. 41) and described as follows:

> There were two doll protagonists, Sally and Anne. First, we checked that the children knew which doll was which (Naming Question). Sally first placed a marble into her basket. Then she left the scene, and the marble was transferred by Anne and hidden in her box. Then, when Sally returned, the experimenter asked the critical Belief Question: 'Where will Sally look for her marble?'. If the children point to the previous location of the marble, then they pass the Belief Question by appreciating the doll's now false belief. If however, they point to the marble's current location, then they fail the question by not taking into account the doll's belief. These conclusions are warranted if two control questions are answered correctly: 'Where is the marble, really?' (Reality Question); 'Where was the marble in the beginning?' (Memory Question).
>
> (Baron-Cohen et al., 1985, p. 41)

Although there are noted variations across cultures in the development of theory of mind, the research is consistent in showing that the ability to understand others' minds is established during childhood (Harris et al., 1989). There is some evidence (McAlister & Peterson, 2007) suggesting that the presence of older siblings in the home can speed up the progression towards success in the false-belief task. However, there is consistent evidence that for children under the age of 3, and those diagnosed with autism, that the 'Sally–Anne' task is beyond their cognitive capacity.

Further reading

About investigating theory of mind in children with autism:

Baron-Cohen, S., Leslie, A. M. & Frith, U. (1985) Does the autistic child have a theory of mind'? *Cognition*, 21(1), 37–46.

Influence of siblings on theory of mind development:

McAlister, A. & Peterson, C. (2007) A longitudinal study of siblings and theory of mind development. *Cognitive Development*, 22(2), 258–270. doi: 10.1016/j. cogdev.2006.10.009.

More recent theory of mind research suggests that children as young as 3 to 4 years old are able to understanding other people's role and dispositions. For example, young children were able to notice when people were telling the truth, and use this information to decide on whom they base their trust (Koenig et al., 2004). These findings have potential implications for professionals involved in direct work with children: to foster a trusting relationship, young children need to be given truthful explanations regarding facts and decisions, at their level of understanding. The following views from a young person in care shows how perceptive young people are.

The voice of the child: Carrie, ex-foster child

> When I was taken into foster care after my mum took an overdose I knew that the woman I was placed with was lying to me when she said 'You'll just be here for a day or two – treat it as a holiday'. I was only five years old at the time and had been in foster care twice before and knew how long these things take – to a kid it feels like forever. I always knew as well when mum said a new bloke in our house was just her friend. I knew he would be in mummy's bed and that she wouldn't be bothered about me while he was on the scene. Adults need to know that young kids are canny in these things and know what's true. You just do.

Parents and carers with learning disabilities

Historical views were prejudiced against people with learning disabilities becoming parents and sterilization of young adult females, regardless of issues of consent, was commonplace (Campion, 1990). More recent policies of equal opportunities and anti-discrimination have led to people with learning disabilities living in the mainstream community rather than in institutional care and attitudes towards their right to parenthood have mellowed. Wharton and colleagues (2005) stated there is some association between intellectual ability and parenting capacity and that this is why many parents with learning disabilities come to the attention of children's social care. There has been a history in social work of focusing on a deficit, rather than a strengths, model (Saleebey, 1996), but there are signs that this situation is changing, despite the trend whereby the deaths of children known to social workers have led to significant increases in the numbers of children coming into care (Jones, 2014).

However, the UK evidence suggests that the changes in the percentages of children removed from the care of parents with learning disabilities has changed only slightly in recent practice – Booth and Booth (2004) stated that up to 40–60% of parents with learning disabilities had their children removed into alternative care, whereas Tarleton and colleagues' (2006) review estimated that some 50% of parents with learning disabilities have their children removed. There is a difficult balance for professionals to strike, between empowering learning disabled parents to live independently in the community and their children being protected from harm. There is conflicting evidence also about how much support is given to learning disabled parents, Booth and Booth (2004) having found that such parents rarely get any support, whereas Tarleton and colleagues' (2006) review is rather more positive regarding the emergence of appropriate support systems.

Various terms are used to describe the complexities inherent in the fields of learning disabilities – most commonly those of profound, mild, moderate and severe. Such categorizations are not always helpful, however, in promoting holistic approaches to learning disabilities. It should be noted that the use of the term 'learning difficulties' in the UK pertains more strictly to children and adults experiencing cognitive difficulties in terms of educational learning. The Royal College of Nursing (RCN, 2013) stress that learning disability is a common, lifelong condition which is neither an illness nor a disease. In clinical terms, diagnoses of learning disability have been based on having an impairment of intellectual functioning, typically an IQ below 70 (BPS, 2001), and the seminal policy paper 'Valuing People' (DoH, 2001) defines learning disability as being made up of three core criteria, namely significant impairment of intellectual functioning (usually taken as IQ < 70); significant impairment of adaptive/social functioning; and age of onset before adulthood.

For an individual to be given the diagnosis of learning disability, and hence perhaps become eligible or ineligible for services, they must meet all three criteria. These criteria are also those used in the White Paper 'Valuing People' (DoH, 2001), although a person's ability to function well and safely in the community is perhaps dependent more on the availability of familial and social support rather than IQ alone. However, some categorization of individual need is useful in the planning of services and interventions, and while it would be expected that individuals with learning disabilities would always be treated as people first, the terms 'mild', 'moderate', severe' and 'profound' are widely used at present. Hardie and Tilly (2012) articulate that that learning disability is a culturally determined, social construct, while acknowledging that some categorization can be helpful provided that the approach by social workers and others is a holistic one. Hardie and Tilly (2012, pp. 6–7) provide the following definitions:

> ➤ Profound learning disability – intelligence quotient (IQ) is estimated to be under 20 and therefore they have severely limited understanding. In addition, individuals may have multiple disabilities, which can include impairments of vision, hearing and movement, as well as other challenges such as epilepsy and autism. Most people in this group need support with mobility, and many have complex health needs requiring extensive support.

> ➤ Severe learning disability – people with a severe learning disability often use basic words and gestures to communicate their needs. Many need a high level of support with everyday activities such as cooking, budgeting, cleaning and shopping, but many can look after some, if not all, of their own personal care needs.

> ➤ Moderate learning disability – people with a moderate learning disability are likely to have some language skills which means they can communicate about their day-to-day needs and wishes. People may need some support with caring for themselves, but many will be able to carry out day-to-day tasks with support.

> ➤ Mild learning disability – a person who is said to have a mild learning disability is usually able to hold a conversation, and communicate most of their needs and wishes. They may need some support to understand abstract or complex ideas. People are often independent in caring for themselves and doing many everyday tasks.

Reflective point

Helen, student social worker, has been allocated two parents in their 20s, who both have mild learning disabilities. The couple are about to have their first child together.

> ➤ What would Helen need to know about the couple's cognitive abilities in order to best safeguard their forthcoming child?

> ➤ Where might she seek best advice on this issue?

McGaw and Sturmey (1993) have stated that professionals have difficulty in applying the standard forms of assessment of risk when parents have learning disabilities; this is due to problems being able to define what constitutes 'good enough' parenting. Any assessment that focuses on parents with learning disabilities and their ability to parent should take into consideration a number of factors. McGaw and Sturmey (1993) stated these assessments should not be based around IQ levels, or looking at any forms of written information, if an individual cannot read. Morris and colleagues (2007) argued that when doing an assessment it should be multi-professional and competency-based rather than IQ-based. Such assessments should take into account the level of cognition in the parents, and the aim of the assessment should be focused around what can be done to support the children and family, rather than the parents' inadequacies. Morris and Wates (2007) emphasized that parents should be allowed enough time to take into account what is being asked of them, rather than being rushed through any process, because of their often slower cognitive response abilities.

Wharton and colleagues (2005) argued that when assessing parenting capability, McGaw's Parent Assessment Manual should be used if possible (McGaw et al., 1998). This tool is a broad framework which guides professionals when using the Framework for the Assessment of Children and Families in Need (DoH, 2000). Gough and Stanley (2004) found that some professionals have been unsure about how to collate information, which is regrettable given that the use of this type of tool can help raise self-esteem in parents, and can clarify areas where support is needed, providing a common focus for parents and professionals.

Unfortunately, many of the families who are subject to intervention by social services are at the point of crisis, a crisis which could often be avoided if sufficient support and advocacy was put in place initially (McMillan, 2006). Morris and Wates (2007) point out that to enable parents with learning difficulties to feel empowered, and to also be protective, then the simple things should be tackled in the first instance – starting with clarity and level of information and communication. Frequent changes in personnel, and the conflicting advice given by different professionals, can be particularly difficult for a parent with learning disabilities to comprehend.

Case study – New parent with moderate learning disabilities

Helen, student social worker, is working with Joanne Cairncross, who is 19 years old and has moderate learning disabilities. She lives at home with her single mother, Iris Cairncross, 42 years, and her 12-year-old brother, Jason. Joanne has quite well-developed speech although she tends to repeat people's questions back to them

▶

◀

rather than answering any question: she is prone to temper tantrums if she does not get her favourite snacks or meals and she has had to have her mobile phone taken off her by Iris because unknown men were contacting her and asking her to send them photos of herself.

Joanne spends most of her days watching TV and has refused to attend college courses due to problems with bullying, especially about her weight. There had been an incident at her last college course 6 months ago when other students had shown her images of oral sex on their phone and asked her if she would like to suck one of the male student's 'lollipops'. Joanne said she would and gave oral sex to the male in question while her classmates filmed this on their mobile phones. The police were involved and a prosecution of the male perpetrator followed, but since that time Joanne has become reclusive, only going out occasionally to the local shops and neighbours' houses.

The family was amazed when, taking to her bed saying she had tummy ache, Joanne turned out to be in labour, her pregnancy not having been noticed by her mother or the wider family.

Joanne was unable to comprehend the 999 call to the ambulance service and the rush to hospital, and could tell no one how she became pregnant. She viewed her baby daughter, Skye-Leigh, as a little doll and, supported by her mother who said she would give up her part-time job to care for Skye-Leigh, insisted she wanted to keep the baby.

Task

➤ What reassurance might Helen seek that Joanne, as a mother, had sufficient cognitive ability to be able to keep Skye-Leigh from risk of significant harm over her first 3 months? It might be considered unfeasible to envisage Iris being on 24/7 duty.

➤ How might Helen draw up a working agreement with Joanne and Iris regarding the care of Skye-Leigh in a way that included Joanne?

➤ What levels of comprehension might Helen expect Joanne and her mother to have in respect of wider safeguarding throughout Skye-Leigh's wider childhood?

Exercise

Read the leaflet below which is based on one used by a Children's Social Care Department to inform parents about what is involved in child protection:

The aim of this leaflet is to give you some guidance about the purpose of Initial Child Protection Conferences, how they are organized and the possible outcomes. If you or your advocate wants to know more about the Safeguarding Children Board and how it works, you can get details from their website or ask your Social Worker. What are Child Protection Conferences? They are meetings to discuss children and young people where there are concerns that they may be at risk of significant harm and what steps can be taken to keep them safe. They are attended by parents or carers, family members and, depending on their age and understanding, the child or young person, as well as agencies who know your child or the family.

Who will attend the Conference?

Your child, as with all children, will be known to a number of professionals, such as teachers, police, health visitors, doctors or social workers. Information about your child will be shared by the agencies with you present, so a full picture of the concerns can be put together. Some of the key people you will know, but others you may not but they will have important information or knowledge useful to the meeting.

What is the purpose of the Conference?

The purpose of the Conference is to share all the relevant information about your child and your family, to consider whether your child is at risk of significant harm and, if so, how best to help. Only after a full discussion of the pertinent circumstances will any decision be made. Conference may recommend to Children's Services that legal action is taken to protect children.

Can I appeal against my child/ren being made subject of a Child Protection Plan?

The Child Protection Conference is not a court of law so technically there is no right of appeal against a decision to make your child the subject of a Child Protection Plan. You can, however, complain about the process or the decision of the Conference. Should you wish to complain, you can ask your social worker to tell you how to do this.

Are the discussions at the Conference confidential?

Yes. At the start of the meeting the Chair will remind those attending the Conference that all the information is confidential. The information will only be shared with the minimum number of people necessary for the protection of the child(ren).

Reflective point

➤ How helpful do you think the above leaflet would be to Joanne and Iris Cairncross in the preceding case study?

➤ How might you restructure this leaflet to take into account differences in cognitive levels within a range of families?

Looked-after children and educational outcomes

Recent government initiatives (e.g., DfE, 2014) have looked seriously at the problem of educational school achievement for looked-after children and report that educational attainment is clearly affected by placement stability and the emotional upheavals in foster children who are not in settled placements (defined as being in the same placement for a 12-month period). Exclusion levels are far higher again in looked-after children and the question arises whether it is the care system itself with its stigma, its changes of placements and social workers, the attitude of some educational staff about looked-after children, or is it the damage done to looked-after children before they enter the system that affects their cognitive abilities around memory and concentration or do the overwhelming emotions swamp any cognitive potential? The 'Virtual Head' (DfE, 2013) system was introduced in England with one person responsible for the educational attainment and school welfare for all looked-after children within the locus of an Education Authority. This system has been well received and there is some emergent evidence of success having been produced by this role according to Ofsted in respect of educational attainment, attendance and exclusions (Maddern, 2012).

Case study: The Kelly family

Helen, student social worker, is working with Paul Kelly, a 12-year-old looked-after child, who tells her he does not want to go to school anymore, threatening to run away (see Chapter 2 for more detail on the Kelly family). Helen tries to put herself in Paul's shoes, and thinks back to when she had just started secondary school – a time of anxiety, loss and anticipation. Paul tells her that, at a recent break time, an older boy told him his dad beat up Paul's dad in a pub the previous week, and was going to burn out the house where Paul's dad lived with Paul's mum, whom the older boy

▶

◀

called a 'whore'. Paul did not tell any school staff about this and has been so worried that he has got into trouble with teachers for not paying attention.

TASK

- How might a child's emotional state impact on their cognitive ability to learn in class?
- How might Helen best respond to Paul's situation?

If you can imagine such vignettes as the one above happening on a regular basis throughout a looked-after child's life, is it any wonder that looked-after children do not fare well in school settings? The reasons for this are very complex, however, but emotional factors are perhaps core. O'Higgins and colleagues (2015) conducted a systematic literature review of factors associated with the educational outcomes of children in the looked-after system, noting the complex interplay of some 80 different variables. Her findings were:

➤ Consistently lower educational outcomes are found in the older ranges of looked-after children.

➤ Boys tend to do worse than girls, with some exceptions.

➤ Children of minority ethnic groups (e.g., Black, Aboriginal) tended to do worse with some exceptions (e.g., Chinese).

➤ There is a very high prevalence of children in care with behavioural problems and these children tend to do worse.

➤ Placement instability was not consistently linked to worse outcomes.

➤ Overall, the longer the children spent in care, the worse their outcomes.

➤ High caregiver expectations and support were associated with better educational outcomes.

➤ Educational attainment of caregivers was not associated with the child's outcomes.

Reflective point

➤ Do any of above findings surprise you?

➤ Why do you think boys might fare worse than girls in educational terms?

The above findings about placement stability contradict received wisdom and government data, as well as contradicting research which indicate a strong correlation between parental education and children's educational attainment (Goodman & Gregg, 2010). What is evident is that the educational challenges facing looked-after children are considerably greater than those facing children outside of the system. Contemporary pressures in schools regarding attainment and league tables often mean that such children's emotional and pastoral needs are neglected.

The theoretical perspectives discussed above offer different views on understanding children's cognitive development, and continue to be highly influential in various areas of practice in working with children. By their very nature, theories of cognitive development are mostly applied in the learning and educational fields, but have great relevance to the field of social work with children and young people. At times offering competing views of how cognitive development happens, the perspectives discussed above build and complement each other in an attempt to offer a multifaceted view of development.

In the following section the focus will be upon memory as a cognitive process underpinning cognition. In light of recent research into children's memory, the implications for life-story work with children will be discussed.

Memory and life-story work with children

Understanding how memory develops is of crucial importance in understanding cognitive development: memory provides the knowledge that is processed through various cognitive processes. There are several types of memory identified.

Short-term memory – or working memory – is the conscious area of memory. The amount of information that a person can hold in short-term memory at any one time – memory span – is limited; but this limit changes with development. However, changes in short-term memory development can be interpreted differently: as simple capacity changes or changes that are influenced by the use of increasingly sophisticated strategies (such as interest or motivation or rehearsing strategies) that facilitate being able to hold more in the memory.

Long-term memory stores information and knowledge retained for long periods of time. Long-term memory includes the knowledge and facts a person possesses, called semantic memory, as well as knowledge of events, called episodic memory. The episodic memory is predominantly autobiographical in nature, including events and experiences lived by an individual.

Memory develops from infancy through the increased ability to use encoding processes, with young children creating scripts that help them remember what to do in a common occurrence situation or through the process of rehearsal (repeating information in order to remember it). Elaboration is another memory strategy that involves creating extra connections that can tie the information together for easier recall (such as using images).

Further reading

Infantile amnesia – how much children may really be storing in the first 3 years of life?

Howe, M. L. & Courage, M. L. (1993) On resolving the enigma of infantile amnesia. *Psychological Bulletin*, 113(2), 305–326. doi: 10.1037/0033-2909.113.2.305.

Autobiographical memory is of particular relevance to development as it stores knowledge about self and the events experienced through one's life. Autobiographical memory emerges in the early years (at about 2 years of age) and it develops substantially over childhood during family interactions in which parents also talk directly to children about the past or reminisce about the past in children's presence. Children begin to make contributions to this process of shared past from about the age of 3. Through such reminiscing and sharing memories within families, children acquire information about themselves, others and their social world knowledge which is crucial to the development of self – both historical and cultural self, which communicates cultural values to the child. Research has shown that family practices of personal storytelling and reminiscing occur in all types of families and cultures (Miller, 1995). The content of these conversations seems to emphasize the values salient in a particular culture. For example, Chinese children are believed to recall memories on social aspects of their lives, whereas American children recall more individual experiences and feelings (Wang, 2004).

Particular challenges are presented for the development of children who do not have shared memories and reminiscence, such as children who have been separated from their families, and adopted or fostered at an early age. For children with histories of early abuse and neglect, such memories may prove difficult to process and integrate in the child's sense of self because of their negative nature.

'Life-story work' is a practice intervention to support such children make sense of their past histories and experiences. It usually involves the development of a 'life-story book' prepared by the child with the support of an adult (social worker or foster carer/adoptive parent) in which the child records significant information and events such as the information about their birth family, significant people and events in their lives and their care history. However, recently life-story work has been expanded, and used with people in residential settings across the life course, and people with dementia.

Case study

Helen, student social worker, is working with Shane, who is 9 years old and has been in care since the age of 6, after a history of parental neglect and drug abuse. His mother and father have not contacted him for two years and, unbeknown to Shane, his mother has since had two more children with a different man. These two girls are also in care due to issues of neglect. Shane does not know about these half-sisters and neither does he know that his father is currently serving a 15-year jail sentence for the sexual exploitation of children on the internet. Shane is now asking more and more about his background and his foster carers do not know the right answers to give.

As a student social worker, Helen is not a specialist in life-story work, but has a colleague available to do such work. However, there is a waiting list for this specialist service and Shane seems to need answers now. How might Helen go about exploring what work she, and Shane's foster carers, might be able to carry out themselves?

Further reading

Baynes, P. (2008) Untold stories: A discussion of life story work. *Adoption & Fostering*, 32(2), 43–49. doi: 10.1177/030857590803200206.

Hussain, F. & Raczka, R. (1997) Life story work for people with learning disabilities. *British Journal of Learning Disabilities*, 25(2), 73–76. doi: 10.1111/j.1468-3156.1997.tb00014.x.

McKeown, J., Clarke, A. & Repper, J. (2006) Life story work in health and social care: Systematic literature review. *Journal of Advanced Nursing*, 55(2), 237–247. doi: 10.1111/j.1365-2648.2006.03897.x.

Summary

In this chapter, we explored some of the key theoretical perspectives in understanding cognitive development, such as Piaget's stage theory and Vygotsky's socio-cultural theory, including how 'theory of mind' develops and underpins children's understanding of the 'social world'. Various applications for practice in educational, social care, health and forensic settings have been highlighted, providing the reader with a platform to further explore these aspects. It is recommended that readers delve more deeply into the theoretical roots of psychology by reading textbooks such as those by Nicholson (2014) and Sudbery (2009).

Further resources

Lamb, M. E., La Rooy, D. J., Malloy, L. C. & Katz, C. (eds.). (2011). *Children's Testimony: A Handbook of Psychological Research and Forensic Practice.* Chichester: Wiley.

An edited volume bringing together research on children's testimony and practice on interviewing children.

Nunes, T., Schliemann, A. D. & Carraher, D. W. (1993). *Street Mathematics and School Mathematics.* New York: Cambridge University Press.

A classical text discussing the research on the role of culture in cognitive development.

Rogoff, B. (2003). *The Cultural Nature of Human Development.* New York: Oxford University Press.

This book analyses patterns of similarities and differences across many cultural communities in children's opportunities to participate in activities and the role of such participation in children becoming competent members of their community.

Web resources concerning parents with intellectual disabilities:

www.intellectualdisability.info/families/parents-with-intellectual-learning-disabilities (Accessed: 30 January 2018)
www.bristol.ac.uk/media-library/sites/sps/migrated/documents/rightsupport-summary.pdf (Accessed: 30 January 2018)

4

Social development: From childhood to adolescence

Key learning outcomes

Following the study of this chapter, successful learners will have an understanding of:

➤ The main contemporary theories of adolescent development.

➤ The role of peer relationships in adolescence.

➤ How these psychological theories and research can be applied to settings in social work.

Introduction

This chapter will review contemporary theories on social development through childhood and adolescence, and their relevance for social work practice with young people. Major themes in adolescent development will be explored, such as peer and romantic relationships, identity formation (including ethnic and gender identity), the pressures of contemporary media and social networking. The particular relevance of these theories for working with adolescents living in substitute forms of parental care, such as foster care, will be examined in detail. The issues will also be explored from a cross-cultural perspective as applicable.

Case study: Darren

Jennie Izon, foster carer, has told Helen, student social worker, the following information about Darren, her foster child, aged 15 years:

Over the past 12 months, Darren has seemed to get in with the 'wrong crowd'. It started with him spending a lot of time with friends outside school and being secretive

▶

> ◄
>
> about who these friends were. Jennie suspected that these outings involved heavy alcohol consumption and Darren appeared to bring home new, luxurious objects that he would not have the means to buy – such as new smartphones and designer clothes. When not with 'friends', Darren would spend a lot of time online and on social media such as Facebook.
>
> Jennie is rather uneasy about these observations but is unsure what to make of them.

Task

> ➤ How might Helen best advise Jennie? – Are Darren's behaviours mentioned above any cause of concern or they are just normative risk-taking behaviour? Argue your position with reference to relevant theoretical perspectives.

Adolescence is the period of transition bridging childhood and adulthood, largely covering the teenage years. Biologically marked by the onset of puberty, the period of adolescence comprises changes across multiple domains of development, biologically and neurologically as well as psychosocially. These changes include growth spurts, body fat and muscle development; sexual development of both primary and secondary sex characteristics; and brain development, especially brain-matter growth (Fuhrmann et al., 2015). Much attention has been paid to how physical changes in adolescence induce psychological and behavioural effects. For example, puberty is brought about by hormonal changes which in turn can activate behavioural effects, such as increased emotional distance from parents and adolescent autonomy, parent–child conflict, moodiness and aggression.

Adolescence: 'Storm and stress'?

Overall, adolescence can be construed as a developmental period of reorganization at the biological, psychological, social and cognitive processes level, enabling children to transform into young adults. The beginning of the twentieth century saw the emergence of adolescence as a field of study, with the beginning marked by Hall's work (1904), one of the first theorists to study adolescence. Hall considered adolescence to be a time of crisis and emotional and behavioural upheaval, and he coined the popular phrase of adolescence as a time of 'storm and stress'. This view was later criticized, when research findings challenged the view of adolescence as a crisis. For example, Rutter and colleagues (1976) argued that the myth of adolescent turmoil emerged from clinically biased studies, whose findings which are not replicated in community samples.

Further reading

A critical review of the original work around adolescence storm and stress:

Arnett, J. J. (2006) G. Stanley Hall's adolescence: brilliance and nonsense. *History of psychology*, 9(3), 186. doi: 10.1037/1093-4510.9.3.186.

Rutter and colleagues' seminal study which paved the way to considering adolescence as a normal transition:

Rutter, M., Graham, P., Chadwick, O. F. & Yule, W. (1976) Adolescent turmoil: fact or fiction? *Journal of Child Psychology and Psychiatry*, 17(1), 35–56. doi: 10.1111/j.1469-7610.1976.tb00372.x.

Nevertheless, complaints about adolescents' behaviour 'getting worse' have been and continue to be around in common perception. A potential interpretation of such concerns may be found in epidemiological studies showing trends of mental health problems increasing in adolescent populations since the 1980s, both in the UK (Maughan et al. 2008) and, to a lesser extent, in the USA. However, the factors underlying such time trends in child and adolescent mental health are largely unknown (Maughan et al., 2008).

Brain and cognitive development

Recent developments in cognitive neuroscience have made important contributions to our understanding of both social and cognitive development in adolescence. For example, changes in brain structure affect emotion regulation, response inhibition and planning. Maturation of the brain continues until the mid-20s in most individuals, resulting in advances in abstract reasoning, metacognitive thinking, decision-making, working memory and response inhibition. However, it is important to note that the development of the brain occurs in an irregular, uneven pattern, and as the brain is still developing, adolescent emotional regulation is not yet fully mature. For example, the main changes in the prefrontal cortex during adolescence include:

➢ Increased functional connectivity, referring to the way in which various parts of the brain activate together in the performance of a task.

➢ Synaptic pruning, the process of eliminating extra and weak or poorly developed synapses.

➣ Myelination increases, making speed of processing faster and enabling brain networks to interact more efficiently.

In terms of cognitive development, adolescence coincides with Piaget's period of formal operational thought, with adolescents being increasingly able to think about abstract issues and hypothetical situations. The transition to using abstract thought sees an increase in argumentativeness, self-consciousness, idealism and difficulty in making everyday decisions, and these can be observed as adolescent behaviours.

Elkind (1967) suggested that a kind of 'egocentrism' appears in adolescence, illustrated by observations that adolescents often imagine how they would appear to an 'imaginary audience' and some adolescents become bound up or obsessed with their own feelings, constructing a 'personal fable', an imaginary story of their own life.

Further reading

Elkind, D. (1967) Egocentrism in adolescence. *Child Development*, 38(4), 1025–1034. doi: 10.2307/1127100.

Oda, A. Y. (2007) David Elkind and the crisis of adolescence: review, critique, and applications. *Journal of Psychology & Christianity*, 26(3), 251–256.

Schwartz, P., Maynard, A., & Uzelac, S. (2008) Adolescent egocentrism: a contemporary view. *Adolescence*, 43(171), 441–448.

Accessible syntheses of brain development during adolescence:

Dumontheil, I. (2016) Adolescent brain development. Current opinion. *Behavioral Sciences*, 10, 39–44. doi.org/10.1016/j.cobeha.2016.04.012.

Fuhrmann, D., Knoll, L. J., & Blakemore, S. J. (2015) Adolescence as a sensitive period of brain development. *Trends in Cognitive Sciences*, 19(10), 558–566. doi: 10.1016/j.tics.2015.07.008.

Risk factors for brain development in adolescence:

Castellanos-Ryan, N., Pingault, J. B., Parent, S., Vitaro, F., Tremblay, R. E. & Séguin, J. R. (2017) Adolescent cannabis use, change in neurocognitive function, and high-school graduation: a longitudinal study from early adolescence to young adulthood. *Development and Psychopathology*, 29(4), 1253–1266. doi.org/10.1017/S0954579416001280.

Squeglia, L. M., Tapert, S. F., Sullivan, E. V., Jacobus, J., Meloy, M. J., Rohlfing, T. & Pfefferbaum, A. (2015) Brain development in heavy-drinking adolescents. *American Journal of Psychiatry*, 172(6), 531–542. https://dx.doi.org/10.1176%2Fappi.ajp.2015.14101249.

Whittle, S., Lichter, R., Dennison, M., Vijayakumar, N., Schwartz, O., Byrne, M. & Allen, N. B. (2014) Structural brain development and depression onset during adolescence: a prospective longitudinal study. *American Journal of Psychiatry*, 171(5), 564–571. https://doi.org/10.1176/appi.ajp.2013.13070920.

Reflective point

> What might be the implications of the notion of 'adolescence ego-centrism' for adolescents growing up separated from their parents and cared for in foster or residential care?

Many children in the care system develop their own life narratives to fit in with peers. For example, fostered children will ask their foster carer to pretend to be their gran or aunty, and will construct narratives for themselves and peers regarding their backgrounds. These backgrounds might involve a father who has an important overseas job, which is why he is never seen with the child, or an elder sibling who is a high-flying business person. The egocentrism of vulnerable adolescents who may also have experienced a life of rejection makes them particularly vulnerable to sexual predators, as evidenced in England's child sexual exploitation scandals (e.g., Jay, 2014). Grooming of such vulnerable young people is made easier by their reaction to being told how attractive they are and how much they are loved and appreciated by men whose only goal is to abuse and exploit such young egos, sometimes for financial gain.

Attachment in adolescence: From parents to peers

A critical developmental task in adolescence is to achieve the transition from reliance on parents as attachment figures to functioning with greater emotional, social and practical autonomy from parents. Traditional beliefs of adolescents' purposeful flight away from their attachment with parents have been replaced in past decades to the realization that successful autonomy in adolescence is not achieved at the expense of the relationships with parents, but supported by a secure attachment with them (Allen & Land, 1999). The relationships with parents are likely to sustain well into adulthood for most young people.

Longitudinal studies on adolescence (Allen et al., 1994, 1998) support the idea of this gradual change. Indeed, by early adolescence, friends, teachers and other people with whom the child is close may be used as 'secure-base' figures in specific contexts (Waters & Cummings, 2000). Thus it is of crucial importance to take into consideration multiple attachment relationships that adolescents experience both within and outside the family (e.g., in school or care settings).

In adolescence and adulthood, a person's attachment is conceptualized as a mental representation of self and relationships based on experiences with several 'attachment figures' over time (Armsden & Greenberg, 1987; Bartholomew & Horowitz, 1991; Hazan & Shaver, 1987). There is a lack of systematic investigation of the relationships children and adolescents have with non-family adult figures to whom they may become attached, especially in the case of young people who might use such 'parent surrogates' (Ainsworth, 1991) and which may include an older sibling or other relative within the family, such as grandparents, or a supportive teacher.

Reflective point: Conflict with parents – myth or reality?

A commonly held stereotype about adolescence is that, in this period, families are plagued by persistent and often intense conflict between parent(s) and their adolescent children.

> ➤ In your experience – personal and or observed in others – is this the case?

Recent studies show that parents and younger adolescent children actually agree on many things and that often areas of disagreement can be exaggerated. There is, however, agreement on a general decline in emotional closeness to parents in adolescence, and an increase in conflicts which may be over a range of issues, but mainly concerning boundaries and discipline. Often, such conflicts can be explained by the different points of view that parents and adolescents take in relation to an issue – for example, conflicts around household chores; parents may see these as matters of social convention, but adolescents often view them as being issues of personal autonomy.

Cross-cultural perspectives on adolescence

Adolescence is not a universally accepted term, or even a life stage. In some cultures and societies, children enter adulthood directly through a ritual or 'rite of passage'. Moreover, different cultures contrast in their treatment of adolescents. For example, initial evidence supporting this came from a seminal anthropological study; Mead (1928) reported adolescence in traditional Samoan society as being easy and without turmoil, thus the antithesis of the 'storm and stress' notion in Western societies.

A particular focus in the UK has been on forced marriages among certain Asian communities, this traditional custom being resisted by westernized young people who wish to assert their own choice of marriage partner rather than have such unions forced upon them by their families. In 2014 the UK introduced new legislation regarding forced marriage as part of the *Anti-social Behaviour, Crime and Policing Act*; there was only one successful prosecution in its first three years of operation even though the government's Forced Marriage Unit issued 246 Forced Marriage Protection Orders in 2016 (Dodd, 2017).

The UK government's Forced Marriage Unit estimate that 80% of the cases they become involved with concerned young women and 20% young men (Dodd, 2017). Young women and young men who resist the cultural practice of arranged marriage (with its associated forms of consent), or who seek boyfriends/girlfriends and spouses from other ethnic backgrounds, have been either 'forced' into such marriages or ostracized and even murdered by their families. 'Honour killings' is the unfortunate phrase sometimes used to describe such situations. There is, however, nothing honourable about such criminal practices, which transgress criminal law and ignore the rights and welfare of children and young people.

In certain parts of the UK, social workers specialize in this type of safeguarding work, and there are some limited counselling/accommodation services available – the NSPCC estimated that over 200 counselling sessions took place in 2015/16 in respect of fear of forced marriage (Dodd, 2017). Forced marriages exemplify the challenges of diverse communities, and present psychological and physical dangers to young women which are very challenging for both psychologists and social workers.

Regan and colleagues (2012) noted, that in many modern arranged marriages there is the possibility of using a 'veto', by which a prospective partner might be able to refuse a chosen spouse, such a hybrid model of arranged marriages perhaps reflecting more the realities and westernized aspirations of young people today regarding self-determination. Research in this culturally sensitive area is particularly problematic, given cultural pressures and consequences for research participants, who may be viewed as transgressing cultural norms. Chantler and colleagues (2009) note that research studies have taken place across many different countries and cultures, thus making firm conclusions difficult to establish, especially regarding the psychological consequences of both arranged and forced marriages. They make a persuasive case for greater nuancing of the debate and definitions of forced marriage due to its complex and multidimensional nature.

Reflective point

> What type of counselling services might be most effective for young women and men at risk of being forced into marriage?

> What would be the particular challenges for such services and who do you think is best placed to provide such services?

> Should the service providers come exclusively from cultures where forced marriages are the cultural norm, or might staff with different cultural backgrounds also be effective?

Further reading

Chantler, K., Gangoli, G. & Hester, M. (2009) Forced marriage in the UK: religious, cultural, economic or state violence. *Critical Social Policy*, 29(4): 587–612. https://doi.org/10.1177/0261018309341905.

Dodd, V. (2017) NSPCC reports large rise in forced marriage counselling for children. *The Guardian*, 30 July. www.theguardian.com/society/2017/jul/30/nspcc-reports-large-rise-rise-in-forced-marriage-counselling-for-children (Accessed: 21 January 2018).

Regan, P., Lakhanpal, S. & Anguiano, C. (2012) Relationship outcomes in Indian-American love-based and arranged marriages. *Psychological Reports*, 110(3): 915–924. doi:10.2466/21.02.07.PR0.110.3.915–924.

The importance of peers in adolescence

Research on adolescent autonomy processes (Allen & Land, 1999) suggests that increasing autonomy from parents during this period creates 'healthy' pressure to use peers as 'attachment figures', ensuring that their attachment needs are met during this process of establishing autonomy in relationships with parents.

From this perspective, adolescence may be viewed as a period in which attachment needs are gradually transferred to peers, so that by mid-adolescence interactions with peers begin to take on functions such as the provision of sources of support, intimacy, social influence and, ultimately, attachment relationships (Markiewicz et al., 2001). Often, by late adolescence, long-term relationships can be formed, in which peers (both as close friends and romantic partners) serve as 'attachment figures', providing the needed emotional resources, role models and self-esteem support (Cassidy et al., 1996; Felsman & Blustein, 1999).

Research that has examined attachments in adolescent peer relationships suggests that the nature of peer attachment relationships derives from prior attachment relationships with parents as well as from prior relationships with peers. As discussed in Chapter 2, attachment towards parents forms the blueprint for all further relationships. There is research suggesting that there is a correlation between the quality of attachment towards parents and peers, and that this relationship is manifest both in infancy (Fagot, 1997) and in childhood (McElwain et al., 2008). Children who were assessed as having secure attachments towards parents tend to have more confident interaction with peers and thus higher quality friendships with peers. There is also some evidence suggesting that not only can infants and children form relationships with other children, but that these relationships resemble attachment relationships in the absence of parents. Such evidence comes from studies of children brought up in orphanages, where it appears that, given the lack of opportunities to form attachments towards adult figures, peers become 'substitute' attachment figures (Freud & Dann, 1951; Kaler & Freeman, 1994; Misca, 2014a).

Reflective point

> Can children who have not made secure attachments to adults make strong attachments to peers?

Further reading

Freud, A. & Dann, S. (1951) An experiment in group upbringing. *Psychoanalytic Study of the Child,* 6: 127–168.

In this classic study, Anna Freud and Sophie Dann document the peer attachment demonstrated by children who were orphaned in World War II and lived in group care nurseries.

Kaler, S. R. & Freeman, B. J. (1994) Analysis of environmental deprivation: cognitive and social development in Romanian orphans. *Journal of Child Psychology and Psychiatry,* 35: 769–781. doi: 10.1111/j.1469-7610.1994.tb01220.x.

In a unique 'natural experiment' Kaler and Freeman document a group of children raised in orphanages in Romania. Although the majority were severely delayed in cognitive and social functioning, the children's greatest capability was in peer social interaction.

Development of peer relationships from childhood into adolescence

As early as infancy there are apparent signs of 'social encounters' whereby babies respond to each other's behaviour. The initial interactions of infants manifest as imitating each other: before 6 months a baby may cry in response to other babies' crying, and in tandem with the development of their motor skills they will imitate each other's behaviours. Gradually the imitation becomes mutual, creating the sense that they are having fun together. With the emergence of language, which allows coordination of activities and use of symbols, children begin to use pretend or make-believe play, which is claimed to be of crucial importance in child development by enhancing children's social skills and enabling them to express and explore their feelings (Dunn, 2004). In early childhood children begin to show preferences for particular playmates, and gender begins to play an important role in peer preference: after the age of 3 to 4 years gender segregation seems to occur and children show distinct preference for same-gender playmates, whereas older children will favour cross-gender interactions.

As children acquire gradual competence in interaction with peers, they also show a distinct preference for playing with peers rather than adults, although they might imitate adult behaviours. Pretend or make-believe play refers to children's play in which they take on different identities and re-enact roles observed in the real world (such as pretend family or pretend visits to the doctors) or imaginary ones such as acting out of stories.

Further reading

Pretend play has been claimed to be crucial to children's healthy development. The article below examines the evidence for this position:

Lillard, A. S., Lerner, M. D., Hopkins, E. J., Dore, R. A., Smith, E. D. & Palmquist, C. M. (2013) The impact of pretend play on children's development: A review of the evidence. *Psychological Bulletin*, 139(1): 1–34. doi:10.1037/a0029321.

The peer group influences child development through the same processes as parents do: modelling, reinforcement and opportunities for learning and socializing. Peers act as social models and children learn from observing the actions of their peers (modelling). Children also reinforce – positively and negatively – the behaviours of their peers by praising or criticizing their behaviour. Illustrated by the well-known concept of 'peer pressure', peers can be a very convincing force in engaging in risk-taking and delinquent behaviour. However, peers can be a wealthy source of learning opportunities, particularly those that are within the 'zone of proximal development' (as discussed in Chapter 3). This is apparent in school games and sports activities, and in certain cultures older peers teach and act as caregivers of younger children (Rogoff, 2003).

Friendships develop with the emergence of a clear preference for specific playmates, albeit at this stage the friendships are based on less sophisticated criteria such as enjoying the same play activities rather than trustworthiness, which becomes important in friendship at later ages. As children develop friendships some of them will be rejected or rejecting others, thus acquiring a *social status* (the individual's accept- ance or rejection within his/her peer group) aspect which becomes par- ticularly salient during school years. Research has examined the factors that influence the social status of children in an attempt to understand what makes some children popular while others are rejected or simply neglected within the peer groups. Research has shown that popular chil- dren are seen as more helpful and cooperative, while rejected children tend to be aggressive or depressive and withdrawn or socially unskilled (Dunn, 2004). However, aggressiveness per se may not necessarily result in rejection. For example, 'antisocial popular' individuals are seen as aggressive but also 'cool', which attracts a high status within certain peer groups.

Reflective point: Friendships in multicultural societies

Recent decades have seen a rapid increase in immigration across Europe. For immigrant children, an important aspect of acculturation and adapt- ing to their new country and culture will be the friendships they make in their school and neighbourhood.

➤ What factors might influence a successful friendship? (For example, language proficiency and attitudes on both sides).

➤ What might be the advantages associated with inter-ethnic friendships on both sides?

Overall, peer group rejection has been associated with difficulties in adulthood; however, these effects may be mediated by the individual's rejection sensitivity. A child with high rejection sensitivity may be more prone to interpret peers' responses to them as hostile and become angry or anxious in their dealings with peers, which creates a circle perpetuating the child's rejection that the child comes to expect. Thus rejection-sensitive children may benefit from interventions helping them to control their responses to their peers and interpret their peers' reaction in a less threatening manner.

Bullying

Bullying is usually considered to be aggressive behaviour characterized by an imbalance of power and repetition (Olweus, 1994), and has been defined as a systematic abuse of power. Different forms of bullying have been identified including:

> 'Traditional' forms of bullying: physical, verbal as well as relational bullying.

> 'Identity-based bullying': gender-based bullying, racist bullying, disability bullying, homophobic bullying.

> 'Cyberbullying': bullying using electronic devices, mainly mobile phones and the internet. Cyberbullying has become prevalent since the 1990s and has, as distinctive features, the extent of audience and the anonymity of those committing the bullying.

Bullying can happen in many contexts but research on school bullying has been a focus of attention since the early 1980s, with longitudinal research highlighting the negative consequences bullying can have for victims' self-esteem and mental well-being (Takizawa et al., 2014). The growth in knowledge about understanding its causes and identifying bullying has led to the development of interventions to prevent bullying as well as supporting victims (Merrell et al., 2008).

Different causal factors have been identified, including societal, community, school and peer group factors, as well as individual factors. For example, individuals committing the bullying may lack certain abilities such as social skills or empathy while factors affecting the victims of bullying may include their temperament, social skills, friendship status or having a disability. It is important to also note that there can be interactions among these factors.

Case study: Angeline

Helen, student social worker, is working with Angeline, a 12-year-old in long-term foster care with single gay carer, Jane Goulding. How could knowledge of the roles of peer relationships help Helen understand the behaviour of Angeline in the case scenario below?

Angeline's brother, Ronnie, lives separately with his foster carers, Mr and Mrs Prag. Contact with Angeline's birth parents, and with Ronnie, is patchy and she is often let down with contact arrangements. Angeline had to change schools when she went into foster care, and has always been careful to keep it a secret that she is fostered.

She has told schoolmates that Jane is her aunty and that her parents both work abroad for long periods.

Up until the past month Angeline has been happy for Jane to drop her off at the school gates but now insists that Jane drops her off every morning a few streets away from her school, so that her peers do not see her with Jane. Two weeks ago Angeline had got into a scuffle with some other girls over a mobile phone, which subsequently went missing. This phone had previously always been 'glued' to Angeline, but now she has told Jane she does not want a replacement as they are just used for 'stupid' things. Angeline has also begun to spend increasing amounts of time in her bedroom alone, only coming down for meals.

Task

During a visit by Helen to the foster home, while Angeline was in her bedroom, Jane mentioned the above behavioural changes.

➢ What advice might Helen give to Jane in respect of normative social development and the risks present to young people today, particularly from social media/cyberbullying?

➢ How could knowledge of the role of peer relationships help Helen and Jane understand the behaviour of Angeline in the case scenario?

Peers and risk-taking behaviours

Adolescents coming into contact with social workers are likely to come from difficult family circumstances, have strained parent–child relationships and thus may look outside the family for a sense of belonging and identity as well as identify social gains from becoming involved with peer groups/gangs that bring personal benefits. Adolescents spend more time with peers and increasingly look to them for social support as they become less dependent on their families. There is more fear of rejection by peers, and the presence of peers may reinforce risk-taking behaviour, although there is also an increasing potential for autonomy and resistance to peer influence. Some degree of deviant or risk-taking behaviour is quite common in adolescence, and peer groups may reinforce risk-taking behaviour.

Decker and Van Winkle (1996) identified both 'push' and 'pull' factors in leading young people, primarily male, to join gangs. There are no agreed definitions of what constitutes a 'gang', but there is perhaps a distinction to be made between 'groups' of young people who band together for friendship and solidarity as compared to 'gangs', the common perception of which might be a street-based group of young people engaged in crime and anti-social behaviour (Fitch, 2009). Decker and Van Winkle (1996) identified that 'pulls' related to social, economic and cultural forces in terms of the gang's opportunities for prestige and status. Criminally oriented gangs can also provide income in socio-economic backgrounds where opportunities in the job market may be low or non-existent. 'Push' factors might include the need for a sense of identity (Vigil & Long, 1990) or a safe haven in which to ride out the storm and stress of adolescence. Fraser (2010) urges caution not to pathologize youth gangs, noting the potential of their role in social development and pointing out that membership may only constitute one part of a young person's identity. Much of the literature on gangs is from the USA (e.g., Decker & Van Winkle, 1996). The culture of territorial and criminal gangs in the USA (e.g., The Cripps and The Bloods) is more established than in the UK, where subcultures ('Mods and Rockers', 'Skinheads'), rather than gangs, began to appear among youth in the post-World War II years, as young people sought freedom of expression. However, in more recent years, gangs in the UK have perhaps grown closer to the US model in terms of criminality, knife crime and involvement in the drug trade in certain cities. The UK government policy regarding gangs has been based on a tough regime of sanctioning and law enforcement (e.g., *Tackling violence action plan. Saving lives. Reducing harm. Protecting the public. An action plan for tackling violence 2008–11* [HM Government, 2008]). Such a stance reflects growing political concern regarding high-profile criminal gangs like Birmingham's 'Burger Boys' and 'Johnson Crew', with UK policies placing law enforcement agencies in the lead roles with UK gangs. The NSPCC have criticized the UK's punitive approach to gangs in the UK (Fitch, 2009), and have called for a more holistic approach to the issues involved in young people joining gangs. Such an approach is partly evidenced in *Ending gang violence and exploitation* (HM Government, 2016), a policy document which acknowledged the vulnerabilities of young people being preyed upon by gangs for purposes of sexual exploitation and selling drugs.

Reflective point

The NSPCC (Fitch, 2009) have suggested that the UK response to gangs has concentrated on punishment rather than on holistic approaches to the problem.

➤ Do you think that policies should adopt approaches that consider the problems young people face rather than the risks they pose?

➤ How would you devise a programme that would encourage young people to take up services which addressed their psychological challenges?

➤ To what extent do you think psychological approaches might be effective against socio-economic backgrounds of poverty, joblessness and cuts to public services?

Further reading

Bellis, M., Hughes, K., Anderson, Z., Tocque, K. & Hughes, S. (2008) Contribution of violence to health inequalities in England: demographics and trends in emergency admissions for assault. *Journal of Epidemiology and Public Health*, 62 (July): 1064–1071. doi:10.1136/jech.2007.071589.
Bennett, T. & Holloway (2004) Gang membership, drugs and crime in the UK. *British Journal of Criminology*, 44(3), 305–323. doi: 10.1093/bjc/azh025.
Fitch, K. (2009) Teenagers at risk: the safeguarding needs of young people in gangs and violent groups. www.nspcc.org.uk/globalassets/documents/research-reports/teenagers-at-risk-report.pdf (Accessed: 18 January 2018).

Emergence of intimacy and adolescent romantic relationships

The emergence of intimacy and romantic relationships are seen as normative aspects of development in adolescence and early adulthood. Generally, intimate relationships in adolescence are seen as transient and superficial but nevertheless they are important in adolescents' lives and play a crucial role in shaping the adolescent's development. For example, romantic and intimate relationships play an important role in shaping the identity.

Collins (2003) suggested there are five aspects of adolescents' romantic relationships; these include:

➢ involvement – the timing and duration of such relationships

➢ partner selection – characteristics of preferred partners

➢ content – what kind of shared activities were engaged in

➢ quality – aspects such as intimacy, affection and nurturance

➢ cognitive and emotional processes.

Romantic relationships in adolescence and memories of 'first love' are often a positive feature of development in adolescence. However, there can be a 'dark side' to romantic relationships, as recent research has highlighted young people's experiences of 'dating' violence and abuse. For example, US research studies found a high prevalence of teenage partner violence (Jackson et al. 2000; Hickman et al. 2004) and it is suggested that this is often bilateral (Roberts et al., 2005), although girls are more likely to be the victims of serious physical and sexual violence than boys (Arriaga & Foshee, 2004) and the impact of violence appears to be greater on girls than on boys (Sears et al., 2006).

The limited number of UK studies on teenage domestic violence confirms its significant negative impact on young people's well-being (Hird, 2000); despite this the research showed that the young people affected by teenage dating violence do not feel that professionals are taking these issues seriously or responding appropriately (Barter et al., 2009).

The development of the self: Identity development

The term identity refers to an organized sense of self, which includes personal beliefs, goals, values and commitments. Erikson (1956) argued that, while identity is developed and transformed throughout life, adolescence is the time when most advance in this area is made, with adolescents seeking to develop a self-identity and a sense of their role in society. Erikson's term of 'identity crisis' refers to the intense exploration of potential and at times conflicting identities during adolescence. Failure to achieve a coherent and satisfying identity may lead to confusion about their adult roles – hence the term 'identity crisis'. Erikson's ideas were based on his own observations and were tested against empirical findings.

Case study

Helen, student social worker, is working with a 15-year-old foster child, Jaime, who has been displaying aggressive behaviours at school and in his foster home. His foster carers, Joanne and Fred Smith, say that he has occasionally shouted out at them that he does not belong there as they are white and he is dark-skinned. Helen discovered that, in the multiple moves Jaime had experienced in care, nobody ever seemed to have talked with Jaime about issues of colour and that the foster carers knew nothing about his heritage.

Helen delved into Jaime's extensive file and found that Jaime's mother was aged 15 when she gave birth to him and that his father was of African-Caribbean descent. His mother was white. In his permanency plan, however, Helen noted that a mixed ethnic couple had been sought, ideally on an adoption basis, to provide Jaime with the appropriate support towards meeting his cultural needs. No adoptive parents had ever been found, however, and the cultural matching issue seemed to have dropped off the agenda as Jaime moved between a series of foster homes.

Mr Smith recalled:

At around the age of 11 Jaime was very upset and for a period of time refused to go to school. After several attempts to understand what was going on, he told us that other children in school made cruel remarks based on his skin colour and the fact that we are both white and he is of mixed ethnicity. He always insisted that we do not tell school that he is not our child. We thought that it is just a phase and it will pass ... children can be cruel like that when they grow up.

Task

> In light of the information discovered by Helen, how might Jaime's behaviour be interpreted and what steps might Helen and the foster carers take to help with Jaime's distress?

Ethnic and racial identity

Marcia (1980) developed a model of identity involving two dimensions: exploration and commitment. He developed an interview technique to assess 'identity status' and described it in four stages: diffusion, foreclosure, moratorium and achievement, although some later studies suggest movement to and fro between moratorium and achievement. Identity diffusion characterizes an individual who has not yet begun to engage in the process of identity formation, and has neither explored goals, values and beliefs nor made commitments to them. The identity foreclosure is the status of an individual who has made commitments without exploring goals, values and beliefs – for example, this status characterizes individuals in traditional or religious close-knit cultures, where a young person takes on the identity of their group or parents without questioning it. Identity moratorium is the status of an individual who is in the process of exploring goals, values and beliefs but has not yet made commitments to them. Identity achievement is the status of an individual who has explored goals, values and beliefs and made commitments to them.

Ethnic identity refers to the social identity derived from membership in a particular ethnic group. Building on Marcia's ego identity statuses, Phinney (1989) proposed three stages of ethnic identity formation:

> **Unexamined ethnic identity** – conceptualized as either *diffusion* (referring to a lack of interest in ethnicity) or *foreclosure* (referring to ethnicity based on the views of others)

> **Ethnic identity search** – equivalent of identity *moratorium*

> **Achieved ethnic identity**.

Racial identity is the identity associated with membership in a group based on a socially constructed designation of race.

Adolescent immigrants show four possible patterns of identification:

> Integration: strong identification with both cultures

> Assimilation: strong identification with the mainstream culture

> Separation: strong affiliation with the culture of origin

> Marginalization: weak identification with both cultures.

Radicalization and identity crisis in adolescents

Radicalization of young people in the UK and worldwide has become a serious concern, and there exist arguments similar to those above regarding why young people join gangs. Joining a group at a mosque or joining with like-minded friends and then going abroad to Syria or Afghanistan to join Jihadist fighters might be seen as a rational choice to seek a different way of life, a way that offers more to individuals in areas of the UK where jobs and educational prospects are poor. Alternatively, it might be the case that individuals are vulnerable psychologically, possibly because of a lack of secure attachments, or possibly because they are seeking validation and status which cannot be found within their families. The UK Government's strategy on anti-radicalization, the *Prevent Strategy* (HM Government, 2011) drew much criticism. This criticism (e.g., O'Toole et al., 2016) holds that the atmosphere brought about by the surveillance and reporting culture in schools, universities, workplaces and in the wider community adds to feelings of alienation and discrimination. Such outcomes can increase the numbers of young people who become radicalized and therefore make our communities less, rather than more, safe.

Case study

In the 'Further resources' section at the end of the chapter, you will find details of the *Prevent Strategy* (HM Government, 2011) and the revised *Prevent Duty* (HM Government, 2015). Please read these and then consider the following:

Imagine you are a university student on a social work course and your friend on the same course mentions her concerns that her 17-year-old unemployed brother, Ali, has begun wearing military-style clothes and attending very frequently a mosque some miles away, never having previously attended the mosque. Your friend also mentions that he has been very abusive to her recently, calling her a 'slag' for wearing make-up and skirts rather than traditional Muslim clothing. You advise that she should have a word with her father and mother in the first instance, as this may just be part of his adolescence.

Reflective point

➢ Do you think your advice was adequate and in accordance with the above guidance?

➢ How did you balance concerns for what might be a vulnerable person with the civic responsibilities inherent in the 'Prevent' advice?

Sexual identity

Sexual identity refers to a sense of self as heterosexual, bisexual, homosexual (gay or lesbian), transgender or 'curious' about a blend of sexualities. Since the 1980s researchers have specifically explored the processes of homosexual identity formation. Several models have been put forward to describe the process for gay and lesbian identity development; among these Cass's model (1984) has since been widely accepted. Applicable to both female and male homosexual individuals, the model proposes six discrete stages for individuals' successful coming-out transition. These stages are identity confusion, identity comparison, identity tolerance, identity acceptance, identity pride and identity synthesis. The progression is towards achieving positive homosexual identity, and is based on an individual's perceptions of his/her own behaviour and their actions as a consequence of this perception.

Tolerance of homosexuality has increased greatly in Western societies in recent decades, and there is evidence of relatively tolerant attitudes to casual homosexual acts during adolescence in many traditional societies (Schlegel & Barry, 1991). Research has found that homosexual adolescents usually start to become aware of their attraction to members of the same sex between ages 10 and 15, and that self-labelling as lesbian or gay tends to happen around age 15, with first disclosure at around 16.5 years.

Normative and non-normative developmental challenges in adolescence

Much psychological theory is based upon children and young people from mainstream populations, where developmental milestones are measured against established thresholds and patterns. However, there are substantial populations of children and young people, such as children in the looked-after system or disabled children, whose development does not accord with such patterns. A large-scale quantitative study by Chatzitheochari and colleagues (2015) found that disabled children suffered substantially higher risks of being bullied, physically and psychologically, at all stages in their development compared with non-disabled children. Disabled children had also been largely absent from the extensive body of research literature on bullying. A significant finding of this study was that disabled children and young people in England were faced with the double disadvantage of suffering bullying in respect of the lessened socio-economic circumstances associated with disability, and bullying associated with certain critical transitions times in their childhood, such as changing classes. The effect of bullying on later life chances has been established as having a stronger effect even than factors such as the socio-economic background of parents (Takizawa et al., 2014), and hence is an issue for psychologists and social workers to address in their practice.

Reflective point

In the light of the above information, reflect on disabled children whom you have known in either a personal or workplace capacity.

➢ To what extent did you ever consider their susceptibility to bullying?

➢ In retrospect, might you have noticed bullying taking place by non-disabled peers?

➢ What strategies might you attempt to use to encourage resilience in a disabled child who was being bullied?

➢ What community/group-type initiatives might you introduce to lessen bullying, especially bullying of disabled children?

Summary

Throughout this chapter the challenges of transitioning during adolescence have been explored. Among the normative challenges explored are those related to achieving autonomy for parents, establishing peer relationships, romantic encounters and exploring identity. Some adolescents will face additional challenges related to their ethnic origins, sexual orientation or disabled status. For example, an additional developmental task for homosexually oriented adolescents is adjustment to a socially stigmatized role.

Further resources

HM Government (2011) *Prevent Strategy.* www.gov.uk/government/uploads/system/uploads/attachment_data/file/97976/prevent-strategy-review.pdf (Accessed: 18 January 2018)

HM Government (2015) *Revised Prevent Duty Guidance in England and Wales.* www.gov.uk/government/uploads/system/uploads/attachment_data/file/445977/3799_Revised_Prevent_Duty_Guidance__England_Wales_V2-Interactive.pdf (Accessed: 18 January 2018)

Kids Matter website – www.kidsmatter.edu.au/mental-health-matters/social-and-emotional-learning/social-development (Accessed: 18 January 2018)

An Australian website which covers a range of developmental issues including mental health.

5

Parenting

Key learning outcomes

Following the study of this chapter, learners will be able to:

➤ Critically analyse parenting styles.

➤ Reflect on theoretical parenting models.

➤ Reflect on the role of diversity.

➤ Apply attachment theory to practice.

Introduction

There is no single textbook to help parents bring up their children, despite a plethora of 'how-to' guides and internet blogs which can confuse the new parent, especially those that claim to hold all the answers. In reality, parenting is a mix of learned behaviour, social influence and instinct. When the state, in the form of social workers and other professionals, becomes involved, it is even more difficult to make decisions about acceptable or 'good enough parenting' (Cleaver et al. 1999, 2011; Caldwell & Taylor, 2017). This chapter will present a historical and theoretical view of parenting before going on to explore some of the psychological challenges in contemporary parenting.

A historical perspective on parenting

It is important for social workers to understand the pressures and psychologies of parenting and it is instructive to begin with a historical overview of parenting in the UK. Traditionally, children in England were the 'property' of their parents who could inflict whatever living conditions or punishments they felt appropriate. The coming of the industrial revolution in the nineteenth century brought the plight of the urban poor into public focus, with charitable organizations beginning to 'interfere' in ways that protected children from the excesses of abuse within families and from a capitalist system that used children as cheap labour in factories and elsewhere. The London Society for the Prevention of Cruelty to Children (London SPCC) was founded in 1884 as a response to such concerns. Parliament passed the first ever UK law to protect children from abuse and neglect in 1889 and the London SPCC was renamed the National Society for the Prevention of Cruelty to Children (NSPCC), having spread across Britain. The first child cruelty case in Britain was brought by the Royal Society for the Prevention of Cruelty to Animals (RSPCA); the court charge list described the affected child as 'a small animal', because at the time there were no laws in Britain to protect children from mistreatment, only animals were protected in law. Physical mistreatment of children in Victorian and later times was commonplace in family settings and schools, as portrayed in modern times through novels such as *Oliver Twist* (also adapted as a film). This culture might be captured best in the old adage 'spare the rod and spoil the child', meaning that unless children are physically punished they will develop bad behaviours. We will return to the theme of physical chastisement later in the chapter.

Failures of the state

The scandals of the mass deportation of children and young people in times of war or civil unrest have been ever present on a worldwide scale, and post-war it is estimated that some 50,000 British children, often from very poor backgrounds, were taken from their parents (sometimes without consent) and shipped out to the British Commonwealth under the promise of a new and fulfilling life. Many of these children will have been sent over to Australia by British authorities, partly to ease pressure on welfare services at home and also to boost the population across the Commonwealth. These children often ended up poorly educated, exploited as cheap labour and many were physically and sexually abused. Recent Inquiries, such as the *Independent Inquiry into Child Sexual Abuse: The Protection of Children outside the United Kingdom* (2017), have shown that promises were rarely met and exploitation and abuse were often the realities for such deported children and young people. An Australian Inquiry into historic child sexual abuse (*Royal Commission into Institutional Responses to Child Sexual Abuse*, 2017) found that, between 1950 and 2010, more than 20% of religious orders had allegations of child sexual abuse against them, allegations that were largely covered up.

More recent moves towards assuring rights for children are exemplified in the work carried out by the United Nations (UN), whose Convention on the Rights of the Child (1989) is the most well-known and adopted international human rights treaty in history. Essentially, this Convention declared that children had a range of civil, political, economic, social, health and cultural rights, and was designed to improve children's life chances and quality of life in all countries. Not all westernized countries that signed up to these rights, however, meet them – for example, the UK has been criticized by the UN in respect of its failure to uphold the right of disabled children to mainstream education (Bulman, 2017). Some attitudes towards children across the world remain hard to change – for example, a survey commissioned by The Valuing Children Initiative (VCI, 2017) found that some 70% of Australian parents still believed that children 'belong' to their parents, suggesting that traditional attitudes have changed little. State parenting in the UK, recently known as 'corporate parenting' (Children and Social Work Act 2017, s.1), has also demonstrated a historical disregard for children's voices and rights over the years, the concept of a corporate parent being that the state (as represented by bodies such as local authorities and health authorities) should treat the children in its own care as they would their own children, having regard to the need to:

➢ Act in their best interests and promote their physical and mental health and well-being.

➢ Encourage them to express their views, wishes and feelings.

➢ Take into account their views and wishes and feelings.

➢ Help them to gain access to and make the best use of services provided by the local authority and its relevant partners.

➢ Promote high aspirations and seek to secure the best outcomes for them.

➢ Ensure they are safe, and have stability in their home lives, relationships and education or work.

➢ Prepare them for adulthood and independent living.

(Children and Social Work Act 2017, s.1 (1))

The above act brought in provision to help improve the life chances of looked-after children, particularly in the areas of aftercare and educational attainment, where outcomes have consistently been far below those of children and young people outside of the care system (see Chapter 3 for more details). Psychologists and social workers are all part of this corporate body and, as such, share the obligations outlined above under the Children and Social Work Act 2017.

Parenting and children in contemporary perspective

Family diversity

In recent decades, Western societies have experienced unprecedented increases in family diversity. What was traditionally seen as a family unit headed by two heterosexual married parents and their biological children has given way to a variety of family forms, where children grow up in contemporary societies: single-parent families – single father or single mother; stepfamilies; adoptive families; foster care families; same-sex parent families; families with children conceived through assisted technologies; and global surrogacy where children may be partially or not at all biologically related to their parent(s). Immigration and the exodus of the greatest number of humans ever from war-torn countries such as Iraq and Syria have introduced multiculturalism into previously traditionally settled cultures. These mass movements have brought with them tensions and racism, with economic migrants and their issues often being conflated with the fates of refugees fleeing war and terror. The challenges to parenting amid all this diversity and social upheaval are very considerable.

Increasingly liberal attitudes in the West have resulted in the breakdown of traditional hierarchies and patriarchies, despite rises in right-wing support in some countries calling for a return to old-fashioned values. Such 'old-fashioned' values do not stand up to scrutiny when one considers the oppressions of children, women and minorities which characterized these 'old-fashioned' times. Parents of challenging children and young people have sometimes been demonized in the media, and it is important that psychologists and social workers do not fall into this trap. Parents often have to cope with poverty and unhappy or abusive relationships, and may have had poor nurturing or abuse in their own childhoods. The work of Unwin and Stephens-Lewis (2016) highlights the negative health impact on parents of children caught up in child sexual exploitation (CSE). The predominant findings were that parents often sacrificed their own mental and physical health in trying to combat the perpetrators of CSE. However, professionals often judged parents to be the part of the problem, rather than part of the solution.

Theoretical perspectives on understanding parenting

Parenting styles

Parenting style is a psychological construct relating to the strategies adopted by parents in bringing up their children. Despite the huge improvements in child welfare in the UK in recent decades, the financial support available to working parents, equal opportunities policies and the proliferation of convenience shopping and modern housing, parenting seems to have become an increasingly stressful role, especially for parents who also need to work outside of the home. Many schools now have pre-school and after-school provision to facilitate working parents, and children's lives are often filled with activities and outings, run by police-checked and fully vetted staff. The days when children played out all day and were perhaps wary but not afraid of strangers have now largely gone, fuelled by media-induced fear of abduction and sexual abuse. Parents are bombarded with 'How-to Parent' guides, websites such as Mumsnet and the mainstream media, many of which paint unrealistic and idealized models of parenting. These models of parenting, complemented by a range of latest accessories and fashions, present parents as always coping, as highly successful and driven to achieve. Parenting seems to have become somewhat of a competition and a false image of the joys of parenting dominates popular culture. Social workers and psychologists are often parents and grandparents, who have added insight gained from the realities of working with parents who have often not benefited from stability and role modelling in their own childhoods.

There are many ideas about how to rear children. Some parents adopt the ideas their own parents used (Foley & Leverett, 2008), whereas others may get advice from friends; some may follow websites/blogs or read 'how-to' books about parenting; while others may take classes offered in the community, ranging from breastfeeding to baby yoga. No one has all the answers, yet somehow adults are expected to 'get it right', as illustrated by the quote below:

> Imagine an education system where none of the educators are trained, indeed, where training is seen as a sign of 'weakness'. There is no curriculum, but the amount to be learnt is vast and it is assumed that everyone knows what it is. There is no assessment, but if people fail, the penalties are severe. This is not any old education system but the foundation for every course, job, and profession in the UK. It is of course the family.

> (Cosin & Hales, 1997, p. 77)

Social work deals with the most vulnerable children in our society and the knowledge and insights of social workers and foster carers cannot afford to follow the 'trial and error approach' that might suffice in the parenting of one's own birth children. Such an approach is by no means adequate for the complex needs of foster children, many of whom will have been previously exposed to negative and inconsistent styles of parenting. Most UK children who are looked-after are in foster care (Fostering Network, 2016), and the particular dynamics of foster care are highlighted in the following section. Foster 'parents' gradually became known as foster 'carers' in UK policy and practice, this terminology being changed to reflect the reality that very few looked-after children were now orphans without parents, and that the role of fostering often involved a rehabilitative core, with most foster children having a least one known parent. This new 'professionalized' role brought with it dilemmas for foster carers which will be highlighted later in the chapter, using the literature regarding parenting practices. Ideas about child-rearing can be theorized in different ways, and we will explore the parenting models put forward by Baumrind (1967) and Belsky (1984). Baumrind (1967) identified three main styles of parenting – authoritarian, permissive and democratic:

Authoritarian parenting

An authoritarian parenting style would be one whereby parents try to be in control of their children. Such parenting will be directive and consistent and may lack affection and warmth. Choices or options are unlikely to characterize this style of parenting, parents needing to be obeyed because they are the adult and often an unquestioning compliance is called for by these types of parents. Such a form of parenting is not appropriate for children known to social workers who are, however, likely to benefit from consistent parenting regimes. An approach that is **authoritative** instead of authoritarian, based on clear boundaries but having some 'give and take', is more likely to produce positive outcomes. Sanctions would play a part in authoritative parenting, but with reasons and explanations being given as many children respond to a sense of fairness. Authoritarian parenting styles that include smacking would not be permissible within foster care, and sanctions such as being sent to one's bedroom would also be discouraged, the latter because certain children may associate bedrooms with abuse. Similarly, the deprival of food and drink is not permitted as a sanction in foster care and pocket monies cannot be withdrawn, only postponed, as such income is the right of a foster child in the UK (DoH, 1991). Appropriate use of authoritative parenting in foster care, which balances control and support with high parental sensitivity/interest, has been seen to lead to positive development outcomes. King and colleagues (2007) studied 191 foster parents in the USA and discovered that authoritarian styles of parenting were predominant in foster homes, going on to debate the relative influence of confidence levels, experience and the belief in the efficacy of a certain parenting style as the key factors influencing the style of their parenting. An appropriate, authoritative parenting style might be more able to keep a balance between what should be high expectations for foster children, while also providing appropriate structures of control, responsiveness and care, which are also necessary to balance and heal previously chaotic, and often abusive, experiences (Cairns, 2004).

Permissive parenting

Permissive parents tend to give up the majority of control to their children, making few, if any, rules – rules that are usually not consistently enforced. Permissive parents may not want to be tied down to routines; they want their children to feel free. The permissive parent may not set clear boundaries for their children's behaviour and tends to accept a child as they are, even where they find certain behaviours unacceptable. Permissive parenting styles may give children choice, even where the early years child may not yet be able to exercise informed choice. Clearly, such a style of parenting would not be suitable for foster children (who are often seeking boundaries), and could indeed be counterproductive, especially in short-term foster care scenarios, where children will return confused to a previous setting, and much of the work of previous carers may be undone. This dilemma perhaps exemplifies some of the tensions between the 'personal' and the 'professional' in contemporary foster parenting.

Democratic parenting

Democratic styles of parenting encourage personal responsibility and explain, rather than authoritatively expect, certain behaviours. They teach, rather than sanction, and reward via affection and praise. The restrictions to fully embracing this model in fostering are the policies and procedures within foster care that discourage close physical contact and demonstration of affection, for fear of allegations of impropriety. The idea of 'hands-off' caring has been fuelled by sex abuse scandals in foster care (e.g., BBC, 2006) although the growing impor-tance of attachment theories (e.g., Cairns, 2004; Golding, 2007) have countered this trend in their acknowledgement of closeness and touch as core to the nurturing of any child. Further challenges to the foster carer come from the positions taken by different professionals, as exemplified in the case study below.

Case study

Kane, a 7-month-old boy, was in a pre-adoption placement and was terrified of baths. The foster carer, Mary, had tried various techniques but still Kane screamed in a most distressing manner at every bath time; Mary reverted to bathing him in a baby bath and not using the bathroom but was anxious that he conquered this fear before mov-ing on to his adoptive placement. The Health Visitor suggested Mary get in the bath with him as a calming strategy, the social worker absolutely saying that this should not happen.

Task

➢ Whose advice was the most child-centred and why do you think the social worker took her prohibitive stance?

Reflective point

Less stark examples from contemporary foster care that deter closeness are advising that foster carers should not read a child stories while in the bed-room (rather, they should read them downstairs before bed) and that any male partner should not get involved with personal care nor spend time alone with children, for example car journeys.

➢ Do you think that such advice is appropriate and protective or does such a prohibition of 'normative' parental closeness deprive foster children of a key part of their development into loving adults, as well as give the wrong messages about men and indeed about children's own bodies?

Baumrind's (1967) Three Models of Parenting were further developed by Maccoby and Martin (1983), as in Figure 5.1.

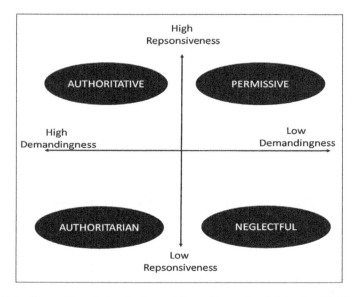

Figure 5.1   Parenting styles (adapted from Maccoby & Martin, 1983)
Source: Maccoby, E. & Martin, J. Socialization in the context of the family: Parent-child interaction in *Handbook of Child Psychology*, Wiley, Copyright © 1983, John Wiley & Sons, Inc.

Neglectful parenting was seen by Maccoby and Martin (1983) to constitute a very significant parenting style, responsible for problems in child development and later life adaptation. In contemporary times neglect has become the largest single reason for children coming into state care worldwide (NSPCC, 2015). Chapter 6 discusses the contemporary issues of neglect in more detail.

Belsky's (1984) Model of Parenting (see Figure 5.2) provides another useful conceptualization of parenting, distinguishing three main influences on parental functioning:

➣ Personal psychological resources of parent

➣ Contextual sources of support

➣ Characteristics of the child.

Belsky's model (Figure 5.2) views parenting as being affected by factors of external stress and support (partner relationship, social network, employment situation) which are in turn seen as influencing a parent's sense of psychological well-being. The personal and psychological resilience of the parent are seen as key to shaping the nature of parenting rather than being primarily shaped by the behaviours and characteristics of the child/children being parented. Good social networks, personal

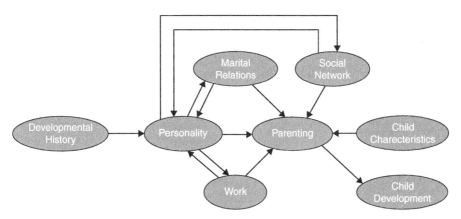

Figure 5.2   Belsky's model of determinants of parenting (Belsky, 1984)
Source: Belsky, J. The determinants of parenting: Process model in *Child Development*,
Wiley, Copyright © 1984, John Wiley & Sons, Inc.

relationships and employment status are seen as leading to a better sense
of parental well-being that lends itself to more sensitive and empathic
forms of caring. If any of these 'external' factors are unhealthy, in terms
of emotional demands, then parenting will consequently suffer.

Case study: The Kelly family

Returning to the case study introduced in Chapter 2 about Paul and Ria Kelly, you
will recall that their parents Mohammed Ishbal and Mary Kelly had a volatile relationship, characterized by heavy drinking and subsequent neglect of the children.
Mohammed and Mary were socially isolated, had no family support and little money.
When Paul was aged 11, he entered another period of foster care but began to use
physical violence against his foster carers, Mr and Mrs Walton, if he did not get his
own way. Paul had average intelligence but was very angry about spending periods
in foster care, and did not understand why his parents kept reverting to their drinking.

Task

> Using Belsky's model of parenting, what kind of parenting might Paul
  have experienced at this stage of his development?

> Can you picture how a typical day might look for Paul, particularly
  thinking about critical times – getting ready for school, coming home
  after school, getting ready for bed?

> How might these experiences be different when Paul was back home
  with his parents or in foster care?

Attachment theory and the parent–child relationship

Social work and psychological practice have increasingly incorporated attachment theory (Bowlby, 1969) into their practice with children and young people. Much attention has been paid in attachment theory research to the development of attachment in the first few years, which are believed to provide the blueprint to all subsequent relationships (see Chapter 2).

Schaffer and Emerson (1964) identified four phases in the development of healthy attachment:

➤ A social stage (up to 6 weeks of age) when the infant orientates without discrimination.

➤ Indiscriminate attachment (6 weeks to 6 months) when the infant preferentially orientates to and signals at one or more discriminated persons, but these do not crystallize in full attachments and infants did not show 'fear of strangers'.

➤ Specific attachment (7 months onwards) when the infant maintains proximity preferentially to a specific person and begins to show separation anxiety (e.g., crying) when their primary attachment figure leaves; they also begin to show fear of strangers.

➤ Multiple attachments (10–11 months onwards) when the infant begins to make multiple attachments, towards grandparents and/or nursery staff.

Case study: The Kelly family

Returning to the case study about the Kelly family, let us imagine how Paul and Ria Kelly might have experienced the above phases when they lived in a volatile home environment prior to coming into foster care.

Task

➤ How might their experiences have compared, say, to children of a similar age who were brought up in a calm and stable home environment?

➤ What might the particular effects have been if allegations about them having been cared for at times by a succession of unsuitable adults and children were true?

To whom are children attached?

Early research within attachment theory tradition has focused on the attachment relationship with the mother. Bowlby's 'maternal deprivation' hypothesis (Bowlby, 1951) originated in the 1950s and was very influential at the time, propositioning that children should not be deprived of contact with the mother during a *critical period*, thought to be during the first 3 years, when the first attachment relationship is being formed. This assertion drew on evidence on the effects of 'broken homes', children separated from their mothers during hospitalization periods, and children abandoned by and brought up in orphanages.

However, later research shows that early attachments are usually multiple and that separation from the mother can be compensated for by the presence of other attachment figure(s). It is now accepted that infants form attachments with adults who interact with them on a regular basis, usually the mother, but also the father, or a grandparent, or child minder/carer. This position is also supported by findings from cross-cultural research with children brought up in cultures where communal childcare is the norm, such as in some agricultural societies. For example, in Israeli Kibbutzim young children develop attachments to both their mother and the kibbutz childminder (Sagi et al., 1995).

Further reading

Seminal studies on multiple attachments in Israeli Kibbutzim children:

Aviezer, O., Van IJzendoorn, M. H., Sagi, A. & Schuengel, C. (1994) 'Children of the dream' revisited: 70 years of collective early child care in Israeli kibbutzim. *Psychological Bulletin*, 116(1), 99. http://dx.doi.org/10.1037/0033-2909.116. 1.99.
Sagi, A., IJzendoorn, M. H., Aviezer, O., Donnell, F., Koren-Karie, N., Joels, T. & Harl, Y. (1995) Attachments in a multiple caregiver and multiple infant environment: the case of the Israeli kibbutzim. *Monographs of the Society for Research in Child Development*, 60(2–3), 71–91. doi: 10.1111/j.1540-5834.1995.tb00198.

Attachment theory (Bowlby, 1980; Cairns, 2004) has recently become high-profile in the social work profession. Bowlby's (1980) original perspectives on attachment theory were predicated on a stereotypical model whereby mothers who stayed at home produced the best adjusted and happy children; recent changes in family diversity are challenging such a view. The more recent work of Cairns (2004) and Golding (2007) view attachment as a need for a child to have one or more core figures, of any gender, with whom the child can make attachments. This view accords with Klaus and colleagues (1996), who defined attachment as being a lasting bond between two individuals. Attachment theorists are nuanced in their perspectives on attachment, but agree that secure attachment is desirable for all children, with fostering and adoption situations presenting particular challenges as bonds will have been disrupted, often several times, before a child has a plan for adoption or some other form of permanent substitute family care.

Moreover, research has shown that the (maternal) deprivation effects may not be irreversible, as originally thought. This is supported by evidence from research on children rescued from 'orphanages' and consequently brought up in families, such as the children 'rescued' from Romanian orphanages in the early 1990s and adopted into Western families. Research indicates that the majority of children showed remarkable resilience and their development, although stunted because of the lack of stimulation in the institutional environment, caught up significantly after adoption, with majority of children functioning within expected norms within a few years (Misca, 2014a, 2014b).

The main attachment styles discussed in depth in Chapter 2 are avoidant, secure, ambivalent and disorganized. Original ideas argued that attachment security – or the lack of secure attachment in early years – may predict some later developmental outcomes. However, such predictions have been criticized from a cross-cultural perspective, with research indicating that secure attachment is not normative or predominant across different cultures. For example a meta-analysis of attachment studies conducted cross-culturally (Van Ijzendoorn & Kroonenberg, 1988) showed that while in North American studies the secure attachment pattern was predominantly found, in German and Japanese samples insecure attachments patterns were highly represented.

Further reading

Van Ijzendoorn, M. H. & Kroonenberg, P. M. (1988) Cross-cultural patterns of attachment: a meta-analysis of the strange situation. *Child Development*, 59(1), 147–156. doi: 10.2307/1130396.

These findings raised questions about the way in which attachment is conceptualized, understood and applied in practice. Contemporary approaches propose attachment as a characteristic of the relationship between caregiver and the child – and not a characteristic of the child. As such, different attachment types, rather than being seen as positive or negative, play an adaptive role in different situations or environments. For example, secure attachments are adaptive strategies for the child to relate to trusting and reliable carers, in environments with adequate resources;

whereas an insecure attachment may be more adaptive when the carers are inconsistent or abusive. In research with Romanian children adopted from orphanages in Canada, Chisholm (1998) highlighted that the predominant feature of these children's attachment relationships was indiscriminate friendliness as in the orphanages, being friendly to any adult was an adaptive strategy that these children used to get attention and stimulation from adults. After adoption into Canadian families, such indiscriminate friendliness towards strangers becomes non-adaptive and potentially endangers the safety of the child, illustrating how a particular type of attachment can be useful in one environment and potentially dangerous in another.

In similar fashion, children abused by their carer(s) would typically develop a disorganized attachment style characterized by ambivalence towards their carers, alternating between displaying fear/rejection towards the abusive parents and closeness. In this context, being aware of the abusive parents is useful, enabling the child to protect themselves from the abuse (e.g., a punch), yet at the same time the child will also seek closeness to the parent to satisfy their needs (e.g., for food).

Attachment in diverse family types

Contemporary family units often use outside childcare facilities – such as childminders and day care provision. Debates on these issues are complex and a child's outcomes depend on the quality of care, quantity of care and the age of the child. For example, the National Institute Health and Human Development (NICHD) Early Child Care Research Network (2002) suggested that high-quality day care is beneficial for children's language development and cognition but early full-time day care may be related to aggression and disobedience. Recent times have seen an increase in fathers' involvement in childcare (Lamb, 2011), although most research has concentrated on maternal perspectives. By way of contrast it has been noted (e.g., Shapiro & Krysik, 2010) that the father is often absent from social work interventions where there are issues about childcare standards or safeguarding, this phenomenon either being because social workers do not actively seek to engage fathers or because fathers avoid such professional contact. One result of such a culture is that it is the mother who tends to take any blame or responsibility on her own.

Reflective point

➢ How might you strive to better engage men within families on your caseload?

➢ What might be the benefits/disadvantages of men's fuller involvement?

Family breakup is always stressful for children, the extent of these effects being dependent on age. Children in their early years may be very upset but able to accept some rationalization of a new situation, those of primary school age might be able to express wishes around solutions, and adolescents may express anger and resentment, sometimes 'taking sides' with the parent deemed to have been 'wronged' in the breakup. Many reconstituted families now have step-parents as part of their composition who may be perceived as intruders by children, step-parenting bringing with it many challenges regarding history and rights to sanction or a need to portray the parent they have 'replaced' in as positive a light as possible. There is some evidence that the introduction of step-fathers can be beneficial to boys but detrimental to girls (Kinniburgh-White et al., 2010). The effects of divorce and the dynamics in reconstituted families have been researched in some depth, with a particular emphasis on the implications for attachment. Stability in any home environment has been shown to compensate for the upset of family breakdown, and evidence (Mooney, et al., 2009) illustrates that quality of home environment and the quality of the relationship with carers can compensate for any detrimental effects of family breakup.

Social workers increasingly encounter diverse family compositions as part of their everyday work, and it is important that they have sufficient grasp of the dynamics of such families if they are to operate in non-judgemental ways. Social work students often misunderstand quite what is meant by 'non-judgemental' because we do expect social workers to make judgements about a child's safety, but not in ways based on prejudice or ignorance. An ecological approach (Bronfenbrenner, 2005; Misca & Smith, 2014) that takes a child-centred view of children in their own environments is perhaps best suited to the delivery of non-judgemental social work. For example, recent research (Richards et al., 2017) has demonstrated that children thrive in the care of same-sex couples.

Dealing with the losses brought about by family dysfunction is core to all aspects of social work with families and children. Every move a child in care has to make between foster or residential placement brings with it significant psychological stressors – loss of place, loss of adult figures, loss of peers and often loss of school. Family members might be lost to children and young people through death, substance abuse and through chaotic lifestyles. It is important that the turnover rate in social workers is addressed if they are not to mirror the chaos from which many children and young people seek refuge. McLeod's (2010) research clearly demonstrates that children and young people value consistency in their relationships with social workers.

Same-gender parenting

The concept of same-gender parenting has led to controversy, notably in the field of adoption (Wood, 2016). A change in the English Adoption and *Fostering Regulations* (2005) meant that all adoption agencies had to embrace same-gender parenting, leading to some organizations having had their positions on homosexuality challenged.

Little is written about same-gender parenting, as it is a relatively new phenomenon, but the case that is often cited by opponents of same-gender parenting in foster care is that concerning Wakefield Metropolitan Borough's case which involved the first gay foster carers ever appointed by that authority (Brindle, 2007). Essentially, it was the mother of a little boy placed who blew the final whistle on the abusive practice in the fostering household. Previous to the mother's complaint, occasioned when her son had shown her a photograph taken by one of his foster carers showing him urinating into a toilet bowl, the excuse of the foster carer when challenged by social workers was that he had taken the photograph to teach the little boy how to aim and not to make a mess on the floor. However, many more inappropriate photographs came to light and a subsequent Inquiry found that the behaviours exhibited by the foster carers were of a nature unlikely to have been tolerated had they not been a same-gender foster couple. Wakefield Metropolitan District Council were severely criticized for their misguided 'political correctness' which had led them to taking no action over previous complaints for fear of being seen as homophobic. It often only takes one case to distort the reality of similar situations, and much of the limited evidence regarding same-gender foster care is that foster carers who are gay, whether single or in a partnership, often speak of having fewer referrals compared to non-gay foster carers, which can only be due to prejudice.

Summary

Parenting in contemporary society is challenging, and social norms are rapidly changing in respect of increasing diversity within families and in respect of communications and lifestyles brought about by social media. Traditional models and concepts of parenting are changing, but in order to better understand parenting it is important to hold a history of the origins and nature of traditional parenting. It is also important that social workers and psychologists support and recognize parents as experts on their own children, and strive to find ways of helping parents cope with the often very challenging behaviours and lifestyle chosen which they have to live with on an everyday basis. There are no master guides to parenting and, as some of the above models suggest, parenting is best seen as a complexity of factors, ranging across personal resiliencies, external factors and the characteristics and temperament of the child/children in question. Parenting of children in foster care has been explored as being particularly challenging, given that many of these children will have previously experienced fragmented and inconsistent parenting. The extra challenges in contemporary parenting brought about by an ever more materialistic world of advertising, celebrity and sexuality have brought with them new challenges, with social workers and psychologists needing to be aware of such challenges and their threats to the well-being of children and young people. The positive benefits of the knowledge available to children and young people via the internet can be outweighed by the challenges that such contact brings, and the next chapter's focus on safeguarding will consider the nature of this threat.

Further resources

Parenting UK website – www.parentinguk.org/ (Accessed: 20 January 2018)

Contains a wide range of research and information about parenting which is helpful for professionals and parents.

Parents against Child Sexual Exploitation (Pace) website, http://paceuk.info/ (Accessed: 20 January 2018)

This website contains research and guidance to help professionals and parents cope with the problems of CSE.

6

Safeguarding children and young people

Key learning outcomes

Following the study of this chapter, learners will be able to:

➢ Critically reflect on the priorities within their own practice.

➢ Develop critical awareness of the child's perspective.

➢ Develop insights into the dynamics of domestic violence.

➢ Become critically aware of the challenges in working with disguised compliance.

➢ Critically interpret research and serious case reviews for the psychological factors present.

Introduction

Safeguarding children has become high on the political agenda, especially after a series of child tragedies, and all best advice is that professionals should work in preventative, holistic ways. The voice of the child should be the core consideration, with social workers encouraging family integration and involvement (Laming, 2009; Unwin & Hogg, 2012). However, the daily reality for social workers in safeguarding teams is that procedures, protocols and time limits tend to subjugate time spent with the child to the margins, little time and thought being available to get to know their psychological concerns.

The solution for many lay observers is that children should be removed from 'bad families' into care but outcomes for children in care are unfortunately very poor overall (DfE, 2014), and being in care does not by any means guarantee that a child will go on to enjoy good mental health. Children's early experiences significantly impact on their future life chances and looked-after children are at greater risk of a poor quality of mental health both because of their pre-care experiences and because of experiences within the care system.

Performance management of safeguarding systems is not the way forward for safeguarding best practice, and this chapter will claim that the place to look for the answers is in the psychological understanding of children's behaviours and in the relationship that professionals are able to forge with children and families. Children are not 'cases' – they are children with complex emotional and mental health needs that psychologists and social workers must ensure stay at the very heart of their work. The findings of key serious case reviews are presented in this chapter for further reflection and discussion, particularly with a view to highlighting psychological factors.

Background to safeguarding children

In the UK the Children Act 1989, whose principles derived from the Human Rights Act 1998, is the core guiding legislation. The core principle of this UK legislation is that the welfare of the child is paramount, this principle being increasingly challenged when services are under-resourced, voluntary sector support services shutting down and foster place demands outstripping supply (Fostering Network, 2016). The death of Victoria Climbié, a young African girl (discussed further in the chapter), was the catalyst that led to a raft of new government measures aimed at improving child protection, the term 'safeguarding' being introduced to emphasize the preventative role that all professionals and all citizens have in ensuring our children are safe, not just social workers.

Local Safeguarding Children's Boards were set up to represent the formalization of inter-agency responsibilities for the standards of safeguarding across all agencies, and for carrying our serious case reviews when children were killed and seriously injured. The subsequent failure of these Boards to raise standards across safeguarding led to their review (DfE, 2016) and a replacement system being proposed with greater central regulation. *Working Together to Safeguard Children* (HM Government, 2018) is the latest version of key inter-agency guidance for best practice in safeguarding, which was first introduced in 2010. Children and young people who suffer any kind of abuse – physical abuse, neglect, sexual abuse and emotional abuse – all suffer psychological harm and this consideration needs to be at the forefront of professional deliberation, alongside the need to follow protocols and procedures. *Working Together to Safeguard Children* (HM Government, 2018) defines the thresholds for safeguarding and the promotion of children's well-being. In times of austerity, neglect has become the largest single reason why children and young people become subject to child protection plans. Definitions of types of child abuse are given below, followed by an Exercise.

Neglect is defined as:

> The persistent failure to meet a child's basic physical and/or psychological needs, likely to result in the serious impairment of the child's health or development. Neglect may occur during pregnancy as a result of maternal substance abuse.

Once a child is born, neglect may involve a parent or carer failing to:

- Provide adequate food, clothing and shelter (including exclusion from home or abandonment).

- Protect a child from physical and emotional harm or danger.

- Ensure adequate supervision (including the use of inadequate caregivers).

- Ensure access to appropriate medical care or treatment.

It may also include neglect of, or unresponsiveness to, a child's basic emotional needs.

(HM Government, 2018, p. 105)

Emotional abuse is defined as:

- The persistent emotional maltreatment of a child such as to cause severe and persistent adverse effects to the child's emotional development. It may involve conveying to a child that they are worthless or unloved, inadequate, or valued only insofar as they meet the needs of another person.

- It may include not giving the child opportunities to express their views, deliberately silencing them or 'making fun' of what they say or how they communicate.

- It may feature age or developmentally inappropriate expectations being imposed on children. These may include interactions that are beyond a child's developmental capability, as well as overprotection and limitation of exploration and learning, or preventing the child participating in normal social interaction.

> It may involve seeing or hearing the ill-treatment of another. It may involve serious bullying (including cyberbullying), causing children frequently to feel frightened or in danger, or the exploitation or corruption of children.

(HM Government, 2018, p. 104)

Physical abuse is defined as:

> A form of abuse which may involve hitting, shaking, throwing, poisoning, burning or scalding, drowning, suffocating or otherwise causing physical harm to a child.

> Physical harm may also be caused when a parent or carer fabricates the symptoms of, or deliberately induces, illness in a child.

(HM Government, 2018, p. 103)

Sexual abuse is defined as:

> Abuse that involves forcing or enticing a child or young person to take part in sexual activities, not necessarily involving a high level of violence, whether or not the child is aware of what is happening. The activities may involve physical contact, including assault by penetration (for example, rape or oral sex) or non-penetrative acts such as masturbation, kissing, rubbing and touching outside of clothing. They may also include non-contact activities, such as involving children in looking at, or in the production of, sexual images, watching sexual activities, encouraging children to behave in sexually inappropriate ways, or grooming a child in preparation for abuse.

> Sexual abuse can take place online, and technology can be used to facilitate offline abuse.

> Sexual abuse is not solely perpetrated by adult males. Women can also commit acts of sexual abuse, as can other children.

(HM Government, 2018, p. 104)

Child sexual exploitation is defined as:

> A form of child sexual abuse. It occurs where an individual or group takes advantage of an imbalance of power to coerce, manipulate or deceive a child or young person under the age of 18 into sexual activity in exchange for something the victim needs or wants, and/or

for the financial advantage or increased status of the perpetrator or facilitator.

➤ The victim may have been sexually exploited even if the sexual activity appears consensual.

➤ Child sexual exploitation does not always involve physical contact; it can also occur through the use of technology.

(HM Government, 2018, p. 104)

Exercise

Consider each category of abuse and list what type of psychological harm might be occasioned to a child at various stages of development. Consider the long-term effects of each category of abuse on a child's life. How might cultural norms have an influence on social work decisions?

Type of abuse	0–5 years	5–11 years	11–18 years
Neglect			
Emotional abuse			
Physical abuse			
Sexual abuse			
Child sexual exploitation (CSE)			

Attitudes towards safeguarding

Safeguarding children has become a contentious issue in today's society, with polarized views evident regarding whether social workers do enough to protect children, or asking why social workers interfere in family business. Despite public stereotypes about social workers being 'child snatchers', the vast majority of children known to social workers live in their own homes. Moving into care, being either looked-after in a foster or residential placement, is the outcome for a minority of children and plans are usually for rehabilitation. Most young people in care say that their experiences are good and that it was the right choice for them (Biehal et al., 2014). However, more needs to be done to ensure that all children in care are healthy and safe, have the same opportunities as their peers and are enabled to move successfully into adulthood. Concern has been expressed about defensive practice which is leading to children and families being unnecessarily brought into the child protection net. Devine's (2017) research suggested that approximately one in 20 UK families are investigated regarding safeguarding concerns, yet the rates of actual detection of child abuse have fallen. Concern has been expressed also that the rise in children becoming subject to child protection plans due to neglect are victims of austerity and public sector cutbacks. Contemporary evidence from the UK (e.g., Featherstone et al., 2014) clearly links poverty with this phenomenon. Poverty is also closely linked with parental mental illness, domestic violence and substance abuse (Bywaters et al. 2016). Cleaver and colleagues' (1999) seminal work regarding risks to children in domestic settings established that the presence of the 'toxic trio' (a combination of domestic violence, substance abuse and mental ill-health) is a critical indicator.

Parents and families known to social workers have increasingly been 'othered' (Warner, 2015) by press and government rhetoric. Michael Gove (2012), then Secretary for Education, spoke publicly about social workers needing to rescue children from 'a life of soiled nappies and scummy baths, chaos and hunger, hopelessness and despair'. The recent move towards 'fast-tracking' adoptions (Unwin & Misca, 2013) has been criticized as oppressive to parents, who often do not have the resources to challenge decisions made by social work organizations. This suggests an unhealthy and unbalanced approach to safeguarding children, which does not effectively help families most in need of help and protection, and one which often takes a deficit approach, dealing with symptoms rather than solutions.

Signs of Safety (Turnell & Edwards, 1999) is a strength-based process that offers a different approach, this approach having recently gained popularity in the UK. This is partly because of its applied nature, but also because it offers a way of working with families and children in ways that do not pathologize and dwell only on problems and dangers. Rather, this approach brings in the solution-based perspective of what 'more safe' might look like, and explores the approach by way of practical techniques, such as the 'Three Houses' exercises, which are very child-friendly, aiming to capture pictorially the detail of a child's concerns and aspirations in ways that standard social work and counselling interviews may not. There is a growing evidence base relating to the efficacy of *Signs of Safety*, although its authors acknowledge that, despite all families having strengths, some will be unable to sufficiently build on these to enable their children to stay safely in the home environment. Such an approach is a refreshing alternative to the bureaucratic approaches that characterize much safeguarding work, and also gives prominence to the individual social worker's skills in helping children and families look in fresh ways at how they live on a day-to-day basis. The *Signs of Safety* approach might be viewed as a progressive form of psychology, one which seeks to invest in the future by developing family strengths and social networks rather than deal only in the realm of symptoms.

Fear of being responsible for the next Peter Connelly or Daniel Pelka (NSPCC, 2018) can be seen to drive senior management culture, such a culture also ignoring the fact that child deaths at the hands of parents/carers have actually declined in recent years (Pritchard et al. 2013). The harsh reality is that parents/carers have, throughout time, always been guilty of murder and harm to their children. The increasing complexity and pressures of contemporary family life (poverty, unemployment, cuts in public services, lack of pastoral focus in schools, social media pressures) and the pressures on professionals such as social workers mean that future tragedies will inevitably happen. This is not to argue for complacency, however, and certainly the deaths of children such as Peter Connelly and Daniel Pelka, both of whom were well known to a number of child welfare agencies, could have been avoided had professionals acted competently, had the knowledge base, and followed the procedures and protocols in place. There should be no excuses for poor communication, failure to speak to children on their own and for social workers being deceived by parents about the realities in a child's life, all recurring themes highlighted in Brandon and colleagues' (2012) study of serious case reviews. However, social workers do not kill children; parents and carers do. Yet some of the media coverage would imply that social workers are wholly at fault – for example, Booker's (2013) headline in *The Telegraph*: *'Pelka: social workers let down the children who really need them'*.

The following section will illuminate issues related to some of the most high-profile child deaths in the UK, exploring psychological factors that may have influenced outcomes. It will look in more detail at the psychological complexities around the cases of Victoria, Peter, Khyra and Daniel. We will return to these children and the psychological elements of their development, their family circumstances and the professional interventions at key points throughout the book. This is not to forget the other children and young people who have died at the hands of their parents and carers, but these are the cases well known and ones which have led to much published documentation and, hopefully, much learning.

What can we learn from the serious case reviews?

Turning now to look particularly at the psychological elements pertinent to the deaths of Victoria Climbié, Khyra Ishaq, Peter Connelly and Daniel Pelka (NSPCC, 2018), we will address these in chronological order before concluding with some common learning. (Note that the NSPCC website contains a repository of all serious case reviews in the UK and is referenced throughout this book because individual safeguarding boards remove their reviews after certain lengths of time: https://learning.nspcc.org.uk/case-reviews/national-case-review-repository/

The Victoria Climbié Inquiry

The death of Victoria Climbié in Haringey in 2003 has become well known through a Public Inquiry that highlighted major shortcomings in multi-agency child protection work and its associated systems. Victoria, 8 years old at the time of her death, was sent to England from the Ivory Coast with the intention of increasing Victoria's life chances and education. Her parents had arranged for a person known to the family and presented in England as Victoria's great-aunt, Marie-Therese Kouao, to care for her. This private arrangement led to a catalogue of the most horrific abuse once Kouao had met up with Carl John Manning, a local bus driver. Despite being seen by a number of housing officers, social workers, police, child protection teams, NSPCC staff and staff at two hospitals during her 11 months in England, no professional got close enough to really know Victoria, what she was thinking and what she was suffering. Victoria's first language was French, yet the only time she was spoken to in French was by a member of hospital staff, who, meeting her for the first time, asked about whether she had been a victim of sexual abuse. A core factor throughout Victoria's contact with professionals was that Kouao always spoke for her, gave plausible explanations for a range of injuries, and was never challenged appropriately.

Reflective point

➤ Is it likely that an 8-year-old, terrorized by her carers, would disclose anything about sexual abuse to a stranger in a medical setting, even if that child's first language is used?

➤ What better strategies, which would have taken into account Victoria's overall emotional well-being and level of cognitive development, might have been more appropriate and child-centred?

➤ What signs might a professional look for that would indicate that a parent/carer was lying?

➤ Should a child always be spoken to alone by a social worker where there are issues of concern?

➤ Can you think of an appropriate way of explaining to a parent/carer why you might need to speak to a child/young person alone?

The issue of race, the danger of assumption and how to challenge the childcare practices of other cultures were also key concerns in Victoria's case, both black and white professionals having had involvement at various times.

Neil Garnham QC said in his opening statement to the Laming (2003) Inquiry:

Assumption based on race can be just as corrosive in its effect as blatant racism ... racism can affect the way people conduct themselves in other ways. Fear of being accused of racism can stop people acting when otherwise they would. Assumptions that people of the same colour, but from different backgrounds, behave in similar ways can distort judgements.

(p. 12)

This brings up interesting questions about diversity, and how much a social worker or psychologist should know about a culture before they are considered culturally competent. This does not mean that a professional could read a book on, say, the Sikh culture and then be competent to ask about issues as delicate and contentious as child abuse within that culture, but it does show a cultural respect to have tried to understand some of the customs and norms of other cultures. Cultural stereotypes are dangerous in that not every individual conforms to them (e.g., Marie-Therese Kouao), and if you believed unquestionably that all African families come to England with a high value placed on children's education then you may have missed the fact that, despite having been in the country for 11 months, Victoria had still not been to school.

Laming's (2003) Inquiry into the death of Victoria was particularly interesting in its conclusions that, despite systems failings in respect of inter-agency working and managerial incompetence, a basic failure to establish the kinds of relationships with the family lay at the heart of the tragedy. Such relationships could have enabled Victoria to speak out to a professional she trusted and knew well, and such a professional may also have known the adults well enough to know when they were not telling the truth. Laming believed that the answer lay in 'doing relatively straightforward things well' (2003, p. 13), which would have included speaking to Victoria more than once in her native language, following up visits after hospital and having a sound knowledge of child development that told professionals that 8-year-old girls are usually bubbly and full of comments rather than silent and withdrawn.

Peter Connelly serious case review

Unlike Victoria, Peter Connelly (often referred to as 'Baby P') was on the then Child Protection Register in Haringey when he died in August 2007, aged 17 months, at the hands of his carers, one of whom was his mother. The family were seen 60 times in eight months by social workers, police and doctors. Why would a social worker or other health professional not know from their basic child development training that even a poorly child of two will always try to interact and be chatty? Ferguson's

(2011) research was illuminative in that he discovered that some social workers did not think that they could ask to pick up a child. As with Victoria, Peter's mother, Tracy Connelly, and her partner, Jason Owen, lied repeatedly to professionals about Peter's care. One particular missed opportunity that stands out is the social worker's home visit when Tracy Connelly explained that Peter was sitting still on the sofa as he was feeling poorly. The reality was that the terrified little boy had a number of broken bones and was in great pain, yet no professional ever got close enough to this family to know Peter's behaviours and character and so be able to know when he was in danger. Another incident occurred during a home visit when Peter's face was covered in chocolate which was covering up extensive facial bruising, yet the social worker did not insist Peter have his face cleaned.

Reflective point

> What psychological barriers might stop a social worker asking a carer to clean up a child's face so that she could see him fully?

> What techniques might you develop to be an effective practitioner to prepare for situations like a child with a chocolate-covered face that prevented you from seeing any marking?

Subsequent to Peter's death, the government asked Lord Laming to carry out a follow-up to his 2003 Report to evaluate what progress had been made on his original recommendations regarding the need for a less procedural approach to safeguarding children, and for social workers to be better trained and skilled in recognizing child development concerns and dealing with manipulative and collusive carers. In his progress report, *The Protection of Children in England* (Laming, 2009), Lord Laming concluded that safeguarding practices across agencies had made little progress in the six years since the Victoria Climbié tragedy. The bureaucratic systems were seen to have remained as cumbersome as before, senior management remained unaccountable, and social work skills and development had not been sufficiently improved.

Khyra Ishaq serious case review

Khyra Ishaq was a 7-year-old girl starved to death in Birmingham in 2008 by her parents, who had removed her from school. Khyra had a Caribbean heritage and her family had converted to Islam. Many people remember her case from the vignette of her being seen taking food from a bird table by neighbours, neighbours who thought it none of their business to interfere. Khyra's step-father, Junaid Abuhamza, suffered from mental illness and had strong beliefs surrounding evil spirits, as well as being a heavy user of cannabis. Khyra's mother, Angela Gordon, was known as an aggressive woman who threatened, and made, allegations about the racist approaches of education officials enquiring about Khyra's welfare. Gordon also kept her family away from the home, creating numerous excuses why they should not visit. Khyra's parents had taken her and her two siblings out of school, ostensibly for home schooling, but in reality to hide the extent of the starvation and beatings that the children, Khyra in particular, were being made to suffer. Fear of being politically incorrect and challenging other cultures was a key element of failings in Khyra's case, which also drew wider attention to the lack of statutory oversight of children who are home-educated. Khyra's family dynamics were also characterized by the 'toxic trio' (Cleaver et al., 1999) of mental illness, substance abuse and domestic violence – this trio's presence always indicating a high level of safeguarding concern. Again, as with Victoria and Peter, no professional got close to Khyra and her family, particularly after she was removed from school.

Reflective point

> If your manager told you not to visit a family who had complained about you harassing them about the care of their children and made a complaint alleging racism, what would your response be?

> Where might you turn for further advice?

Daniel Pelka serious case review

Daniel Pelka was a 4-year-old Polish boy killed by a blow to the head in 2012 by either his mother, Magdalena Luczak, or her partner, Mariusz Krezolek. Problems of drink and domestic violence were present in the Coventry household in which Daniel and his sister lived. Daniel was not registered with a GP and only became known to any public authorities once he attended primary school where staff saw him deteriorate into a withdrawn little boy constantly scavenging for food. Daniel's school attendance was poor, his mother aggressively telling education welfare officials that she was too ill to always get him to school. She informed the school staff that Daniel suffered from a food absorption disease, which meant he could not gain weight, but that he was receiving specialist consultant treatment. Using this fictitious condition as an excuse, Daniel's mother instructed staff never to allow him access to any food during school time, to which they agreed. School staff proved grossly incompetent in their knowledge of how to use safeguarding procedures, and despite appropriate concern being expressed from Daniel's newly qualified teacher, the school management did not follow procedures. Social workers carried out two core assessments during Daniel's short life, both being undertaken as procedural requirements rather than incisive pieces of work designed to develop a psychological understanding of Daniel and his family's dynamics. A health visitor thought the family was caring, and only very shortly before Daniel's death did he even get to see a specialist consultant who prescribed vitamins, which were never given to him. Further lies from the mother and her partner duped the paramedics, hospital staff and police on the night of Daniel's death, and it was only some days after his death when police records showed up logs of a domestically violent household that Daniel's body was examined properly. Bruising, broken bones and old fractures were found, leading to a police home visit where the house was searched, revealing a urine-soaked 'spare room' that in reality had been Daniel's prison, with no heating and no door handle. The strong smell of air fresheners could not disguise the smell and Daniel's urine-soaked, blood-marked mattress was also found hidden away. The bedroom that he was supposed to have shared with his sister was clearly also a fabrication, and his sister, through the use of the Achieving Best Evidence procedures (ABE), was to eventually prove a reliable and critical witness in the criminal case.

Reflective point

➢ Why do you think Daniel and his sister always insisted that things were alright at home?

➢ What would you have looked for in the house as social workers undertaking a core assessment?

➢ Why do social workers and other professionals so rarely engage with the males in safeguarding cases?

Despite the many failings in the lives of the above children, much work in day-to-day children's safeguarding is effective, despite the bureaucracy that Lord Laming (2003, 2009), the SWRB (2010) and the *Munro Report* (Munro, 2011) so criticized still being ever-dominant. This effective everyday work is confidential in nature, however, and does not reach public or media attention. Procedures are needed to safeguard children, as demonstrated particularly in Daniel's case; but what is so often absent is any deep relationship between key social workers and other professionals who are kept at a distance from the real issues in families, both by deceit on behalf of the adults involved, and by a managerialist preoccupation with proceduralism and performance management.

Exercise

Read one of the above-mentioned child death inquiries online and make a note of how your understanding of the 'facts' of the matter change from any previous understanding you had of this situation.

Ask colleagues what they understand about the case in question and share your learning at a team meeting or in a memo. You might be surprised at how their perceived understanding of what actually happened is quite different from the facts of the matter, many social workers not reading such Inquiry reports, but relying for their information on mainstream media.

Further resources

For details of the above serious case reviews, and others, search the NSPCC repository web resource:

https://learning.nspcc.org.uk/case-reviews/national-case-review-repository/
(Accessed: 14 September 2018).

Signs of Safety website – www.signsofsafety.net/signs-of-safety/ (Accessed: 21 January 2018).

This is a strengths-based programme that originated in Australia. The approach has gained in popularity and focuses on how social workers can work to build partnerships with parents/carers and children, yet still rigorously and safely investigate the risk issues.

Exercise

Choose a serious case review from the above-mentioned NSPCC safeguarding repository or choose a recent one from any local children safeguarding board's website.

> When you read the review ask yourself, could that have been me, my team and my practice being reported on?

> ➤ To what extent were the psychological states of mind of the child/children in the serious case review taken into account by various professionals as the specific events unfolded?

> ➤ Why do you think that the findings of many serious case reviews are similar?

In order to safeguard children, social workers must be both creative and knowledgeable, and read reports such as serious case reviews to learn from them in ways that place hold the child at the centre of practice.

Reflective point

> ➤ Is there any way you could take a lead in promoting learning from reviews and inquiries and thereby contribute to the learning culture, which Munro (2011) was keen to establish? Might you be able to invite others, such as your local psychologists, to contribute their views?

It is essential as practitioners that we are able to build effective, open and honest relationships with the families and children we work with; this can be easier said than done, with various factors influencing this challenge. Many families are resistant to engage in social care support; they may have a fear of stigma, they may feel that, as social workers, our lives are too far distanced from their own, that we do not understand their needs and that we are blaming them for their circumstance. It is vital, as a social worker, that we are sensitive and appropriately attuned to the family's and children's needs and are able to deal appropriately with possible conflict (Frost & Parton, 2009).

Reflective point

In order to establish the basis of a working relationship with children and their parents/carers, how might you openly acknowledge the potential psychological barriers to progress?

> ➤ Might you talk frankly about your different perspectives, roles and responsibilities?

> ➤ Might you acknowledge that the family may have preconceived ideas about 'what social workers do?'

> ➤ Might you acknowledge that some families are resistant and collusive?

Case study: The Kelly family

Returning to the Kelly family (discussed in detail in Chapter 2), let us consider earlier social workers' involvement with the family:

Mohammed had lost his job at the local factory, Paul was aged 3 years and Ria was 2. A neighbour had reported domestic violence on two occasions and the police had also referred the family after a drink-fuelled brawl outside of their home. You are a well-experienced, white social worker and you have written to the Kelly family saying you will visit at a specified time to discuss the domestic violence concerns and risk to the children.

- What do you think would be the psychological concerns for Mary and Mohammed upon receipt of the letter?

- Do you think they will have contrived to 'get their story straight'?

- Would you directly ask them whether they had done this?

- What signs might suggest they are not telling the truth?

- What might their fears be, given their likely media images of social workers?

Paul was only 3 at the time but is he likely to pick up on his parents' anxiety? How would you involve Paul, being aware that his parents may have 'prepped' him about their relationship or threatened him if he said anything bad about them? Ria was only 2 at the time but what signs of safety/distress will you be looking for in her behaviour during your visit?

Depending on your judgements after an initial visit, what factors would indicate to you that a *Signs of Safety* approach based around the three core questions of 'What are we worried about?', 'What's working well?' and 'What needs to happen?' might represent a positive way of moving ahead in partnership?

Issues of diversity

Social work values diversity as a richness in our society but working in safeguarding brings with it particular challenges – Whose cultural norms are appropriate? How are interactions going to be affected by the culture/gender of the investigating social worker? Can interpreters be trusted to accurately represent a situation? Increasingly, UK social workers are directed to approach families with a 'children first, culture second' attitude (Laming, 2003). Effective social work needs to be sensitive to cultural norms but must not shy away from asking any questions that might compromise the guiding principle of the 1989 Children Act, namely that the welfare of the child is paramount. Practices such as female genital mutilation (FGM) are clearly abusive in context of the UK law, although are not seen as such by many families of African origin. Indeed, arranging operations for their female children is seen as good parenting in some cultures. FGM is an extreme example but this is an issue about which social workers, psychologists and school staff have to be clear. Years of re-education programmes have led to very recent signs that the practice of FGM may be losing ground in Kenya and Somalia but unless this issue is clearly confronted UK (e.g., questioning the reasons for young girls spending long periods abroad), then the children at risk will never be safeguarded.

Reflective point

We know that the barbaric physical process of cutting away the outer parts of young girls' genitalia takes place in non-hospital settings across most parts of the world.

Reflect for a moment on the psychological impact of this act on a young girl. Imagine her terror as she awaits the time of the day of her mutilation. What will be the psychological scars she carries throughout her life? What is the message to her about the worth of her body? How will this mutilation affect her future sexuality, especially if she returns to Western society?

Knowledge, investigative lines of questioning and getting to know the communities engaging in FGM are also options open to social workers and psychologists, although it is appreciated that the dominance of procedure and casework militates against such community-based approaches being put into place.

Might you be able to spearhead a community-based approach to the issue of FGM in your area – How might you set about achieving such a goal? What systems might you be able to tap into?

Child sexual exploitation (CSE)

The phenomenon of CSE has had much media interest, particularly with regard to headlines reporting its perpetration by Asian gangs in cities across England. While the majority of sexual abuse is perpetrated by white men against white girls and young women, the nature of group or gang-related CSE has primarily included Asian male perpetrators (Unwin & Stephens-Lewis, 2016). Some parts of the Asian community see such claims as racist, whereas other sections of the same community see this as a serious and unacceptable problem in their midst.

The modus operandi of group CSE perpetrators is to 'groom' vulnerable girls, with false affection and gifts, often related to the night-time economy (taxi firms, takeaway outlets). The 'boyfriend' model of arranging for initial approaches to be made by way of a younger, attractive Asian man may then be followed up by him introducing the girl in question to his friends. Hotel 'parties', group sexual abuse, violence and intimidation follow.

Psychological consequences of CSE

The psychological effects of involvement in any form of sexual abuse are far-reaching, and involvement in CSE brings with it a range of psychological symptoms, compounded by a lack of response from professionals and a dearth of rehabilitative services (Jay, 2014). Some of the victims, many with backgrounds of having been in care, and having experienced domestic violence/mental ill-health problems, also refused to cooperate with the authorities:

> I know he really loves me ... (about a perpetrator convicted of very serious offences against other children) ...
>
> He may have other girlfriends but I am special.

> (Jay, 2014, p. 37)

There are echoes of the Stockholm syndrome above (Jameson, 2010), whereby victims develop close bonds with their perpetrator.

A significant number of the victims in the Rotherham case, and others, also had backgrounds of neglect and/or sexual abuse when they were younger. Consider the following vignette, taken from Jay (2014):

> Child N (2013) was 12 when extremely indecent images of her were discovered on the phones of fellow students. There were suspicions that older men and one woman had groomed her via Facebook. Her family were very shocked by photos and video images that had been taken of her, and have co-operated fully with the Police and the support offered by the CSE team. Child N was very angry at the agencies trying to help her. She showed no understanding of the risks of online contact with strangers and was not willing to disclose anything about those who have groomed and exploited her.

> (p. 34)

Exercise

Consider the following questions in respect of the sexual exploitation of children such as Child N:

➤ What do you think the psychological effect will be on a child such as Child N for the rest of their lives and for their sexual lives?

➤ Why do some abused young women go back to their abusers and insist that they are 'loved', despite abusive episode after abusive episode?

➤ Some of the sexually exploited children discussed in the chapter clearly had deep needs for attention and affection. How could social workers or a psychologist find ways to work with such children and prevent them being further harmed?

The example of Child N above portrays the effects of CSE on parents who wanted to be protective, an area which warrants further debate. As the sources of CSE, as opposed to other forms of sexual abuse, emanate from outside of the family, it can be seen as a lost opportunity if social workers do not swiftly assess parental capacity for safeguarding and bring them on board. However, many social work teams seem reluctant to do this and research carried out by Unwin and Stephens-Lewis (2016) found that parents who wanted to work in partnership were often excluded from key meetings and discussions. Interviews with parents of CSE victims found that living with CSE was causing some families to adopt extreme lifestyles. For example, the physical and psychological impact on adults and children included the following narratives:

> It has had a huge impact on the relationship not only with me and my child, but my eldest child as well ... Their estranged father and my relationship with my partner, now separated.

> Husband now has depression, second daughter had depression and self-harmed, and son has high anxiety and has stopped school.

> I'd have to get up and check they were all in their beds ... Yeah, and also yeah, I'd have to do a pillow sweep. I don't know if you've done pillow sweeps. Where they're in bed and they're asleep, but you have to do a pillow sweep underneath just to check there's no knives there because they used to take knives to bed to protect themselves. Getting my sleep pattern, which you can't always do because if you're worrying about the door opening, or not even that, just getting out of bed; she'll go and find a sharp object to cut herself because she self-harmed too.

These above perspectives bring home the all-pervasiveness of CSE and its far-reaching effects, with even less therapy being available for parents and other family members than for the direct victims.

Bullying via social media, such as Facebook, is endemic among today's children and young people. Parents, social workers and foster carers need to be up to date and competent in understanding how social media works and how it can be a tool of manipulation and perpetration. The complexities of CSE are such that all professionals need to have a sound knowledge about culture, diversity, human growth and development, and partnership working. We must treat each individual family and child and not make assumptions about them without evidence (Unwin & Hogg, 2012).

Current policy dictates the importance of child-centred work, with the 'voice of the child' being paramount. However, policy recommendations do not always translate into the necessary resources for professionals to implement them effectively at ground level (Laming, 2009). Recent initiatives encourage social workers to work alongside parents as partners in parenting/safeguarding children, but the reality for many statutory social workers is that parents are resistant or collusive (Brandon et al., 2012). Infamous child deaths such as those of Daniel Pelka and Peter Connelly (NSPCC, 2018) were characterized by carers deceiving social workers with regard to the risks present to their respective children. Social workers and psychologists need to be inquisitive and authoritative when involved in safeguarding. Peter Connelly's case involved a social worker who was unsure about picking him up and, although Daniel's mother was asked to clean his face in order that the skin could be clearly seen. This request was not complied with and the social worker left the house without seeing the bruises hidden beneath the chocolate smears on Peter's face. Working with some families can be a frightening experience for social workers, who often visit alone, and it is imperative for the mental health of social work staff that they are afforded backup and appropriate lone working support as a right, rather than as an exception.

It is not only adults who might be mistrustful of working with professionals but the children of some families will have absorbed their own parents' antipathy towards officialdom and will also sometimes collude/hide the truth from social workers and psychologists. Sometimes children may have been threatened with consequences such as a beating and other times perhaps by threats of being 'taken away'.

Domestic violence and safeguarding

Domestic violence or intimate partner violence is defined by UNICEF (2006) as:

> a pattern of assaultive and coercive behaviours including physical, sexual and psychological attacks, as well as economic coercion used by adults or adolescents against their current or former intimate partners.

The effects on children and young people witnessing such abuse, even if not directly physically hurt, are captured by the following testimony of a 9-year-old girl:

> Me and my sister are scared ... Our parents fight a lot and we fear they might split up. They fight when we're upstairs. They don't think we know what's going on, but we do.

(Childline, 2004)

Children within violent homes are often forgotten, despite the general public now having higher degrees of awareness about the unaccept-ability of domestic abuse between partners, in whatever form. There is a greater likelihood that a child living in a domestically abusive home will be physically abused, and it is now known that the psychological effects on children of such environments are considerable and long-lasting. Such children may suffer from depression, anxiety and suicidal tendencies. Social development will also be affected, whereby children lose empathy for others and become socially isolated and unable, for example, to bring friends home (UNICEF, 2006).

Unfortunately, there is also evidence that children who grow up in such abusive environments are more likely to be abusers or victims as adults (Baldry, 2003). This reality makes it all the more imperative that psychologists, social workers and all other professionals are alert to circumstances of children who may be caught up in such lifestyles.

Reflective point: The smacking debate

Organizations such as the NSPCC have long argued that smacking should be banned in England, where current law allows 'reasonable punishment' (Children Act, 2004). There are strict guidelines covering the use of rea-sonable punishment, and it will not be possible to rely on the defence if a person uses severe physical punishment on a child which amounts to wounding, actual bodily harm, grievous bodily harm or child cruelty. Smacking children in ways that cause wounding, grievous or actual bodily harm is likely to be a criminal offence.

Further reading

Gardiner, B. (2012) *Should smacking be banned?* https://yougov.co.uk/news/2012/02/22/should-smacking-be-banned/.

Reflective point

Some of the parents and carers known to psychologists and social workers will smack their children. Access the You.Gov UK website given above, consider the debates presented by Gardiner (2012) and then reflect on the following:

➤ How would you arrive at a decision that a certain level of smacking constituted abuse, or even a criminal matter?

➤ If an 8-year-old child suffered reddening of the skin, swellings, grazing or scratches as a result of physical punishment, what action would you take as a student social worker on placement?

➤ What do you think would be the psychological effect on a child who is always being hit as a regular occurrence, several times daily, but not in ways that mark or physically injure?

Children in the looked-after system

Variously referred to as being in care or in the 'looked-after' system, some 85% of the UK's current care population are placed in foster homes (The Fostering Network, 2016). The world of the foster family is even more complicated than that of the 'normal' family unit, with its unique combinations of dynamics and histories, foster children's lives often being very fragmented and lacking in stable friendships and relationships. Social workers and psychologists need to understand the psychologies of foster care if they are going to be able to most effectively understand the lives of children and young people.

The importance of stable relationships for children is increasingly recognized; friendships early on in a child's life can help build resilience and well-adjusted adults (Foley & Leverett, 2008). Friendships are particularly important for young children because they allow them to learn social skills in equal relationships, skills such as cooperation. There is an obvious difficulty for children who are fostered in that they are often not in a single place for long enough to allow themselves to make attachments with too many people. This lack of attachment is then associated with a range of other problems – for example, emotional problems, poor co-operative play and a tendency for conflict, poor sociability and poor school adjustment.

Dowling (2005) states:

> A child's home needs to have a level of consistency within it so that the child can value themselves and increase their self-esteem. Optimal conditions to

promote children's self-esteem include care and respect for their ways of thinking and appreciation of difference which enables children coming from different backgrounds and cultures to experience feeling good about themselves. Self-esteem is only likely to be fostered in situations where all aspects of all children are esteemed.

(p. 10)

To do this there are strong arguments that foster parents need the time and the 'professional expertise' to become effective. They need to present themselves as responsive and to establish conditions that establish a relationship of trust, caring and acceptance, thereby increasing the child's likelihood of accepting therapeutic fostering inputs (Howe, 2011). It is interesting to note that the dropping of the word 'parent' and substituting it with 'carer' does not reflect much of the role that actually is at the core of fostering. This is not to pretend that fostering is adoption, and it is fully understood that children in foster care need to have clarity about their birth parents, but does calling people who foster 'carers' and not 'parents' really help children and were children threatened or comforted by the terminology of 'foster parent' in the first place? Children seem to cope with knowing that they have grandparents, step-parents, step-grandparents and all kinds of different relationships in contemporary society – would reintroducing the term 'foster parent' be that confusing for children, many of whom may prefer the concept of a more familial type description rather than the more professional or bureaucratic term 'carer'?

For many children who are fostered, they want fostering to provide them with a 'normal' life (Sinclair et al,. 2005) – they want to belong in the foster family; to be treated the same as the other children; to be loved, listened to and encouraged. They want respect for their backgrounds, no matter what. They want to be able to influence their future and to be successful at school, to go on to get a good job, to have a happy family and children of their own.

We discover who we are, learn how others feel about life's important issues and find out how to live together by forming intimate relationships; the security and warmth derived from initial close relationships with a loving parent (or parent figure) gives us a 'base' from which we can develop. The theory of attachment (see Chapter 2) is concerned with these relationships, which may have been denied to fostered children, whose fragmented early lives make ongoing relationship formation difficult. Why should a foster child 'settle' in a new foster home when all of their experience says they will soon be moved on? Far preferable to take control and break down the placement. The pushes and pulls on the emotions of children in foster care are highly volatile, children having split loyalties to parents and to foster carers, and contact times being fraught with anxiety as the child tries to keep both sides happy. How difficult it must be for a young child to find that balance between these sometimes opposing forces (e.g., mum says you are coming home soon while your foster carer is talking about your holiday planned for next year).

Consider the reflections of Leon, an ex-foster child:

> As a young child of around 5–6 years, I felt an unbreakable and eternal bond with my birth mother. I felt an unfaltering sense of loyalty and support for her despite what others said to me retrospectively throughout my life consisting of 'your mother doesn't want you?', 'You're an orphan now'.

> I would defend her at every opportunity which would often lead me into fights and arguments with other children and sometimes adults. I listened to my mother and soaked up everything like a sponge as children do. I listened to the false promises, the sure fantasy that one day my mother would leave my step-father, Malcolm, who was no textbook father substitute. My birth father was out of the picture. Thus it felt like I had no father at all. I would wonder if this hole in my life would ever be filled and it made me feel separate and isolated in a way from other children and families, well … I felt different.

Reflective point

- ➢ If Leon was a child you were working with as a field social worker, how might you prepare him and his foster carers for what his psychological challenges were likely to be?

- ➢ How would a foster carer in your area of work access appropriate skilling-up to meet such needs?

- ➢ Do you think that this type of planning is routine in foster placement set-ups or do other, more procedural, pressures take over?

- ➢ What could you do to change any such state of affairs?

It is increasingly important that foster parents are able to help promote their foster children's psychological needs and help ensure that they do indeed get equality of opportunity out of the system, rather than see the very foster care status of a child as meaning they get a second-rate service. However, foster carers are in a different position to birth parents and do indeed need to take on a form of educative modelling in order to help redress previous lack of developmental attainment in their foster children. Living in a foster home is not easy even for young children, especially with their 'baggage' of previous experiences, and issues of difference can lead to bullying. It is interesting that many foster children actually ask if they can call their foster carers 'mummy' or 'daddy' as they want to appear 'normal' to their peers.

Some of these experiences are likely to have adversely affected foster children's development in social, emotional, moral and psychological terms which will affect the child's self-concept and shape their presenting behaviour. Foster carers and other professionals such as psychologists need to have a sound understanding of child development, of how the concept of self develops, and of what the management of behaviour involves. With such a complex array of individual needs evident in young children, the ways in which foster carers work together should reflect this diversity and promote a balanced approach between 'teaching' modelling and learning. Such modelling includes being open and honest with a foster child.

Consider Leon's reflections below about the dishonesty he experienced in a social worker, such dishonesty setting the foster placement up to fail from the outset:

> The night I was separated from my mother I was almost 6 years old and at this time the bonds were so powerful that I would not let go of my mother as I was pulled away from her. I think this was the reason why I kicked and screamed with rivers of tears running down my face. I was about to be taken away from everything I knew and placed into a world I did not know. I had never felt so alone especially when my social worker told me that I would not be with my sister after all, after being told I would be. I had felt in such high hopes to be together with my sister but all of those hopes came crashing to the ground. I think my buzzword had always been 'disappointment'.

Leon did indeed go on to quickly break down this placement, and many more, often taking advice from his mother while on contact about how to misbehave so that he would come back to her. Leon is now an adult and has enjoyed much success, most of which he ascribes to eventually finding two older foster carers who stuck with him and always took him back after periods of breakdown. Leon is an intelligent man but still recognizes that he will fall for any stories his family tell him about the past, although he knows in his heart of hearts that they are untruthful. The point is, as his first extract above indicates, he wants to believe them; he did not want to be different – he wanted the 'normal' life identified above by Sinclair and colleagues (2005).

The key challenge for foster carers would seem to be that they must attain certain personal and professional levels of both competence and confidence if they are to best promote the developmental needs of their foster children, and advocate for them in a system that can be oppressive and not child-centred.

For children who come into the care system carrying the needs associated with a lifetime of distress, uncertainty, no consistency and confusion, the primary aim of a parent/carer and any other significant adult should be to provide them with positive experiences and opportunities. There is a key role for foster carers, supported by social workers and psychologists as necessary, in helping achieve these ends and hopefully changing the poor patterns of outcomes regarding mental health currently associated with care-experienced children and young people.

It is important to add here that foster care is not necessarily a panacea, breakdowns in placement unfortunately remain too common and not all children, especially teenagers, share the political and professional preference for foster care – some children (especially those with previous negative and abusive experiences of family units) may prefer the 'anonymity' of residential care. Children who are under 8 are less likely to be able to articulate such views and may only be able to express their fears via negative behaviour while in a foster home (as was the case with Leon above), such behaviour calling for particularly skilful parenting interventions. Some children may have very had complex needs of such a challenging nature (violence to adults and children, or perpetrators of sexual abuse of children) that would make a residential placement preferable (Green et al. 2005). *Every Child Matters* (DfES, 2003) stated:

> A residential care placement by itself is unlikely to give a young person a secure sense of attachment but it may help secure a permanent placement. It can also be suitable for young people who are unable to live with their families but reject being fostered.

The foundations for good psychological health are laid in early childhood. The development of autonomy has been described as one of the key developmental tasks for a toddler; the importance of getting it right in early years foster care is all the more important. Those children who have to adapt to stress and trauma by becoming passive or who have particularly low self-esteem may have little or no sense of their own potential for happiness, and therefore the challenge to foster parents is to find ways of creating opportunities for young children to experience feelings of success.

Kinship or family and friends care

A fascinating area of care and one which has grown in popularity in recent decades is that of kinship or family and friends care. This means that, should a child or young person need to come into care, social workers first explore friends and family as carers. As the old saying goes 'blood is thicker than water', and in many cases kinship care means less upset for the child or young person as they would usually know the proposed family. Also, in these times of austerity, it is by far the cheaper option to mainstream foster care or residential care.

Older children in particular may vote with their feet and decide by their behaviours about the acceptability of placement, but psychologically it must be comforting to a child or young person, even if a placement does not work out, to know at least that your family or friends cared. Critics of kinship care say that family and friends are unlikely to be able to put in place the necessary boundaries to keep children safe, thinking of issues such as supervised contact. There is little documented evidence to support such claims, and kinship care would seem to be no more or no less successful in terms of length of placements offered, but it does have this extra psychological boost for a child or young person later in life that they will know their family was there for them.

A more radical approach, put forward by Ritchie (2005), proposes that the very ideology of 'saving children' by removing them from their birth families should be questioned. She states that:

> The advantages of children staying in their birth families, with appropriate support are clear: the child's sense of identity, self-esteem and cultural heritage is affirmed; the child remains in touch with wider family, including siblings, cousins and grandparents; remaining within the family solves the difficult shortage of minority ethnic foster placements.

(p. 765)

Ritchie (2005) further highlights that abuse occurs in all forms of public care and suggests the risks of children staying at home are no greater than entering the looked-after system; far more children are at risk of death and serious injury as a result of accidents every year than they are at the hands their own parents.

Case study: The Kelly family

Helen, student social worker, had begun to work with Ria Kelly, 11 (for more detail on the Kelly family, see Chapter 2), who had been settling with her single foster carer, Annie Brown, when she started secondary school. Classmates there teased her about being in foster care and said that all foster children were 'sluts' who had sex with

▶

> ◄
> Asian lads. Ria was naïve in terms of sexual issues, but knew enough to tell Jane that some older girls at school were putting naked pictures of themselves on mobile phones because it was what their boyfriends liked. The girls had said they were going to strip Ria at school and send pictures of her out on social media to show her mum and the whole world she is a 'foster slut'.

Task

> ➤ What might be the best way for Helen and Annie to respond, and what kind of parenting skills – advocatory, reassuring, educative, emotional, nurturing and resilient – are called for in this distressing situation?

Summary

Safeguarding is at the core of social work, although safeguarding is everybody's business. Psychological knowledge has much to offer to the understanding of risks posed to children and young people, and all human services professionals need to be aware of safeguarding policies and practices, and learn from serious case reviews and national Inquiries. Safeguarding interventions and the particular cases of children in the care system and those involved in CSE were explored in this chapter with a view to encouraging debate aimed at improving practice. The complexities in safeguarding and in interdisciplinary working were also explored in this chapter and a series of key public domain cases analysed.

Much day-to-day practice in safeguarding is effective and child-centred, but such practice is essentially confidential in nature and does not make the headlines. Social workers in particular suffer from a negative press, mainly because the only time social work is profiled is in regard to failure. Munro's (2011) expressed wish for a learning culture to become part of social work has not yet been realized, particularly in the light of public sector cutbacks, and there has been governmental criticism of safeguarding boards and serious case reviews for not having been effective in preventing repeated mistakes across safeguarding. However, the pressures on parents and carers, together with the increasing complexity of young people's lives means that, even with the best trained social workers and psychologists, safeguarding children and young people will continue to pose great challenges for future generations of parents and professionals.

Further resources

Child Exploitation Online Protection (CEOP). National Crime Agency. www. ceop.police.uk/safety-centre/ (Accessed: 20 January 2018)

Excellent guide for professionals, parents and children regarding the spectrum of potential online abuse and ways to take action.

Coram Voice website. Getting young voices heard. www.coramvoice.org.uk/ (Accessed: 20 January 2018)

Consistently missing from the myriad of Serious Case Reviews and Inquiries is the voice of the child. This website contains a wealth of resources for young people and professionals.

NSPCC website. www.nspcc.org.uk/ (Accessed: 20 January 2018)

A comprehensive website with up-to-date safeguarding advice and issues. Research reports and the repository of serious case reviews are located here.

Real Safeguarding Stories website – Bradford M.B.C. and Collingwood Learning. http://realsafeguardingstories.com/index.php/danis-story/, http://realsafeguardingstories.com/index.php/tashs-story/ (Accessed: 29 January 2018)

The above are video clips which present narratives from young actors and illuminate a range of safeguarding issues from young persons' perspectives.

7

Understanding child and adolescent mental health

Key learning outcomes

Following the study of this chapter, successful learners will be able to:

➤ Critically appreciate the context and pressures surrounding contemporary experiences of mental health in childhood and adolescence.

➤ Recognize assessment and diagnoses associated with common child and adolescent mental health disorders.

➤ Develop an understanding of the workings of Child and Adolescent Mental Health Services (CAMHS).

➤ Be able to explain the how multi-disciplinary teams operate in CAMHS settings.

Introduction

The Mental Health Taskforce (NHS England, 2015) concluded that mental health services for young people had been undervalued, underfunded and underprioritized for far too long, and made a strong case for greater investment in mental health services. Wide-ranging evidence collected included a significant service user voice and the report highlighted the role of social inequalities in relation to usage rates of mental health services. The government response was to pledge further investment into services and undertook to work in partnership with young people and their organizations to bring about a much-needed transformation. The children and adolescents who will form part of social workers' caseloads grow up with the same societal pressures as their mainstream peers, despite a tendency for society to pathologize children who are in the looked-after system, children in need and children subject to child protection plans. The main difference between the children known to social workers is that such children have often experienced high levels of trauma and dysfunction and abuse, largely through having non-protective parents/carers. The 'system' itself might be seen to further abuse children and young people by failing to provide the continuity, consistency and competence (McLeod, 2010) of care as evidenced in the number of placements looked-after children experience, the attitudes of some professional staff (Jay, 2014) and in the waiting times for CAMHS appointments (Children's Commissioner for England, 2016).

Societal pressures that stem from social media and peer pressure are particularly significant in modern-day childhood and the all-pervasive images of sexuality, body image and material success are additional pressures that can severely affect a child or young person whose genetic inheritance may predispose them to experiencing poor mental health. There exist particular challenges for children with backgrounds of domestic violence or sexual abuse, who are refugees and for those children in state care who strive for psychological and relational maturity, but receive distorted messages about what is 'normal' and about how to become accepted by peers. Black, Asian and minority ethnic (BAME) people, lesbian, gay, bisexual and transgender people, disabled people, and people who have had contact with the criminal justice system, many of whom will be living in poverty, are particularly disadvantaged in terms of access to mental health services. BAME households are more likely to live in poorer or overcrowded conditions, increasing the risk of developing mental health problems.

These environmental issues will all be discussed alongside clinical factors in this chapter, and it is essential that all professionals pay full regard to the effects of wider societal factors as they go about their professional practices.

Psychopathology

Psychopathology is the scientific study of mental health disorders, focusing on deviation from what is termed 'normal' psychological functioning (Marshall, 2013). Over half of all mental ill-health starts before the age of 14 years, and 75% of mental ill health has developed by the age of 18, hence early diagnosis and intervention are crucial (Murphy & Fonagy, 2012).

It is important that social workers have a basic grasp of common mental health disorders that are prevalent in the child and adolescent population, including the major diagnostics and assessment tools used by professionals in the field and how these mental health disorders are treated in practice. Contemporary research in the field of child and adolescent psychopathology will be explored below, with a view to raising awareness that can enable professionals from different disciplines to both understand and respectfully challenge each other. No one profession holds a straightforward explanation for psychopathic behaviour, as it comprises an ever-changing mix of genetic, social, environmental and cultural factors.

Reflective point

> - If you were a social worker in a case conference dominated by psychologists and members of the medical profession, how would you ensure your voice was heard?

> - How might you champion the need to profile a child or young person's social situation if the conference was focusing only on clinical issues?

The context of child and adolescent psychopathology

For decades, the mental health of children and young people in the UK was not given due priority, and attitudes towards young people were often judgemental and dismissive. This culture began to change with a series of reports that highlighted the moral, social and economic costs of such neglect. The Office of National Statistics (1999) conducted a UK-wide survey to establish prevalence rates and impacts of what were seen as the three key areas of children and young people's mental health – conduct disorders, emotional disorders and hyperkinetic disorders. This survey was followed up in 2004 and found similar levels of prevalence, with one in ten children and young people (10%) aged 5–16 having a clinically diagnosed mental disorder. This report also highlighted the correlation between social factors and children and young people's mental health. For example, mental disorders were more prevalent among children in lone-parent families (16%) compared with two-parent families (8%); in reconstituted families (14%) compared with families containing no stepchildren (9%); where parent(s) had no educational qualifications (17%) compared with those who had a degree-level qualification (4%); and in families where neither parent worked (20%) compared with those in work (8%) (Green et al., 2005, p. 9).

No Health without Mental Health (DH, 2011) was a very significant milestone for children's mental health, as it represented the first time that mental health and physical health were included together as policy. Greater importance was placed on early intervention and good parenting, recognizing the effect that parental mental health has upon children's mental health. Hagell and colleagues (2013) examined key data on adolescence and found that many mental health problems of later life began before age 14. A further government report – *Future in mind promoting, protecting and improving our children and young people's mental health and wellbeing* (DH, 2015) – found continuing increases in the prevalence of mental health problems among children and young people and brought heightened focus to preventive ways of working, envisaging that mainstream settings such as schools were well-placed to carry out such roles. Additional investment of £1.4 billion as part of a planned transformation of children and young people's mental health was announced to support this report. However, it was acknowledged that there remained very significant shortfalls in England's mental health services in this field, CAMHS being subject to a 'Lightning Review' in 2016 (Children's Commissioner for England, 2016), the findings of which will be discussed later in this chapter. The delivery of timely and appropriate mental health services to our children and young people continues to offer a huge challenge to all of us, citizens and professionals alike.

Reflective point

> What are the factors which you think may have caused this rise in mental health problems among young people?

Might it be the effects of recession and austerity, with so many families and children living in poverty, or might it be the complex demands placed on children and young people today in terms of school pressures, body image pressures and the relentless usage of social media which promote distorted images of life and relationships? Or is it that children and young people are more aware of their own states of mental health these days? Or are professionals across the mainstream health, social care and education services more aware of mental health and therefore able to refer cases on, in greater numbers than before?

Range of mental health conditions and their meaning

Stages in a child's lifespan development are often related to any psychopathological disorder that may be experienced. Carr (2006) outlines (Table 7.1) what disorders may be related to the developmental stage of the child or adolescent.

Table 7.1   Disorders associated with developmental stages (adapted from Carr, 2006)

Infancy and early childhood	Middle childhood	Adolescence
Sleep problems	Conduct disorders	Drug abuse
Toileting problems	Attentional disorders	Mood disorders
Intellectual, learning and communication disabilities	Fear and anxiety	Eating disorders
		Schizophrenia
Autism and Pervasive developmental disorders	Repetition problems	Self-harm
	Somatic problems	Suicidal ideation

Assessment and diagnostic tools used in psychopathology

The two major classifications for the diagnosis of mental health disorders are the American Psychiatric Association's (2013) *Diagnostic and Statistical Manual of Mental Disorders* (DSM-V) and the World Health Organization's (2013) *International Classifications of Diseases* (ICD-11), the latter being favoured in the UK. These classifications change as society changes and such medicalized 'labelling' of conditions can be criticized for its failure to capture holistic representations of individuals and for not acknowledging ecosystems and the effects of environment. Both of these sources provide diagnostic tools which are intended to focus on specifics and distinguish them from other disorders. Thresholds are set regarding 'what is normality', a hotly debated construct, in conditions ranging across all types of mental distress. Mental health professionals have led the development of these classification systems with the aim of improving the worldwide reliability, validity and usefulness of clinical interventions. There has, however, been little service user or patient input into the compilation of such classification systems, although such classifications have an important role to play regarding administrative and clinical purposes.

There are links between psychopathology in parents leading to similar conditions in children but there are no definitive conclusions regarding this link, the complex interplay of genetics, caring regimes, relationships and the wider environment making explicit, causal links too difficult to make (Mordoch & Hall, 2002; Ramchandani & Stein, 2003; Maughan & Kim-Cohen 2005). Clearly, if a child experiences significant health problems which are not addressed, these are likely to perpetuate into adulthood, even though they may manifest in different forms. The double bind that many children of mentally ill parents may experience is that the parents may overlook a child's needs because of their own needs, and thus make it all the more unlikely that they will ever be referred on for help and support.

Common psychopathological disorders in children and adolescents: Assessment and treatment

When diagnosing child or adolescent mental health disorders, there can be differences between the diagnostic criteria for adulthood. This factor is due to the disparity in research findings in those emotional disorders with a childhood onset; they do not continue on into adulthood and many adults who develop a disorder may not have had a childhood diagnosis of the sort. In the following section we will present the common disorders that are found within children and adolescents, and explore ways in which these disorders might be treated, using the National Institute for Health and Care Excellence (NICE) guidance as the basis for this section (www.nice.org.uk/). NICE guidelines are regularly reviewed against new evidence and offer best practice advice to a range of practitioners. All follow a 'stepped' format though which interventions escalate, depending on the severity of the presenting condition. It is important that social workers, many of whom will be working on a daily basis with children suffering from poor mental health conditions, acquaint themselves with the essence of the various therapies offered. This knowledge can be used to support a child and their family, or to advocate for a different type of intervention.

Depression and suicide

Depression is considered present when a low mood causes severe and lasting misery (Meltzer et al., 2003) which affects everyday living as all interest in life dissipates. When severe in nature, depression can lead to suicidal thoughts. Various forms of depression are an increasingly common problem among today's children. A study in the USA (2015) estimated that 12.5% of the US population aged from 12 to 17 suffered from at least one major depressive episode per year; UK rates of depression in the UK Wellbeing Survey (2013) estimated that nearly one in five people in the UK aged 16 and older showed symptoms of anxiety or depression. This percentage was higher for females (21%) than for males (14.8%).

Advice on treatment for depression is differentiated depending on the severity of the reported condition, all advice stressing the importance of sharing good information, being culturally sensitive and careful assessment of frequency and severity. Explorative approaches to moods and feelings and signposting to support groups can be beneficial, and CAMHS should always be involved if other risk factors, such as the length of depression or suicidal ideas, are present. A child or young person presenting with self-harm should always be escalated, and again a careful history taken of precipitating factor(s), home environment, support systems and the severity of the self-harming behaviour. Medication such as fluoxetine also has a part to play in young people suffering from depression but this should always be alongside other forms of psychological therapies. Inpatient care remains rare for children and young people but those most at risk will benefit from the safe, monitoring environments provided in such facilities.

Depression often emerges in adolescence and can persist into adulthood (Lewinsohn et al. 1994). Recently identified risk factors for depression are those of eating and weight-related issues such as beliefs that popularity is directly related to weight, thinness equating with popularity. Binge eating and comfort eating are maladaptive strategies employed by young people in the face of such image pressures, perpetuated and exacerbated by the media (Crow et al., 2008). Suicidal thoughts can also stem from beliefs about being overweight as well as lead to extreme behaviours such as overuse of diet pills or steroids in a search for an idealized body type by both males and females. Other risks of depression during adolescence include substance abuse, suicidal ideation and relationship problems.

It seems inconceivable that a society that is as knowledge-risk and materially advanced as the UK would have produced a culture of childhood wherein increasing numbers of young people see their life as without purpose, love or meaning and so fall into suicidal thoughts. The bombardment of social media images, an ever-demanding school curriculum and the general pace of childhood as children grow up more quickly, particularly in relation to sexuality, are doubtless factors in the continued high rate of suicides.

Suicide and suicidal attempts carry with them great stigma, a historical legacy from the days when suicide was illegal in the UK. Self-harming children and young people use inflicted pain to let out feelings they are in touch with, whereas suicidal attempts often occur when a child or young person loses touch with feelings and with reality and sees death as a desirable outcome. A suicide strategy for England was produced (HM Government, 2012) and a progress report (HM Government, 2017) included a commitment to further resourcing, with a spotlight on educational settings, including colleges and universities. The overall rate of suicide in England fell slightly in 2015, although suicide rates for children and young people aged between 15 and 19 rose between 2013 and 2016, either suggesting that the resources directed into suicide prevention were inadequate, or that the increasing pressures on young people today are insurmountable for many. A recent study by the University of Manchester and the Health Care Quality Improvement Partnership (2016) explored the suicides of the 145 young people who died between January 2014 and April 2015. This study found significant factors in suicide that included academic pressures, bereavement, bullying, alcohol/drug misuse and childhood abuse. More than half of those who died had a history of self-harm, and 27% had expressed suicidal thoughts in the week prior to death.

Reflective point

There is a belief that people who say they are considering suicide will not be the people to carry such an action. It is a core part of safeguarding practice that a child or young person should always be told that any such concerning discussions will always be passed on for further advice and action. Secrets have no place in this arena, even if a child or young person pleads with you to keep a secret.

➢ Where do you stand on the 'If they talk about it, they won't do it' belief?

Conduct disorders

Conduct disorders, and associated anti-social behaviour, are the most common mental and behavioural problems in children and young people, with 5% of children and young people between the ages of 5 and 16 years being affected. The Office of National Statistics (2004) found that almost 40% of looked-after and abused children had a conduct disorder. The ICD-11 breaks down conduct disorders into a number of subsections but essentially these disorders equate to harmful non-age-appropriate forms of behaviour and are more common in boys than girls.

Conduct disorders are often associated with other conditions such as attention deficit hyperactivity disorder (ADHD) and are also associated with a significantly increased rate of mental health problems in adult life. Culturally, there is a marked difference in the prevalence of such disorders. For example, children and young people of South Asian background are less likely to suffer such forms of disorder whereas young people from African-Caribbean backgrounds are more likely to have them present. Conduct disorders are commonplace among children known to social workers, and account for the greatest percentage of referrals to CAMHS, the educational, health and anti-social consequences of these disorders often meaning that a multiplicity of agencies become involved with children.

Medication such as Ritalin is frequently used for serious cases of conduct disorder and has its advocates and opponents, many parents finding that medication is sometimes the only way they can manage some of their children's behaviours.

Parenting programmes focusing on younger children and multisystemic approaches focused on older children are common interventions in the field of conduct disorders. Practice places a strong focus on working with parents and families, although the success of a range of interventions is not fully evidenced in research. The successes claimed by the UK government's *Troubled Families* initiative (Cameron, 2010), which invested heavily in parenting schemes, tackling anti-social behaviour and school absenteeism, were severely criticized as overclaimed in a report by the National Institute of Economic and Social Research (Bewley et al., 2016).

Anxiety

YoungMinds (https://youngminds.org.uk/), a UK-based charity committed to improving the emotional and mental health of young people, defines anxiety as:

> Anxiety is a feeling of fear or panic. Feeling generally anxious sometimes is normal. Most people worry about something – money or exams – but once the difficult situation is over, you feel better and calm down. If the problem has gone but the feeling of fear or panic stays or even gets stronger, that's when anxiety becomes a problem. With as many as one in six young people experiencing anxiety at some point, it is very common to have anxiety.

Depending on the severity of a child or young person's anxiety, and its effect on stopping them participating and enjoying everyday activities, there are three general ways in which treatment might be delivered. Medication, via a general practitioner, may be used alongside cognitive behavioural therapy (CBT) inputs delivered on either a one-to-one or group basis or self-help groups/relaxation regimes may also be effective. CBT has been specifically adapted to treat anxiety disorder in children and young people, and there are a range of psychological therapies designed to counter obsessive-compulsive disorder (OCD), body dysmorphic disorder and post-traumatic stress disorder (PTSD) in children and young people. Individual CBT sessions might consist of 8–12 sessions of approximately 45 minutes, and would include exposure to social situations causing the anxiety, role-playing and support in working through issues. In the case of younger children, parents would be part of such therapeutic programmes. Group CBT might consist of 8–12 sessions of 90 minutes working through fear scenarios with peer support and encouragement.

Eating disorders

Anorexia nervosa is well recognized as a problem across Western societies, sometimes due to problems of body dysmorphia and sometimes as a strategy to appear unattractive and hence be less likely to be a victim of abuse. The Adverse Childhood Experiences (ACEs) study (Felitti et al., 1998) is a seminal US study, which discovered that many cases of obesity could be linked back to experiences of childhood abuse, the gaining of excess weight partly being attributable to comfort eating, but also as a subconscious response to making one's body unattractive to abuse.

Eating disorders were once considered to be conditions of the upper and middle classes but the complexities of young people's lives across all cultures and classes mean that eating disorders are known to most psychologists and social workers. A young person's relationship with food is reflective of their state of psychological health, their body image, relationships with peers, friends and culture as well as a means of exercising control and their wish to conform to media stereotypes and also to gain peer approval.

Social work theory and practice, alongside specialist psychological theory and practice, are well suited to work with eating disorders in young people. The eating disorders most evidenced in young people are anorexia nervosa, bulimia nervosa and binge eating. Anorexia nervosa has been associated with the body image of being thin, which has so influenced today's young people, women in particular, although its causes and effects are far more complex than merely a desire for thinness. Affected young people (predominantly females) eat very little at all, often have distorted perceptions of how their body looks and have irrational fears about gaining weight. In extreme cases, anorexia nervosa can cause serious medical problems. Bulimia nervosa is a condition largely associated also with young women who eat excessive amounts but purge themselves afterwards by vomiting or by the self-administration of laxatives or diuretics. Such behaviours are usually kept secret and are often accompanied by psychological complexities such as depression and anxiety (NICE, 2017a). Amianto and colleagues (2015) reviewed 71 studies of binge-eating disorder and found that the disorder frequently starts in the late teenage years, often together with conditions such as mood disorders and substance abuse. Binge eating has been recognized since 2013 as a discrete mental health condition, and involves frequent bouts of excessive overeating, followed by periods of shame and disgust. In contrast to bulimia nervosa, however, weight loss is not part of this syndrome.

Eating disorders are notoriously difficult to work with and no single intervention holds the key to success. Psychologists and social workers' joint efforts, using combinations of CBT, interpersonal therapies and family therapies, all have their advantages, although, without the young person's cooperation, and some kind of relationship base to work from, prognoses can be bleak.

Case study

Helen, student social worker, is working with Kristen, a 17-year-old girl, who was admitted to hospital suffering from anorexia, with a very low bodyweight and a serious kidney infection. She was initially very uncooperative and dismissive of all offers of therapy or activities, and engaged in very little conversation.

Helen spoke by chance with Kristen's boyfriend, Matt, as he was leaving the ward after a visit, and he told her that he might have sparked off this recent episode when he had joked with Kristen that she was getting a bit 'cuddly' around her thighs and tummy, during a recent trip to the beach.

Helen mentioned her chance meeting with Matt to Kristen, and suggested that perhaps she would be able to engage him in some counselling alongside Kristen.

Task

➢ Should Helen tell Kristen what Matt had told her or leave this for the planned counselling session?

➢ What are the advantages and disadvantages to involving Matt in such a session?

➢ What other interventions might Helen suggest to Kristen alongside counselling?

Psychosis and schizophrenia

Zubin and Spring (1977) define psychotic states of mental ill-health as consisting of a person having distorted thoughts and perceptions, often accompanied by hallucinations, delusions and sometimes by social withdrawal. The onset of psychosis or schizophrenia in childhood or adolescence can lead to serious mental ill-health throughout a lifetime and NICE guidelines emphasize the importance of early recognition and treatment. Psychosis in children and young people is usually treated with anti-psychotic or neuroleptic medication, and should be offered alongside therapies such as CBT or counselling. As a social worker, your role is not to be an expert on medication but you do need to know and understand what medication one of the young people with whom you work might be on and, for example, whether there are any associated side-effects.

Schizophrenia is a specific type of psychosis where a person loses touch with reality, often accompanied by 'hearing voices'. This condition is not often found in young children, and tends only to develop in later adolescence. Its causes are not fully understood and may be attributable to a chemical imbalance in the brain, genetic inheritance, extreme stress or usage of drugs such as cannabis, LSD and ecstasy. Sufferers may withdraw from everyday activities, such as school attendance, and exhibit unexplained periods of anger and rage. Most young people recover from a single schizophrenic episode, particularly when intervention is early, treatment regimens are adhered to and escape into drink or drugs avoided. As with all types of psychopathology, the existence of a support network and a caring home environment provide great aids to recovery. Unfortunately, many young people do not have access to such networks and support as in the case study that follows.

Case study

Jimmy was an unpopular pupil at primary school, known as 'Jimmy No Mates'. Secondary school proved difficult for him, both intellectually and as regards making friends. He was rather a scrawny boy, last to be picked at sports and preferring to get detention by 'forgetting' his games kit than be kicked to bits on the football field. Home life was characterized by domestic violence, with Jimmy's salesman father drinking excessively, at weekends in particular.

One Saturday night, when Jimmy was aged 14, he received a broken nose while stopping his father from beating his mother. Jimmy's father left home that night and has never been seen since. Jimmy is an only child and he feels guilty that he was partly the reason why his father left, neighbours having called the police during the fight. Jimmy had subsequently given a statement, though his mother refused.

▶

◀

Jimmy's mother blames him for her husband leaving and says she still loves her husband. The family receive no Child Support monies and the house is now rather rundown, food banks having become a necessary part of monthly household routine. Desperate for friends, Jimmy shoplifted cider from a local supermarket and started smoking cannabis most nights with older youths, for whom he also delivered 'packages' across the estate. At weekends Jimmy spent a lot of time in his room where his fascination was with *Star Wars*, various versions of which he would watch on repeat after repeat on DVD. Sometimes, his mother heard him talking and thought he had friends round, but the voices were all Jimmy's. Jimmy began to stop going to school, stopped hanging around with the cannabis smokers and got very angry with his mother when she pleaded with him to get up and go to school.

Jimmy eventually went to his GP after a bad bout of the flu and the doctor picked up on his anger, Jimmy having become very hostile to innocuous questioning about his lifestyle.

The GP contacted Jimmy's mother, who spoke about Jimmy's behaviour of late and said she would try to get him to come back to the surgery to discuss these behaviours, especially the anger and the 'voices'.

Task

Let us be positive and imagine that Jimmy agrees that he is unhappy and says he will visit the GP. Helen, student social worker, is spending some of her placement at the surgery and has been asked by the GP to meet with Jimmy prior to a GP consultation. The GP thinks Helen is more 'down with the kids' than he is!

➢ What might Helen do to prepare for this meeting?

➢ How could Helen use her social work skills to attempt an initial discussion?

➢ What advice might Helen give the GP about interventions that could run alongside any medication regime suggested?

➢ What wider factors might Helen consider if Jimmy is to avoid a lifetime of mental ill-health?

Further reading

www.youngminds.org.uk/training_services/policy/mental_health_statistics
    (Accessed: 20 January 2018)

Helpful website reflecting the views of young people with lived experience of mental health difficulties.

www.mentalhealth.gov/talk/young-people (Accessed: 20 January 2018)

Government website for young people seeking help with mental health issues.

www.mind.org.uk/information-support/types-of-mental-health-problems/depression/#.WSMKDpLysdU (Accessed: 20 January 2018)

This is MIND's generic website with specific areas concerned with children and young people. Practical advice and personal stories are present.

Who's who in Child and Adolescent Mental Health Services (CAMHS)?

CAMHS in England were developed after a Health Advisory Service Report (Williams & Richardson, 1995) that recommended the bringing together of hitherto disparate services, which were located in child guidance clinics and sometimes within adult services, with no national policy direction. CAMHS are based around a four-tier system. Table 7.2 illustrates the staff and roles at each tier.

Table 7.2   Tiers within Child and Adolescent Mental Health Services (CAMHS)

Tier 1 – Practitioners who are not mental health specialists	Tier 2 – Specialists working in community and primary care settings in a uni-disciplinary way	Tier 3 – Multidisciplinary team service working in a child psychiatry outpatient service	Tier 4 – Services for children and young people with the most serious problems
GPs, Health Visitors, School Nurses, Teachers, Social Workers	Psychologists, Counsellors, Psychotherapists	Child and Adolescent Psychiatrists, Clinical Psychologists, Community Psychiatric Nurses and Occupational Therapists	They have day units, highly specialized outpatient teams and in-patient units. They usually serve more than one district or region
General advice and treatment for less severe problems; mental health promotion; more preventive work	Consultation to families and other practitioners; assessment; outreach to identify severe or complex needs; training to practitioners at Tier 1	Specialized service for children and young people with more severe, complex and persistent disorders	Day units, highly specialized outpatient teams and in-patient units. Usually serve more than one district or region

How CAMHS are performing

The Children's Commissioner for England's Review (2016) found a very diverse pattern of services across England in respect of some 3,000 referrals to CAMHS in 2015, waiting times for example varying from over 200 days in one part of the West Midlands to 14 days in one part of the north-west. On average, some 28% of children and young people referred were turned away without a service, and a particular concern noted was that, out of the 3,000 children and young people referred to CAMHS with a life-threatening condition, 14% were given no service and 51% went on a waiting list. The practice of sanctioning children for missing appointments, a 'business efficiency' model quite unsuitable and unethical in this area of work, was also noted as being of great concern – 28% of all CAMHS said that children and young people were stopped from accessing CAMHS if they missed appointments. Social workers' roles as advocates are called for in situations when a child may have been oppressed by such a system, many young people with mental health issues having genuine reasons for missing appointments.

Exercise

> If you were a self-harming young person, or you have suicidal tendencies, would a service with a long waiting list be of any use at all?

> While finance and resources remain limited in times of public austerity, what alternative types of services might be designed to make accessibility less of a barrier?

You might consider dedicated phone services/chat lines or the use of peers who have survived similar experiences. Alternatively, rapid assessment/drop-in clinics might be useful options, even if individualized person to person therapy is the underling need.

As regards who uses, or attempts to use, CAMHS, the Children's Commissioner for England (2016) found that girls were slightly over-represented, as were children of mixed race. Males and Asian children and young people were under-represented in comparison to national demographics. A particularly notable statistic was that 4 of all referrals were from children already looked-after whereas less than 0.1 of England's children are looked-after children.

Exercise

> From your knowledge of contemporary childhoods, diversity and the likely backgrounds of children who are looked-after, how might you explain these above statistics?

Reasons for referral

Only 25% of English CAMHS provided the Children's Commissioner (2016) with data on reasons for referral, partly because such information was not routinely kept at the time. Referrals for psychosis, suicide risk, severe self-harm, severe depression and anorexia nervosa accounted for 25% of all referrals, with conditions leading to severe functional impairments (e.g., anxiety, phobic and panic disorders; autistic spectrum disorders; and complex relationship difficulties) accounting for the largest numbers of referrals at 32%. As regards the ages of children and young people referred to CAMHS, there was a peak of over 90,000 children between the ages 11 and 15 years, with some 12,500 between the ages of 0 and 5 years and some 500 referrals concerning children between 6 and 10 years of age.

A CAMHS provider in the north-west of England stated that their priorities were as follows:

> We focus our resources primarily on children and young people presenting with the most severe mental health difficulties. We consider referrals based on the following factors:
>
> Severity: Is the problem at a level that is causing significant distress or disruption to the child/young person's life?
>
> Persistence: Is the problem ongoing and has not been resolved despite input from other services?
>
> Complexity: Is the problem made worse by other factors making change more difficult?
>
> Risk of secondary disability. State of the child/young person's development.
>
> Presence/absence of protective or risk factors.
>
> Presence/absence of stressful social and cultural factors.
>
> (Children's Commissioner for England, 2016, p. 13)

Reflective point

➢ Do you think that these above priorities are appropriate?

➢ Would you change them at all?

Voices of young people

Although the mental health of children and young people is now recognized in ways it was not in the past, the voices of those living with mental health conditions are rarely heard. The absence of the voices of children and young people is a regular criticism of service development and practice across health and social care, the following vignettes being presented to illuminate the day-to-day realities of living with a mental health condition. Every child and young person is unique but there are common themes running through the testimonies below, themes that psychologists and social workers need to address throughout their work. Adapted from an article in *The Guardian* (2017), these contemporary insights from young people in receipt of services provide reflective points for you to consider, either singly or in groups:

Voice of the child: Mick, 19, Stigma

I've had depression on and off since I was 11. Over the years, I've tried various coping mechanisms: self-harm, restrictive eating, bulimia – you name an unhealthy coping mechanism, and I've tried it.

The one that's been the most constant is alcohol. It's now got to the point where I'm drinking a small bottle of vodka pretty much every day, sometimes as early as 9am. Needless to say, this doesn't help my depression, but I'm too dependent on it to give it up. I know I'm in desperate need of professional help, but it terrifies me thinking of my friends and family knowing I'm depressed. I worry that people will be awkward around me, feel guilty for not being able to help me or utter the dreaded phrase: 'What have you got to be depressed about?'

I hope that one day the stigma surrounding mental health issues will be non-existent and I will have the courage to deal with my problems in a healthy way.

Reflective point

➢ At what stages in Mick's life might referral to a professional have helped?

➢ What advice might you, as a social worker or psychologist, have given Mick when aged 11 about telling his parents about his condition?

➢ Are you always open with those close to you, at home and at work, about your mental state of health? If not, why not and what are the implications for the continuance of stigma if you do not speak up?

Voice of the child: Daniel, 17, Fear of asking for help

At secondary school I was taught about religious education, maths, science, English and a plethora of other subjects. But there was one thing missing. After countless sleepless nights, and episodes of self-harm, depressive thoughts and suicidal ideation, I had no idea what was wrong with me. I went to the top of a car park and watched the people walk past below like nobody in the world cared.

A woman spoke to me and saved me. After that, I got a correct diagnosis. Learning about mental health and that it is OK to ask for help is important.

Reflective point

➢ It is not uncommon to read of young people jumping to their deaths from places such as high-rise car parks. What are your feelings when you read about such a tragedy?

➢ Have you thought through what you might/might not say to a person you came across on the edge of a suicidal attempt?

Voice of the child: Andrea, 23, Let down by professionals

Over the years my depression and anxiety have come and gone in waves. After a friend who was having similar problems was diagnosed with Asperger syndrome, I visited a doctor and told him my symptoms. He laughed at me and said I simply had social anxiety, and put me on beta blockers.

When I was at university, a different doctor suggested I see a counsellor. After the first session the counsellor said she'd follow up and make a second appointment, which never happened. My confidence was shook, and I tried a second service. The session went well, and she said she'd make a second appointment for me. She never did. I was convinced that they didn't think I was worth their time.

I called a mental health charity when my depression got particularly bad. They arranged a time for them to call back and do a full assessment. They never called back.

I have a great family, and got a first in my degree, and a distinction in my postgraduate degree. Still, I constantly feel numb and almost completely emotionless. My few friends have all cut ties with me for unknown reasons.

Reflective point

➤ How much difference might it have made to Andrea's mental health had one of those professionals delivered on their promises of follow-up?

➤ We are increasingly busy in times of austerity in public services but how long does it take to just get a message to somebody/ask a colleague to make the call for you/check you have the right address (maybe one of the professionals did send a message/send out a written appointment but maybe it went to the wrong address)?

➤ How easily could you adapt your professional practice to ensure you always got the person's correct details?

Voice of the child: Laura, 18, Trivialization of OCD

'I'm so OCD about that, I have to have everything straight.' Or, 'I'm such a clean freak, I'm so OCD.'

People don't say these things maliciously, however, they do cause upset to actual sufferers of OCD. There are four main categories of OCD: checking; contamination/mental contamination; hoarding; ruminations/intrusive thoughts.

My OCD falls into the category of contamination/mental contamination. I cannot eat cold savoury food, and without medication I could not even be in a room with cold savoury food without having a panic attack. This is the main feature of my OCD, but I also can't deal with foods touching, or sharing food and drink.

Once (while taking Prozac, which really messed with me), I had to empty my room and paint it white. I knew this was illogical, I was crying because I felt insane, and yet I felt that this was the only way for me to be safe and comfortable. Intrusive thoughts control my life. From basic anxieties to more obscure ones, such as my absolute terror of ever having a child and then starving the child through my OCD. But it can be manageable and, for those who know me, since diagnosis I have taken massive strides.

The main issue with OCD is the lack of understanding in mainstream society. By making statements such as 'I am so OCD about that,' you are trivializing a mental illness that is so controlling, manipulative and horrible, and making the sufferer feel as though their struggle is not real and their feelings are irrelevant. Education is key.

Reflective point

➤ Take a few minutes to imagine what daily life must be like for Laura.

➤ Imagine also how her OCD robs her of the aspirations of so many of her peers, such as becoming a mother.

➤ Do you agree that education is the key to changing attitudes and that casual comments about OCD are really harmful?

Despite some of the criticisms about the classification of mental disorders, Laura was very positive about having a diagnosis and felt able to move forward from that point. Think of all those young people turned away from CAMHS who never get the opportunity to receive specialist help, the scale of their suffering probably being impossible to conceptualize.

Further resources

YoungMinds. Looking after yourself. https://youngminds.org.uk/find-help/looking-after-yourself/

This charity's resources are aimed at schoolchildren, and cover issues such as bullying and resilience in a user-friendly manner.

The role of schools in promoting good mental health

Schools have been increasingly recognized as being the location where many children experience adverse mental health, and various reports have been commissioned to tackle this problem. The problems faced at primary and secondary schools are of a different nature to those of even 20 years ago – the advent of social media has led to a wide range of difficulties for children, with cyberbullying and its 24-hour presence meaning that there is little escape. Bullying around sexuality, body image, race and fashion are commonplace. Violence in schools, the carrying of knives among young men in particular, is a new phenomenon, and society has not found a way to ensure that childhood is a safe and mentally healthy time for every child.

The Public Health England Report (2014), *Local action on health inequalities: Building children and young people's resilience in schools*, came about partly as a consequence of the Marmot Report (2010), which was concerned with health inequalities in general, its headline finding having been that people living in the most deprived areas in the UK lived 7 years less than people living in more affluent areas. The importance of resilience – a child or young person's ability to bounce back from low times – was stressed in the Public Health England Report (2014). Rutter (2012) sees resilience as the key protective factor against poor mental health and describes resilience as a dynamic process which develops across the lifespan. Protective factors (such as stable relationships, self-esteem and skills) increase resilience, and young people are better able to cope with difficulties in living. However, for some children and young people, the risk factors in their lives (such as domestic violence, poor school attendance and bullying) will often outweigh their ability to be resilient. The UK government is funding a £2.8 million programme from 2016 to 2019 specifically to tackle homophobic, biphobic and transphobic (HBT) bullying in schools, all part of an overall strategy to transform our children's lives.

A further document, specifically aimed at promoting best mental health in schools, was produced by Weare (2015). This document examined the non-cognitive side to schooling and was particularly interested to develop interdisciplinary approaches based on sound research evidence which could be of use across the whole workforce.

It can be seen, then, that government in the UK has made serious attempts at redressing the issues that blight the psychological health problems of so many of our children and young people. However, rapidly changing social trends and norms around family compositions, sexuality, materialism, poverty and oppression of minorities are mighty forces, and good intentions in well-meaning schools are unlikely to turn this tide by themselves. Effective challenges to the unacceptable side of modern childhood need to be made at both government and individual levels against unhealthy social media usage, advertising, discrimination and bullying. Professionals such as social workers and psychologists have roles to play at systems levels, not just on individual clinical levels, a good start being to join and campaign in their respective professional bodies (British Association of Social Workers [BASW] and the British Psychological Society [BPS]).

Further reading

Public Health England (2014) Local action on health inequalities: Building children and young people's resilience in schools. www.gov.uk/government/uploads/system/uploads/attachment_data/file/355770/Briefing2_Resilience_in_schools_health_inequalities.pdf (Accessed: 20 January 2018).

Weare, K. (2015) *What works in promoting social and emotional well-being and responding to mental health problems in schools?* Advice for Schools and Framework Document. London: National Children's Bureau.

Partnership for Mental Health and Well-being in Schools. www.mentalhealth.
    org.nz/assets/ResourceFinder/What-works-in-promoting-social-and-
    emotional-wellbeing-in-schools-2015.pdf (Accessed: 20 January 2018).

A useful website regarding ways in which schools can best play a part in
promoting positive mental health

Reflective point

Resilience is a key concept in health and well-being.

> - Do you think that this concept is appropriately used or are we some-
>   times asking children and young people to be more resilient than their
>   years allow?
> - Think perhaps of the young carer or the young person living at home
>   within an atmosphere of domestic violence. To what extent should
>   children and young people be expected to be resilient and to what
>   extent are some of their lifestyles intolerant and needing interventions
>   from outside?
> - You might also consider the position of social workers who are
>   expected to be resilient individuals able to cope on a daily basis
>   with violence, mental illness, poverty, abuse and sometimes with
>   threatening behaviour towards them. How much emotional stress
>   might it be reasonable for a social worker to take from adults or
>   children?

Case study: The Kelly family

Paul (whose family background is outlined in Chapter 2), 15, has been physically
aggressive to his foster carers, Mr and Mrs Walton, and he has recently started
going missing from school, blaming bullying. As part of an intervention plan for
addressing these current difficulties, and in the hope the placement can be saved,
he has been provided with a brief course of counselling/life-story work. Here is
an excerpt from his first session in which he completed the life-story task with his
therapist:

> So many people in my life ... coming and going ... all telling me what to do and I am
> pissed off with this. There is this big gap when I was a baby 'cos I don't remember
> much of my mother ... I do not feel like calling her my mother ... why she could not

▶

> be a good mother so I would not have kept on ending up being with the Waltons on
> and off? Don't get me wrong they are nice people, but they are not my parents ... And
> how about my father? He always lets me down at contact sessions – why couldn't he
> be a good dad to me? And there were so many social workers all my life, that I simply
> lost count! I don't know ... I don't know who I am anymore ... what's the point ...

Task

➤ How do you think that Jason, Paul's fairly recent social worker, might help him identify his main issues?

➤ How might Jason weigh Paul's resilience factors up against his risk factors?

➤ If Jason think risks outweigh resilience in respect of care planning, then how might he set about redressing that balance?

The mental health needs of refugees

The UK, in common with many other European countries, has seen large waves of refugee children come into the country, with unaccompanied minors being placed in foster homes and residential care. Children who have witnessed killing and rape, lost close family members, and endured perilous and abusive sea-crossings have suffered both mentally and physically. The fact that they are safe, warm, fed, housed and clothed is critical, but the next steps, if they are to enjoy full lives, must be to address their mental health needs. Fazel and Stein (2002) and Steventon (2016) found that refugee children suffered high levels of psychological distress manifested in PTSD, depression and wide-ranging behavioural problems, often exacerbated by continuing uncertainties regarding status once in a new country. Steventon (2016) uses the case example of Gulwali, who fled Afghanistan after his family had been killed, travelled across Iran, Turkey and Europe via a series of exploitative smuggling gangs and in dreadful conditions. Gulwali arrived in the UK alone, traumatized and physically scarred, aged only 13 years – 'I felt less than human' is his poignant reflection on this time. His battles then commenced with officialdom within the UK, the scars of these battles also remaining with him to this day as he still struggles with poor mental health, despite having graduated at university and making a new life for himself. Many unaccompanied child asylum seekers also suffer extreme psychological problems; PTSD is far more prevalent in unaccompanied minors than among children who travelled with family. The nature of such trauma is that the consequences are often long-term; Gulwali is still experiencing nightmares and depression some nine years after his arrival in the UK.

Reflective point

> How might you develop the requisite cultural competence to be an effective social worker or psychologist with refuge children and young people?

> How would you be able to find out enough about a culture to show respect and interest, which may open up fruitful areas on which to base any ongoing work?

> Remember that the very concept of therapeutic intervention/state care and having concern for the mental health of a child or young person might be totally alien to a person of refugee status. They may have come from a culture where children have no rights or voice whatsoever.

Care-experienced children and their mental health issues

Young people who are looked-after by the state, in foster homes and in residential care are from the same gene pool as the rest of the population yet their mental health outcomes are very considerably poorer. Partly, this is due to the experiences that led to their coming into care but also the care system itself fails children in terms of stability of many placements, quality education and consistent health care. Looked-after children also need to deal with being separated from their parents and being judged/discriminated against on account of their looked-after status. Meltzer and colleagues (2003) studied the mental health of the UK's looked-after children and young and found that, among young people aged 5–17 years, 45% were assessed as having a mental disorder: 37% had clinically significant conduct disorders; 12% were assessed as having emotional disorders such as anxiety and depression; and 7% were diagnosed as hyperactive. A more recent national review (National Institute for Health and Social Care Excellence, 2017) reported that 40% of looked-after children had been diagnosed with conduct disorders (compared to 6% in the non looked-after population). Similar comparisons for the prevalence of emotional disorders were 12% compared to

6% whereas hyperkinetic disorders were found to be at a level of 7% compared to 1%.

Children in the care system are very much more likely to experience a lifetime's worth of mental ill-health as well as be over-represented in the prison population and among substance misusing populations. Who Cares Scotland (2016), which represents the voices of looked-after children, reported on a study in the Glasgow area which found that almost 50% of young people in their children's residential units had self-harmed at some point. There are interesting studies around the phenomena of self-harm, with social media said to play a role in young people copying behaviours. Suicide clusters in young people, such as the one in Bridgend, Wales (Mickel, 2009), have been partly attributed to the influence of social media.

Reflective point

- ➤ What more could be done to equip foster carers and residential staff to better help the children and young people for whom they care with their psychological problems?

- ➤ What would need to be in place to enable such a culture change?

- ➤ What role might you as a student social worker or other professional play towards changing the psychological health of our looked-after children?

Summary

This chapter does not make for optimistic reading. Despite the UK government having invested considerable resources into mental health services for children and young people, many of the social factors contributing to this very problem are of government's own making. The pressures on children and young people in terms of school exams and curriculum, the all-pervasiveness of sexualized and pornographic material via social media, the failure to eradicate childhood poverty, the endemic nature of school bullying, and the atmospheres of fear and violence that still comprise home and neighbourhood life for many children and young people cannot be changed by social workers and psychologists in terms of their structural causes.

However, there is a wealth of knowledge out there and persuasive arguments need to be continually championed at all levels by front-line workers who, equipped with their own knowledge and values bases, can be effective both as advocates and as therapists. There is, more than ever, a need for professionals and organizations to work together in ways that share and blend each other's knowledge and skills in helping our children and young people cope with mental challenges that are unique in our social history.

Further resources

www.gov.uk/government/uploads/system/uploads/attachment_data/ file/355770/Briefing2_Resilience_in_schools_health_inequalities.pdf (Accessed: 20 January 2018)

A useful Public Health England site on building resilience in children and young people in schools.

MindEd Hub, www.minded.org.uk/

A resource for young people, parents and professionals with an interest in mental health.

Burton, M., Pavord, E. & Williams, B. (2014) An Introduction to Child and Adolescent Mental Health. London: Sage.

8

Conclusions

This book has explored the critical, symbiotic nature of the relationship between the disciplines of social work and psychology and is designed to help practice. There are many textbooks which give much greater detail about psychology in its various manifestations and it is hoped that readers, inspired by the insights of this book, will delve deeper into such works. The need to share knowledge and insights between social work and psychology is essential and there is much that the disciplines of social work and psychology can learn from each other in respect of best practice with children, young people and their families.

A core theme running through the chapters has been that social work with children and young people has become dominated with systems and procedures, children increasingly being viewed as 'cases' rather than as unique, individualized human beings. Psychology has never lost its focus on the individual child but has perhaps not had the necessary social lens through which to locate its clients. The waiting lists and complexities of children and young people are now at such levels that we are beginning to see psychology embrace a social perspective. The beginnings of social movements (e.g., *Psychologists against Austerity*) are finding that they share much common ground with social work.

This book calls for an opening up of more common ground as the children, families and communities with whom each profession works are one and the same. Children's mental health is beginning to get the attention that it deserves, and there has been an effort from Government to achieve parity of esteem with physical health. Evidence shows that children and young people in poverty experience risks that seriously affect their mental health – lack of money/inadequate housing and anti-social behaviour in neighbourhoods (Ayer, 2016). Children in poverty have lower aspirations and the impact of poverty hardly features in the mental health priorities of health trusts. The Blair Government promised to eradicate child poverty in the UK by 2020 but what has actually happened, especially since the banking crisis, is that children's poverty has increased and in recent years there has been a rapid growth in foodbanks, with an estimated rise of 54 between 2012/13 and 2013/14 (Perry et al., 2014).

Applications to the family courts to remove children from their parents' care have also continued to rise over the past few years, with 12,789 applications between April 2015 and March 2016, which represented a 14-fold increase from the previous year (CAFCASS, 2016). The question must be asked regarding how much of this rise, and the rise of the numbers of children on child protection plans for reasons of neglect, is in many ways the direct result of government policies.

This book may have painted a worrying picture of contemporary life for children and young people. Worries about body image, social media bullying and terrorism are new and all-pervasive phenomena for our children and young people, which they have to deal with alongside core issues of developmental changes. Achieving good mental health in the face of these and other pressures amounts to a great challenge for our times – for children and young people, parents and carers, the wider community and professionals themselves. The knowledge in this book, supported by personal narratives wherever possible, is a contribution to helping equip the next generation of social work and psychological professions with some of those insights, skills and value that can make a difference.

There is much that social work can learn from psychology and vice-versa. Social work has been affected more than psychology in terms of its contemporary practice having become increasingly performance-managed and proceduralized. Many psychological practitioners still manage to develop effective working relationships with children and families. Social work has lost much of its relationship-based focus and this book is a call to reinstate that focus, even if (as is often the case in psychology) that relationship might nowadays be relatively brief or time-limited. Many of the deaths of children known to social workers in recent years have come about in families where the social workers (and other professionals) had not developed the types of relationship base that enabled safe practice. How many tragedies might have been avoided had more time been available to social workers to spend with those children and families? During the writing of this book, several more children have died at the hands of their parents, and again, social workers take the blame in the media: for example, a headline in *The Telegraph* read '*Social workers should have spotted mother posed danger to murdered Ayeeshia-Jayne Smith, report finds*' (Sawer, 2017). The truth is a lot more complex than the media ever portray, but until social work and psychology services are resourced in ways that allow professionals the time to invest in their own careers, and work in relationship-based ways, it is likely we will see more tragedies, even when the children are known to services. Social work in the UK has become increasingly focused on child protection, to the detriment of the wider, preventive possibilities of social work.

The psychological professions have suffered less than social work in terms of being subjected to performance management regimes and media vilification, but, as evidenced, for example, in waiting lists and thresholds for services such as CAMHS, psychologists too are increasingly working with more complex children. We can take some comfort in the fact that deaths of children at the hands of their parents/carers have in fact lessened in recent years (Pritchard et al., 2013), and in the further investment in children's mental health services. Furthermore, movements such as *Psychologists against Austerity* and BASW's *Boot Out Austerity* initiative, together with other public sector forms of protest, are challenging the political basis of cuts to all public services, with challenges being stronger together.

Looking back over the content of the chapters, the landscape of contemporary social work has been outlined, based around a key argument that psychological knowledge is essential if best practice is to be realized in these times of austerity and resource constraints. **Chapter 1** – 'The relevance of child and adolescent psychology to social work' – outlined the main concerns within social work relating particularly to issues of child protection, where systems and procedural approaches have eclipsed approaches that drew more on psychological theory and interventions. The need for social workers to follow the PCF and the KSS for Children was emphasized, although these imperatives give limited profile to psychological considerations, emphasizing more the need for compliance with systems. The challenge for social workers is stated as finding ways to work that best ensure individual needs are understood and not lost within such frameworks. The experiences of newly qualified social workers in trying to work in relationship-based ways that are informed by psychological approaches are highlighted, and recent child abuse deaths are critiqued from a range of alternative viewpoints. The need for effective interdisciplinary working within safeguarding was emphasized, sufficient knowledge of other disciplines being the requisite starting point for mutual collaboration. Case studies, including those from the hypothetical caseload of our imaginary student social worker, Helen, were used throughout the book to illuminate experiences of diversity, domestic violence, substance abuse and the care system, which are typical of many families known to social workers. The ways in which Helen might have approached these various challenges, particularly by making use of psychological insights and theories, were presented for debate and reflection throughout the chapters. There is, of course, no one 'right' way to carry out social work, but it is the knowledgeable social worker who is most likely to experience success in working with children and families. Such a worker can also best negotiate and advocate for children in circumstances when other professionals may hold radically different views about appropriate interventions.

Chapter 2 addressed key issues of emotional development and attachment in children and young people, attachment theory having become much embedded in contemporary social work, and providing an excellent example of how psychological theories and insights can influence social work, hopefully with the effect of producing better, individualized outcomes for children. Cross-cultural perspectives on attachment were explored, and the fit of traditional theories of emotional development was critiqued against the lived realities of many children and young people known to social workers. Psychological considerations were weighed against workplace, managerial and societal pressures, and case studies and reflective pieces presented to consider such conflicting realities. The Kelly family case study focused on the likely attachment and emotional issues experienced by their son, Paul, whose young life has been characterized by disruption and loss. Recent research findings from longitudinal research studies on attachment from infancy through adulthood were critiqued from a range of perspectives.

Chapter 3 introduced how theoretical understanding of cognitive development is essential if social workers and psychologists are going to be able to justify their actions and to effectively advocate for children and young people, especially when other stakeholders may have different views about a child's best interests. The chapter explored the seminal cognitive theories of Piaget and Vygotsky, and related their work to the contemporary realities faced by many children and young people known to social workers and psychologists. Application and interpretation of theory are key to the learning in this chapter, where a series of case studies encouraged reflection and debate about a range of issues, including children in the care system and children with learning disabilities. The theory of mind, and children's understanding of the social world, were also explored alongside the particular educational attainments of children in the care system, where extraneous forces were discussed as factors leading to poor achievements.

Chapter 4 examined social development and adolescence within its contemporary environments. Seminal theories about adolescence such as 'storm and stress' (Hall, 1904) were discussed and applied to the new and changing pressures on adolescence. Adolescence has always been a time of challenge psychologically for young people, whose bodies go through changes at a time in their lives when peer influences, attitudes of parents and society all complicate the ways in which young people find their way in life. Social workers and psychologists are largely concerned with those children and young people who have great difficulties in finding their way through these troubled years, and whose family backgrounds and nurturing have often been fragmented. The case study of the Kelly family, which runs through several of this book's chapters, exemplifies many of the challenges such young people face. The added complications of the technological age include the ways in which online relationships have changed concepts of friendship, with virtual friends and virtual communities often posing risks to vulnerable young people in terms of cyberbullying, or even grooming for sexual purposes. Vulnerable young people can be tricked into believing the person they are speaking to online is a peer when they might be an adult, and social media/mobile phones have been used by adults as ways of controlling and bullying young people, particularly in the field of CSE (Jay, 2014). Every generation of adults seems to think that the mores and behaviours of subsequent generations are of great concern, but there is no doubt that the recent all-pervasiveness of social media, celebrity fixation, body image and ready access to online pornography are quantum changes for young people. The increasing diversity of UK society brings with it cultural richness, but also additional complications of identity and belonging for young people from ethnic minorities or mixed heritages. Radicalization and forced marriages are used as examples to illustrate the extents to which the pushes and pulls of such complications can affect the psychologies, and life courses, of some young people from diverse backgrounds. Social workers and psychologists need to be aware of these modern-day challenges, and resources such as those of Child Exploitation Online (CEOP, 2018) and Parents against Child Sexual Exploitation (Pace, 2018) are presented as tools to help both young people and professionals.

Chapter 5 explored traditional models of parenting and related these to the contemporary challenges of parenthood, particularly those regarding vulnerable children and young people. The realities of such disruptive, and often, abusive, backgrounds call for particular skill sets, time and understanding in social workers and psychologists. Diversity in culture and in parenting models were discussed, as were the new challenges to parenting in respect of social media and the lifestyle models it presents. It was concluded that social workers and psychologists need to be aware of such contemporary pressures if they are to be best placed to support parents and carers in their work.

Chapter 6 discussed the complexities of safeguarding children and young people, such a focus having become core to contemporary social work. Definitions of safeguarding and methods/models of intervention were explored, with reference to the challenges faced by social workers and others, in an era of public sector cutbacks and performance management regimes. Several recent case studies were explored, with common themes of failure to listen to the child, failure to communicate across disciplines, and failure to learn from previous cases characterizing such public domain examples. There are far more day-to-day examples of effective safeguarding taking place across the UK, but these cases are never in the media, because they are essentially confidential in nature. The particular challenges of safeguarding children in the care system, and those involved in CSE, were discussed via case studies, which presented opportunities for further debate, reflection and learning about an area of practice where there are no easy answers.

Chapter 7 examined a range of theories, systems and case examples pertaining to the mental health of today's children and young people, whose mental health problems appear more widespread and complex than ever before. The role of CAMHS was explored and the need for effective interdisciplinary working emphasized. Case studies, including the case study of the Kelly family, are offered as platforms for learning. Additional narratives from young people with experience of mental health systems were included, in order to illuminate the chapter's themes.

Tools for diagnosis and assessment were explained and the common psychopathological disorders in children and adolescents discussed, with case studies offering opportunities for further reflection, with particular focus on care experienced by children and refugees.

The need for psychologists to embrace wider systems thinking in their work and for social workers to be aware of the ways in which psychological services work – their value base and theoretical underpinnings – was presented as crucial, if professionals are to effectively work together with a shared focus on the child, the family and the community.

Across the contents of the book, all the requisite PCFs at *End of last placement/completion of qualifying course'* level (Appendix 1) were covered, as were the KSS (Appendix 2) required of newly qualified children and families' social workers. We hope that this book will provide illumination and inspiration for students, newly qualified and established social workers, and psychologists. Hopefully, it will also play its part in bringing the professions closer together for the psychological well-being of us all.

Appendix 1

Professional Capabilities Framework (PCF) (BASW, 2018a)

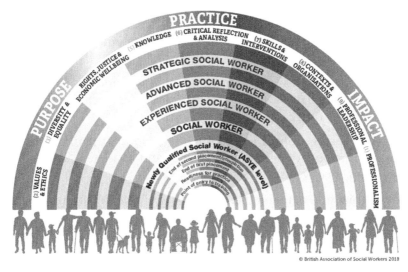

© British Association of Social Workers 2018

Appendix A1. 1 Professional Capabilities Framework (PCF) for Social Workers (BASW, 2018)

End of Last Placement/Completion of Qualifying Course Level

1. **PROFESSIONALISM** – Identify and behave as a professional social worker, committed to professional development.

   Social workers are members of an internationally recognized profession. Our title is protected in UK law. We demonstrate professional commitment by taking responsibility for our conduct, practice, self-care and development. We seek and use supervision and other professional support. We promote excellent practice, and challenge circumstances that compromise this. As representatives of the profession, we safeguard its reputation. We are accountable to people using services, the public, employers and the regulator. We take ethical decisions in the context of multiple accountabilities.

I ...

➢ Am able to meet the requirements of the professional regulator.

➢ Am able to explain the role of the social worker in a range of contexts, and uphold the reputation of the profession.

➢ Understand that social work is an international profession with a global definition.

➢ Demonstrate an effective and active use of supervision for accountability, professional reflection and development.

➢ Demonstrate professionalism in terms of presentation, demeanour, reliability, honesty and respectfulness.

➢ Take responsibility for managing my time and workload effectively, and begin to prioritize my activities including ensuring supervision time.

➢ Recognize the impact of self in interaction with others, making appropriate use of personal experience and awareness, and begin to develop effective use of 'self' in practice.

➢ Recognize and maintain personal and professional boundaries in all contexts and media.

➢ Recognize my professional strengths and limitations and how to seek advice.

➢ Demonstrate a commitment to my continuing learning and development.

➢ With support, take steps to manage and promote own safety, health, well-being, self-care and emotional resilience.

➢ Identify concerns about practice, procedures and ethos in the workplace, and seek support to find appropriate means of challenge and/or offer suggestions for improvement.

➢ Understand the value base of our profession throughout our career, its ethical standards and relevant law.

2. **VALUES AND ETHICS** – Apply social work ethical principles and values to guide professional practices.

Social workers have an obligation to conduct themselves and make decisions in accordance with our Code of Ethics. This includes working in partnership with people who use our services. We promote human rights and social justice. We develop and maintain our understanding of the value base of our profession throughout our career, its ethical standards and relevant law.

I …

➢ Understand and apply the profession's ethical principles (as defined in the Code of Ethics (LINK)) and legislation, taking account of these in reaching decisions.

➢ Recognize and, with support, explore and manage the impact of own values on professional practice.

➢ Manage situations of potentially conflicting or competing values, and, with guidance, recognize, reflect on, and work with integrity with ethical dilemmas.

➢ Demonstrate respectful partnership work with service users and carers, eliciting and respecting their needs and views, and promoting their participation in decision-making wherever possible.

➢ Recognize and promote individuals' rights to autonomy and self-determination.

➢ Promote and protect the privacy and confidentiality of individuals within and outside their families and networks, recognizing the requirements of professional accountability and information sharing.

3. **DIVERSITY AND EQUALITY** – Recognize diversity and apply anti-discriminatory and anti-oppressive principles in practice.

Social workers understand that diversity characterizes and shapes human experience and is critical to the formation of identity. Diversity is multi-dimensional and includes race, disability, class, economic status, age, sexuality, gender (including transgender), faith and belief, and the intersection of these and other characteristics. We understand that because of difference, and perception of difference, a person's life experience may include oppression, marginalization and alienation as well as privilege, power and acclaim. We identify this and promote equality.

I …

➢ Understand how an individual's identity is informed by factors such as culture, economic status, family composition, life experiences and characteristics – and the intersection of such factors – and take account of these to understand their experiences, questioning assumptions where necessary.

➤ With reference to current legislative requirements, I recognize personal and organizational discrimination and oppression and, with guidance, I make use of a range of approaches to challenge them, working in partnership with people using services, carers, families and/or communities where possible.

➤ Recognize and manage the impact on people of the power invested in my role in accordance with our Code of Ethics.

4. **RIGHTS, JUSTICE AND ECONOMIC WELL-BEING** – Advance human rights and promote social justice and economic well-being.

Social workers recognize and promote the fundamental principles of human rights, social justice and economic well-being enshrined in national and international laws, conventions and policies. These principles underpin our practice and we use statutory and case law effectively in our work. We understand and address the effects of oppression, discrimination and poverty. Wherever possible, we work in partnership with people using services, their carers and families, to challenge inequality and injustice, and promote strengths, agency, hope and self-determination.

I ...

➤ Understand, identify and apply in practice the principles of human rights, social justice, inclusion and equality.

➤ Understand how legislation and policy can advance or constrain people's rights and recognize how the law may be used to protect or advance their rights and entitlements.

➤ Work within the principles of human and civil rights and equalities legislation, differentiating and beginning to work with absolute, qualified and competing rights and differing needs and perspectives.

➤ Recognize the impact of poverty and social exclusion and promote enhanced economic status, income and equal opportunities through access to education, work, housing, health services and welfare benefits.

➤ Recognize the value of – and aid access to – independent advocacy.

➤ Demonstrate skills and approaches to practice that promote strengths, agency, hope and self-determination in people using services, carers, families and communities.

5. **KNOWLEDGE** – Develop and apply relevant knowledge from social work practice and research, social sciences, law, other professional and relevant fields, and from the experience of people who use services.

We develop our professional knowledge throughout our careers and sustain our curiosity. As a unified profession, we develop core knowledge that relates to our purpose, values and ethics. We also develop specific knowledge needed for fields of practice and roles. Our knowledge comes from social work practice, theory, law, research, expertise by experience, and from other relevant fields and disciplines. All social workers contribute to creating as well as using professional knowledge. We understand our distinctive knowledge complements that of other disciplines to provide effective services.

I ...

➤ Demonstrate a critical understanding of the application to social work of research, theory, evidence and knowledge from social work and other relevant fields (e.g. sociology, social policy, psychology, technological and digital spheres, and health and human development and from the experience of people who use services).

➤ Demonstrate a critical understanding of the legal and policy frameworks and guidance that inform and mandate social work practice, recognizing the scope for professional judgement and its importance to ethical practice. This may include Knowledge and Skills statements in adults and children's social work.

➤ Demonstrate and apply to practice a working knowledge of human growth and development throughout the life course.

➤ Recognize the short- and long-term impact of psychological, socio-economic, environmental and physiological factors on people's lives, taking into account age and development, and how this informs practice.

➤ Understand the value of systemic approaches and how they can be used to understand and work with the person in their environment, social context and relationships, and inform social work practice.

➤ Acknowledge the centrality of relationships for people and the key concepts of attachment, separation, loss, change and resilience.

➤ Understand forms of harm and their impact on people, and the implications for practice, drawing on concepts of strength, resilience, vulnerability, risk and resistance, and apply to practice.

➤ Demonstrate a critical knowledge of the range of theories and models for social work intervention with individuals, families, groups and communities, and the methods derived from them.

- ➤ Demonstrate a critical understanding of social welfare policy, its evolution, implementation and impact on people, social work, other professions, and inter-agency working.

- ➤ Recognize the contribution, and begin to make use, of research and evidence to inform practice.

- ➤ Demonstrate a critical understanding of research methods.

- ➤ Value and take account of the knowledge and expertise of service users and carers and other professionals.

- ➤ Develop knowledge and understanding of the opportunities and risks of online communications, virtual environments and social media in social work.

6. **CRITICAL REFLECTION AND ANALYSIS** – Apply critical reflection and analysis to inform and provide a rationale for professional decision-making.

Social workers critically reflect on their practice, use analysis, apply professional judgement and reasoned discernment. We identify, evaluate and integrate multiple sources of knowledge and evidence. We continuously evaluate our impact and benefit to service users. We use supervision and other support to reflect on our work and sustain our practice and well-being. We apply our critical reflective skills to the context and conditions under which we practise. Our reflection enables us to challenge ourselves and others, and maintain our professional curiosity, creativity and self-awareness.
   I ...

- ➤ Apply imagination.

- ➤ Select and use appropriate frameworks to assess, give meaning to, plan, implement and review effective interventions and evaluate the outcomes, in partnership with service users.

- ➤ Use a planned and structured approach, informed by social work methods, models and tools, to promote positive change and independence and to prevent harm.

- ➤ Understand and can apply knowledge, skills and interventions in accordance with organizational and national policy while maintaining professional, evidence-informed critical perspectives.

- ➤ Recognize how the development of community resources, groups and networks enhance outcomes for individuals and understand social work's role in promoting this.

➤ Maintain accurate, comprehensible, succinct and timely records and reports in accordance with applicable legislation, protocols and guidelines, to support professional judgement and organizational responsibilities.

➤ Demonstrate skills in sharing information appropriately and respectfully.

➤ Recognize complexity, multiple factors, changing circumstances and uncertainty in people's lives, to be able to prioritize your intervention.

➤ Understand the authority of the social work role and begin to use this appropriately as an accountable professional.

➤ Recognize the factors that create or exacerbate risk to individuals, their families or carers, to the public or to professionals, including yourself, and contribute to the assessment and management of risk.

➤ With support, identify appropriate responses to safeguard vulnerable people and promote their well-being.

7. **CONTEXTS AND ORGANIZATIONS** – Engage with, inform, and adapt to changing organizational contexts, and the social and policy environments that shape practice. Operate effectively within and contribute to the development of organizations and services, including multi-agency and inter-professional settings.

Social workers are informed about and proactively respond to the challenges and opportunities that come from changing social, policy and work contexts. We fulfil this responsibility in accordance with our professional values and ethics, as individual and collective professionals and as members of the organizations in which we work. We collaborate, inform and are informed by our work with other social workers, other professions, individuals and communities.

I ...

➤ Recognize that social work operates within, and responds to, changing economic, social, political and organizational contexts.

➤ Understand the roles and responsibilities of social workers in a range of organizations, lines of accountability and the boundaries of professional autonomy and discretion.

➤ Understand legal obligations, structures and behaviours within organizations and how these impact on policy, procedure and practice.

➤ Am able to work within an organization's remit and contribute to its evaluation and development.

- ➤ Understand and respect the role of others within the organization and work effectively with them.

- ➤ Take responsibility for your role and impact within teams and be able to contribute positively to effective team working.

- ➤ Understand the inter-agency, multi-disciplinary and inter-professional dimensions to practice and demonstrate effective partnership working.

8. **PROFESSIONAL LEADERSHIP** – Promote the profession and good social work practice. Take responsibility for the professional learning and development of others. Develop personal influence and be part of the collective leadership and impact of the profession.

We develop and show our leadership, individually and collectively, through promoting social work's purpose, practices and impact. We achieve this through diverse activities which may include: advancing practice; supervising; educating others; research; evaluation; using innovation and creativity; writing; using social media positively; being active in professional networks and bodies; contributing to policy; taking formal leadership/ management roles. We promote organizational contexts conducive to good practice and learning. We work in partnership with people who use services and stakeholders in developing our leadership and aims for the profession.
   I …

- ➤ Recognize the importance of, and begin to demonstrate, professional leadership as a social worker, promoting our professional purpose, practice and impact.

- ➤ Recognize the value of – and contribute to supporting – the learning and development of others.

- ➤ Begin to contribute to collective/collaborative professional leadership.

- ➤ Recognize own ongoing responsibility to seek, plan and undertake continuing professional development throughout my career.

- ➤ Recognize the significant opportunities and risks of online communications, virtual environments and social media use in social work.

Appendix 2

Post-qualifying standard: Knowledge and Skills Statement (KSS) for children and family practitioners

KSS-1: Relationships and effective direct work

➤ Build effective relationships with children, young people and families, which form the bedrock of all support and child protection responses.

➤ Be both authoritative and empathic, and work in partnership with children, families and professionals – enabling full participation in assessment, planning, review and decision-making. Ensure child protection is always privileged.

➤ Provide support based on best evidence, which is tailored to meet individual child and family needs, and which addresses relevant and significant risks.

➤ Secure access to services, negotiating and challenging other professionals and organizations to provide the help required.

➤ Ensure children and families, including children in public care, receive the support to which they are entitled.

➤ Support children and families in transition, including children and young people moving to and between placements, those returning home, those being adopted or moving through to independence.

➤ Help children to separate from, and sustain, multiple relationships; recognizing the impact of loss and change.

KSS-2: Communication

➤ Communicate clearly and sensitively with children of different ages and abilities, their families; and in a range of settings and circumstances.

➤ Use methods based on best evidence. Create immediate rapport with people not previously known which facilitates engagement and motivation to participate in child protection enquiries, assessments and services.

> Act respectfully even when people are angry, hostile and resistant to change. Manage tensions between parents, carers and family members, in ways that show persistence, determination and professional confidence.

> Listen to the views, wishes and feelings of children and families and help parents and carers understand the ways in which their children communicate through their behaviour. Help them to understand how they might communicate more effectively with their children.

> Promote speech, language and communication support, identifying children and adults who are experiencing difficulties expressing themselves.

> Produce written case notes and reports, which are well-argued, focused and jargon-free.

KSS-3: Child development

> Observe and talk to children in their environment – at home, at school, with parents, carers, friends and peers; including the quality of child and parent/carer interaction.

> Establish the pattern of development for the child, promote optimal child development and be alert to signs that may indicate the child is not meeting key developmental milestones, has been harmed or is at risk of harm.

> Take account of typical age-related physical, cognitive, social, emotional and behavioural development over time, accepting that normative developmental tasks are different for each child.

> Assess the influence of cultural and social factors on child development, the effect of different parenting styles and the effect of loss, change and uncertainty in the development of resilience.

> Explore the extent to which behavioural and emotional development may also be a result of communication difficulties, ill health or disability, adjusting practice to take account of these differences.

> Seek further advice from relevant professionals to fully understand a child's development and behaviour.

KSS-4: Adult mental ill health, substance misuse, domestic abuse, physical ill health and disability

> Identify the impact of adult mental ill health, substance misuse, domestic abuse, physical ill health and disability on family functioning and social circumstances and in particular the effect on children, including those who are young carers.

➤ Access the help and assistance of other professionals in the identification and prevention of adult social need and risk, including mental health and learning disability assessment.

➤ Coordinate emergency and routine services and synthesize multidisciplinary judgements as part of ongoing social work assessment. Use a range of strategies to help families facing these difficulties.

➤ Identify concerning adult behaviours that may indicate risk or increasing risk to children. Assess the likely impact on, and inter-relationship between, parenting and child development.

➤ Recognize and act upon escalating social needs and risks, helping to ensure vulnerable adults are safeguarded, that a child is protected and their best interests always prioritized.

KSS-5: Abuse and neglect of children

➤ Exchange information with partner agencies about children and adults where there is concern about the safety and welfare of children.

➤ Triangulate evidence to ensure robust conclusions are drawn.

➤ Recognize harm and the risk indicators of different forms of harm to children relating to sexual, physical and emotional abuse and neglect.

➤ Take into account the long-term effects of cumulative harm, particularly in relation to early indicators of neglect.

➤ Consider the possibility of child sexual exploitation, grooming (on- and offline), female genital mutilation, enforced marriage and the range of adult behaviours which pose a risk to children, recognizing too the potential for children to be perpetrators of abuse.

➤ Lead the investigation of allegations of significant harm to children in consultation with other professionals and practice supervisors.

➤ Draw one's own conclusions about the likelihood of, for example, sexual abuse or non-accidental injury having occurred and the extent to which any injury is consistent with the explanation offered.

➤ Commission a second professional opinion and take legal advice where necessary.

KSS-6: Child and family assessment

➤ Carry out in-depth and ongoing family assessment of social need and risk to children, with particular emphasis on parental capacity and capability to change.

➤ Use professional curiosity and authority while maintaining a position of partnership, involving all key family members, including fathers.

➤ Acknowledge any conflict between parental and children's interests, prioritizing the protection of children as set out in legislation.

➤ Use child observation skills, genograms, ecomaps, chronologies and other evidence-based tools, ensuring active child and family participation in the process.

➤ Incorporate the contributions other professional disciplines make to social work assessments. Hold an empathic position about difficult social circumstances experienced by children and families, taking account of the relationship between poverty and social deprivation and the effect of stress on family functioning, providing help and support.

➤ Take into account individual child and family history and how this might affect the ability of adults and children to engage with services.

➤ Recognize and address behaviour that may indicate resistance to change, ambivalent or selective cooperation with services, and recognize when there is a need for immediate action, as well as what other steps can be taken to protect children.

KSS-7: Analysis, decision-making, planning and review

➤ Establish the seriousness that different risks present and any harm already suffered by a child, balanced with family strengths and potential solutions.

➤ Set out the best options for resolving difficulties, considering the risk of future harm and its consequences and the likelihood of successful change.

➤ Prioritize children's need for emotional warmth, stability and sense of belonging, particularly those in public care; and identity development, health and education, ensuring active participation and positive engagement of the child and family.

➤ Test multiple hypotheses about what is happening in families and to children, using evidence and professional judgement to reach timely conclusions.

➤ Challenge any prevailing professional conclusions in light of new evidence or practice reflection.

➤ Make realistic, child-centred plans within a review timeline, which will manage and reduce identified risks and meet the needs of the child.

➤· Ensure sufficient multidisciplinary input into the process at all stages.

➤ Apply twin and triple track planning to minimize chances of drift or delay, being alert to the effectiveness or otherwise of current support plans.

KSS-8: The law and the family and youth justice systems

➤ Navigate the family and youth justice systems in England using legal powers and duties to support families, to protect children and to look after children in the public care system.

➤ Participate in decisions about whether to make an application to the family court, the order to be applied for, and the preparation and presentation of evidence.

➤ Seek advice and second opinion as required on legal issues facing children and families involved with statutory services; including immigration, housing, welfare benefits, mental health and learning disability assessment, education and support for children with learning difficulties.

➤ Use the law, regulatory and statutory guidance to inform practice decisions.

➤ Take into account the complex relationship between professional ethics, the application of the law and the impact of social policy on both.

KSS-9: The Role of Supervision

➤ Recognize one's own professional limitations, and how and when to seek advice from a range of sources and disciplines.

➤ Discuss, debate, reflect upon and test hypotheses about what is happening within families, and with children.

➤ Explore the potential for bias in decision-making and resolve tensions emerging from, for example, ethical dilemmas, conflicting information or differing professional positions.

➤ Identify which methods will be of help for a specific child or family and the limitations of different approaches.

> Make use of the best evidence from research to inform the complex judgements and decisions needed to support families and protect children.

KSS-10: Organization

> Operate successfully in a wide range of organizational contexts.

> Maintain personal and professional credibility through effective working relationships with peers, managers and leaders – within the profession and throughout multi-agency partnerships and public bodies, including the family courts.

> Act in ways that protect the reputation of the employer organization and the social work profession, while always privileging the best interests of children.

> Contribute to the organization's role as corporate parent to children in public care.

DfE (Department for Education). (2018) Post-qualifying standard: Knowledge and Skills Statement for Children and Family Practitioners. https://assets. publishing.service.gov.uk/government/uploads/system/uploads/attachment_data/file/708704/Post-qualifying_standard-KSS_for_child_and_family_practitioners.pdf (Accessed: 14 September 2018)

References

Aikins, J. W., Howes, C. & Hamilton, C. (2009) 'Attachment stability and the emergence of unresolved representations during adolescence', *Attachment & Human Development*, 11(5), pp. 491–512. doi: 10.1080/14616730903017019.

Ainsworth, M. D. S. (1991) 'Attachments and other affectional bonds across the life cycle'. In C. M. Parkes, J. Stevenson-Hinde & P. Marris (eds.), *Attachment Across the Life Cycle*. New York: Tavistock & Routledge, pp. 33–51.

Ainsworth, M. D. S. & Bell, S. M. (1970) 'Attachment, exploration, and separation: Illustrated by the behavior of one-year-olds in a strange situation', *Child Development*, 41(1), pp. 49–67. doi: 10.2307/1127388.

Ainsworth, M. S. (1979) 'Infant–mother attachment', *American Psychologist*, 34(10), pp. 932–937. doi: 10.1037/0003-066X.34.10.932.

Ainsworth, M. S. & Bowlby, J. (1991) 'An ethological approach to personality development', *American Psychologist*, 46(4), pp. 333–341. doi: 10.1037/0003-066X.46.4.333.

Allen, J. P. & Land, D. (1999) 'Attachment in adolescence'. In J. Cassidy & P. R. Shaver (eds.), *Handbook of Attachment: Theory, Research, and Clinical Applications*. New York: Guilford Press, pp. 319–335.

Allen, J. P., Hauser, S. T., Bell, K. L. & O'Connor, T. G. (1994) 'Longitudinal assessment of autonomy and relatedness in adolescent-family interactions as predictors of adolescent ego development and self-esteem', *Child Development*, 65, pp. 179–194. doi: 10.1111/j.1467-8624.1994.tb00743.x.

Allen, J. P., Moore, C., Kuperminc, G. & Bell, K. (1998) 'Attachment and adolescent psychosocial functioning', *Child Development*, 69(5), pp. 1406–1419. doi: 10.1111/j.1467-8624.1998.tb06220.x.

American Psychiatric Association (2013) *Diagnostic and Statistical Manual of Mental Disorders* [DSM-V]. Available at: https://doi.org/10.1176/appi. books.9780890425596 (Accessed: 20 June 2018).

Amianto, F., Ottone, L., Abbate, Daga, G. & Fassino, S. (2015) 'Binge-eating disorder diagnosis and treatment: A recap in front of DSM-5', *BMC Psychiatry*, 15(1), pp. 70–92. doi: 10.1186/s12888-015-0445-6.

Amsterdam, B. (1972) 'Mirror self-image reactions before age two,' *Developmental Psychobiology*, 5(2), pp. 97–305. doi: 10.1002/dev.420050403.

Armsden, G. C. & Greenberg, M. T. (1987) 'The inventory of parent and peer attachment: Individual differences and their relationship to psychological well-being in adolescence', *Journal of Youth and Adolescence*, 16(5), pp. 427–454. doi: 10.1007/BF02202939.

Arnett, J. J. (2006) 'G. Stanley Hall's adolescence: Brilliance and nonsense', *History of Psychology*, 9(3), pp. 186–197. doi: 10.1037/1093-4510.9.3.186.

Arriaga, X. B. & Foshee, V. A. (2004) 'Adolescent dating violence: Do adolescents follow in their friends', or their parents', footsteps?', *Journal of Interpersonal Violence*, 19(2), pp. 162–184. doi: 10.1177/0886260503260247.

Atwool, N. (2006) 'Attachment and resilience: Implications for children in care', *Child Care in Practice*, 12(4), pp. 315–330. doi: 10.1080/13575270600863226.

Ayer, D. (2016) *Poor Mental Health: The Links between Child Poverty and Mental Health Problems*. London: The Children's Society.

Baldry, C. (2003) 'Bullying in schools and exposure to domestic violence', *Child Abuse and Neglect*, 27(7), pp. 713–732. doi: 10.1016/S0145-2134(03)00114-5.

Banks, S. (2006) *Ethics and Values in Social Work*. Basingstoke: Palgrave Macmillan.

Barnett, D., Ganiban, J. & Cicchetti, D. (1999) 'Maltreatment, negative expressivity, and the development of type D attachments from 12 to 24 months of age, *Monographs of the Society for Research in Child Development*, 64(3), pp. 97–118. doi: 10.1111/1540-5834.00035.

Baron-Cohen, S., Leslie, A. M. & Frith, U. (1985) 'Does the autistic child have a "theory of mind"?', *Cognition*, 21, pp. 37–46.

Barter, C., McCarry, M., Berridge, D. & Evans, K. (2009) *Partner Exploitation and Violence in Teenage Intimate Relationships*. London: NSPCC.

Bartholomew, K. & Horowitz, L. M. (1991) 'Attachment styles among young adults: A test of a four-category model', *Journal of Personality and Social Psychology*, 61(2), pp. 226. doi: 10.1037//0022-3514.61.2.226.

BASW (British Association of Social Workers). (2012) *The code of ethics for social work*. Available at: www.basw.co.uk/codeofethics/ (Accessed: 22 January 2018).

BASW (British Association of Social Workers). (2018a) British Association of Social Workers (2018a) *Professional Capabilities Framework for Social Work in England*. www.basw.co.uk/system/files/resources/Detailed%20level%20 descriptors%20for%20all%20domains%20wi%20digital%20aug8.pdf. (Accessed: 02 September 2018)

BASW (British Association of Social Workers). (2018b) *Boot out austerity*, www. boot-out-austerity.co.uk/ (Accessed: 30 January 2018).

Baumrind, D. (1967) 'Child care practices anteceding three patterns of preschool behaviour,' *Genetic Psychology Monographs*, 75(1), pp. 43–88. doi: 10.4135/9781473915435.

Baynes, P. (2008) 'Untold stories: A discussion of life story work', *Adoption & Fostering*, 32(2), pp. 43–49. doi: 10.1177/030857590803200206.

BBC (2006). Foster carers jailed over abuse. Available at: http://news.bbc. co.uk/1/hi/england/bradford/5109518.stm (Accessed: 14 September 2018)

Beilin, H. (1992) 'Piaget's enduring contribution to developmental psychology', *Developmental Psychology*, 28(2), pp. 191–204. doi: 10.1037/0012-1649.28.2.191.

Bellis, M., Hughes, K., Anderson, Z., Tocque, K. & Hughes, S. (2008) 'Contribution of violence to health inequalities in England: Demographics and trends in emergency admissions for assault'. *Journal of Epidemiology and Community Public Health*, 62, pp. 1064–1071. doi: 10.1136/jech.2007.071589.

Belsky, J. (1984) 'The determinants of parenting: Process model', *Child Development*, 55(1), pp. 83–96. doi: 10.1111/1467-8624.ep7405453.

Bennett, T. & Holloway, K. (2004) 'Gang membership, drugs and crime in the UK', *British Journal of Criminology*, 44(3), pp. 305–323, doi: 10.1093/bjc/azh025.

Bergin, C. & Bergin, D. (2009) 'Attachment in the classroom', *Educational Psychology Review*, 21(2), pp. 141–170. doi: 10.1007/s10648-009-9104-0.

Bewley, H., George, A., Rienzo, C. & Portes, J. (2016) *National Evaluation of the Troubled Families Programme: National Impact Study Report.* London: National Institute of Economic and Social Research.

Biehal, N., Cusworth, L., Wade, J. & Clarke, S. (2014) *Keeping Children Safe: Allegations Concerning the Abuse or Neglect of Children in Care.* Impact and Evidence Series. London: NSPCC. Available at: www.york.ac.uk/inst/spru/research/pdf/Abuseincare.pdf (Accessed: 9 June 2017).

Black, A. & Ammon, P. (1992) 'A developmental-constructivist approach to teacher education', *Journal of Teacher Education*, 43(5), pp. 323–335. doi: 10.1177/0022487192043005002.

Bolen, R. (2000) 'Validity of attachment theory', *Trauma, Violence, & Abuse*, 1(2), pp. 28–153, doi: 10.1177/1524838000001002002.

Booker, C. (2013) 'Pelka: Social workers let down the children who really need them', *The Telegraph,* 3 August. Available at: www.telegraph.co.uk/comment/10220085/Pelka-social-workers-let-down-the-children-who-really-need-them.html (Accessed: 3 August 2013).

Booth, T. & Booth, W. (2004) 'Findings from a court study of care proceedings involving parents with intellectual disabilities', *Journal of Policy and Practice in Intellectual Disabilities*, 1(3–4), pp. 179–181. doi: 10.1111/j.1741-1130.2004.04032.x.

Bowlby, J. (1951) *Maternal Care and Mental Health* (Vol. 2). Geneva: World Health Organization.

Bowlby, J. (1980) *Attachment and Loss: Vol. 3. Loss.* New York: Basic Books.

Bowlby, J. (1982) Attachment and loss: Retrospect and prospect, *American Journal of Orthopsychiatry*, 52(4), pp. 664–678. http://dx.doi.org/10.1111/j.1939-0025.1982.tb01456.x

Bowyer, S. & Roe, A. (2015) *Social Work Recruitment and Retention.* Dartington: Research in Practice.

BPS (British Psychological Society). (2017) The British Psychological Society website [online] Available at: www.bps.org.uk/ (Accessed: 21 August 2017).

Bradford, A., Burningham, K., Sandberg, J. & Johnson, L. (2016) 'The association between the parent–child relationship and symptoms of anxiety and depression: The roles of attachment and perceived spouse attachment behaviors', *Journal of Marital and Family Therapy*, 43(2), pp. 291–307. doi: 10.1111/jmft.12190.

Bradford M.B.C. & Collingwood Learning (2018) *Real safeguarding stories.* http://realsafeguardingstories.com (Accessed: 30 January 2018).

Brandon, M., Sidebotham, P., Bailey, S., Belderson, P., Hawley, C., Ellis, C. & Megson, M. (2012) *New learning from serious case reviews.* Department for Education. Research Report DFE-RR226. Available at: www.gov.uk/government/uploads/system/uploads/attachment_data/file/184053/DFE-RR226_Report.pdf. (Accessed: 22 January 2018).

Bretherton, I. (1992) 'The origins of attachment theory: John Bowlby and Mary Ainsworth,' *Developmental Psychology*, 28(5), pp. 759–775. doi: 10.1037/0012-1649.28.5.759.

Brindle, D. (2007) 'Extreme prejudice,' *The Guardian*, 12 September, p. 17.

Brinkmann, S. (2016) 'Psychology as a normative science'. In Valsiner, J., Marsico, G., Chaudhary, N., Sato, T., Dazzani, V. (Eds.), *Psychology as the Science of Human Being*. New York: Springer International Publishing, pp. 3–16.

Broesch, T., Callaghan, T., Henrich, J., Murphy, C. & Rochat, P. (2011) 'Cultural variations in children's mirror self-recognition', *Journal of Cross-Cultural Psychology*, 42(6), pp. 1018–1029. doi: 10.1177/0022022110381114.

Bronfenbrenner, U. (2005) *Making Human Beings Human: Bioecological Perspectives on Human Development*. Thousand Oaks, CA: Sage.

Brown, L. S. & Wright, J. (2001) 'Attachment theory in adolescence and its relevance to developmental psychopathology', *Clinical Psychology & Psychotherapy*, 8(1), pp. 15–32. doi: 10.1002/cpp.274.

Bulman, M. (2017) UN denounces British government for failing to protect disabled peoples' rights, *The Independent*, 31 August. Available at: www.independent.co.uk/news/uk/home-news/un-disabled-rights-uk-government-denounced-criticised-united-nations-austerity-policies-a7923006.html (Accessed: 22 January 2018).

Burton, M., Pavord, E. & Williams, B. (2014) *An Introduction to Child and Adolescent Mental Health*. London: Sage.

Bywaters, P., Bunting, L., Davidson, G., Hanratty, J., Mason, W., McCartan, C. & Steils, N. (2016) *The Relationship between Poverty, Child Abuse and Neglect: An Evidence Review*. York: Joseph Rowntree Foundation. Available at: www.jrf.org.uk/report/relationship-between-poverty-child-Theabuse-and-neglect-evidence-review (Accessed: 24 August 2017).

CAFCASS (2016) *CAFCASS care demand statistics: July 2015*. Available at: www.cafcass.gov.uk/leaflets-resources/organisational-material/care-and-private-law-demand-statistics/care-demand-statistics.aspx (Accessed: 22 January 2018).

Cairns, K. (2004) *Attachment, Trauma and Resilience: Therapeutic Caring for Children* (2nd edn). London: BAAF.

Caldwell, L. & Taylor Robinson, H. (2017) *The Collected Works of D. W. Winnicott*. Oxford: Oxford University Press.

Cameron, D. (2010) *Speech on families and relationships*. Leeds: Relate. Available at: www.gov.uk/government/speeches/speech-on-families-and-relationships (Accessed: 22 January 2018).

Campion, M. J. (1990) *The Baby Challenge: A Handbook on Pregnancy for Women with a Physical Disability*. London: Routledge.

Carr, A. (ed.). (2006) *Prevention: What Works with Children and Adolescents*. London: Routledge.

Carraher, T. N., Carraher, D. W. & Schliemann, A. D. (1985) 'Mathematics in the streets and in schools', *British Journal of Developmental Psychology*, 3(1), pp. 21–29. doi: 10.1111/j.2044-835X.1985.tb00951.x.

Carraher, T. N., Schliemann, A. D. & Carraher, D. W. (1988) 'Mathematical concepts in everyday life', *New Directions for Child and Adolescent Development*, 1988(41), pp. 71–87. doi: 10.1002/cd.23219884106.

Cass, V. C. (1984) 'Homosexual identity formation: Testing a theoretical model', *Journal of Sex Research*, 20(2), pp. 143–167. doi: 10.1080/00224499409551214.

Cassidy, J., Kirsh, S. J., Scolton, K. L. & Parke, R. D. (1996) 'Attachment and representations of peer relationships', *Developmental Psychology*, 32(5), pp. 892–904. doi: 10.1037//0012-1649.32.5.892.

Cassidy, J. & Shaver, P. R. (eds.) (2016) *Handbook of Attachment: Theory, Research and Clinical Applications* (3rd edn). New York: Guilford Publications.

Castellanos-Ryan, N., Pingault, J. B., Parent, S., Vitaro, F., Tremblay, R. E. & Séguin, J. R. (2017) 'Adolescent cannabis use, change in neurocognitive function, and high-school graduation: A longitudinal study from early adolescence to young adulthood', *Development and Psychopathology*, 29(4), pp. 1253–1266. doi.org/10.1017/S0954579416001280.

CEOP (Child Exploitation Online Protection). (2018) *Child exploitation online protection: National crime agency.* Available at: www.ceop.police.uk/safety-centre/ (Accessed: 22 January 2018).

Chantler, K., Gangoli, G. & Hester, M. (2009) 'Forced marriage in the UK: Religious, cultural, economic or state violence', *Critical Social Policy*, 29(4), pp. 587–612. doi: 10.1177/0261018309341905.

Chararbaghi, K. (2007) 'Provision of public services in an age of managerialism: Looking better but feeling worse', *Equal Opportunities International*, 26(4), pp. 319–330, doi: 10.1108/02610150710749421.

Chatzitheochari, S., Parsons, S. & Platt, L. (2016) 'Doubly disadvantaged? Bullying experiences among disabled children and young people in England', *Sociology*, 50(4), pp. 695–713. doi: 10.1177/0038038515574813.

Childline (2004) *A ChildLine Information Sheet: Domestic Violence*. Available at: https://search3.openobjects.com/mediamanager/southampton/directory/files/childline_domestic_violence.pdf (Accessed: 12 July 2018).

Children's Commissioner for England (2016) *Lightning review. Access to child and adolescent mental health services, May 2016*. Available at: http://socialwelfare.bl.uk/subject-areas/services-client-groups/children-mental-health/childrens commissioner/179120Children's-Commissioner's-Mental-Health-Lightning-Review-16.pdf (Accessed: 13 February 2018).

Chisholm, K. (1998) 'A three year follow-up of attachment and indiscriminate friendliness in children adopted from Romanian orphanages', *Child Development*, 69(4), pp. 1092–1106. doi: 10.1111/j.1467-8624.1998.tb06162.x.

Chisholm, K., Carter, M. C., Ames, E. W. & Morison, S. J. (1995) 'Attachment security and indiscriminately friendly behavior in children adopted from Romanian orphanages', *Development and Psychopathology*, 7(2), pp. 283–294. doi: 10.1017/S0954579400006507.

Cleaver, H., Unell, I. & Aldgate, J. (1999) *Children's Needs – Parenting Capacity: The Impact of Parental Mental Illness, Problem Alcohol and Drug Use and Domestic Violence on Children's Development.* London: The Stationery Office.

Cleaver, H., Unell, I. & Aldgate, J. (2011) *Children's Needs: Parenting Capacity: Child Abuse: Parental Mental Illness, Learning Disability, Substance Misuse, and Domestic Violence* (2nd edn). London: The Stationery Office.

Collins, W. A. (2003) 'More than myth: The developmental significance of romantic relationships during adolescence', *Journal of Research on Adolescence*, 13(1), pp. 1–24. doi: 10.1111/1532-7795.1301001.

Collins, A. & Laursen, B. (2004) 'Changing relationships, changing youth', *Interpersonal Contexts of Adolescent Development*, 24(1), pp. 55–62. doi: 10.1177/0272431603260882.

Cosin,. B. & Hales, M. (1997), *Families, Education and Social Differences*. London: Routledge.

Crittenden, P. M. (1999) 'Danger and development: The organization of self-protective strategies', *Monographs of the Society for Research in Child Development*, 64(3), pp. 145–171. doi: 10.1111/1540-5834.00037.

Cross, S., Hubbard, A. & Munro, E. (2010) *Reclaiming Social Work. London Borough of Hackney Children and Young People's Services*. London: London School of Economics/Human Reliability Associates.

Crow, S., Eisenberg, M., Story, M. & Neumark-Sztainer, D. (2008) 'Are body dissatisfaction, eating disturbance and body mass index predictors of suicidal behavior in adolescents? A longitudinal study', *Journal of Consulting and Clinical Psychology*, 76(5), pp. 887–892. doi: 10.1037/a0012783.

Decker, S. & Van Winkle, B. (1996) *Life in the Gang: Family, Friends, and Violence*. New York: Cambridge University Press.

DfE (Department for Education). (2010) *Social Work Reform Board: Progress and feedback*. Available at: www.gov.uk/government/publications/building-a-safe-and-confident-future-progress-report-from-the-social-work-reform-board (Accessed: 20 January 2018).

DfE (Department for Education). (2013) *Improving the adoption system and services for looked-after children*. Available at: www.gov.uk/government/policies/improving-the-adoption-system-and-services-for-looked-after-children (Accessed: 22 January 2018).

DfE (Department for Education). (2014) *Outcomes for Children Looked after by Local Authorities in England*. London: Department for Education.

DfE (Department for Education). (2015a) *2010–2015 Government policy: Children's social workers*. Available at: www.gov.uk/government/publications/2010-to-2015-government-policy-childrens-social-workers/2010-to-2015-government-policy-childrens-social-workers (Accessed: 22 January 2018).

DfE (Department for Education). (2015b) *Knowledge and skills statements for child and family social work*. Available at: www.gov.uk/government/publications/knowledge-and-skills-statements-for-child-and-family-social-work (Accessed: 21 January 2018).

DfE (Department for Education). (2016) *Wood report. Review of the role and functions of local safeguarding children boards*. Available at: www.gov.uk/government/uploads/system/uploads/attachment_data/file/526329/Alan_Wood_review.pdf (Accessed: 21 January 2018).

DfE (Department for Education). (2017) *Evaluation of signs of safety in 10 pilots research report*. Social Care Workforce Research Unit, King's College London. Available at: www.gov.uk/government/uploads/system/uploads/attachment_data/file/625376/Evaluation_of_Signs_of_Safety_in_10_pilotspdf. (Accessed: 21 January 2018).

DfE (Department of Education). (2018) *Post-qualifying standard: knowledge and skills statement for children and family practitioners.* Available at: https://assets.publishing.service.gov.uk/government/uploads/system/uploads/attachment_data/file/708704/Post-qualifying_standard-KSS_for_child_and_family_practitioners.pdf (Accessed: 14 September 2018)

DfES (Department for Education). (2003) *Every Child Matters.* CM5860. London: The Stationery Office.

Dodd, V. (2017) 'NSPCC reports large rise in forced marriage counselling for children', *The Guardian.* Available at: www.theguardian.com/society/2017/jul/30/nspcc-reports-large-rise-rise-in-forced-marriage-counselling-for-children (Accessed: 21 January 2018).

DoH (Department of Health). (1991) *The Foster Placement (Children) Regulations 1991.* Available at: www.legislation.gov.uk/uksi/1991/910/note/made (Accessed: 19 August 2018).

DoH (Department of Health). (2001) Valuing people: *A new strategy for learning disability for the 21st Century.* Available at: http://bit.ly/17DUyVN (Accessed: 21 January 2018).

DoH (Department of Health). (2004) *The mental health and psychological well-being of children and young people, CAMHS standard, national service framework for children, young people and maternity services.* Available at: www.gov.uk/government/uploads/system/uploads/attachment_data/file/199959/National_Service_Framework_for_Children_Young_People_and_Maternity_Services_-_The_Mental_Health__and_Psychological_Well-being_of_Children_and_Young_People.pdf (Accessed: 21 January 2018).

DoH (Department of Health). (2011) *No health without mental health a cross-government mental health outcomes strategy for people of all ages.* Available at: www.gov.uk/government/publications/no-health-without-mental-health-a-cross-government-mental-health-outcomes-strategy-for-people-of-all-ages-a-call-to-action (Accessed: 21 January 2018).

Devine, L. (2017) Rethinking child protection strategy: Progress and next steps, *Seen and Heard*, 26(4), pp. 30–49. Available at: http://eprints.uwe.ac.uk/29438 (Accessed: 20 January 2018).

Dominelli, L. (2004) *Theory and Practice for a Changing Profession.* Cambridge: Polity Press.

Dumontheil, I. (2016) 'Adolescent brain development'. *Current Opinion in Behavioral Sciences*, 10, pp. 39–44. doi: doi.org/10.1016/j.cobeha.2016.04.012.

Dunn, J. (2004) *Children's Friendships: The Beginnings of Intimacy.* Hoboken, NJ: Wiley-Blackwell.

Dykas, M. J., Woodhouse, S. S., Cassidy, J. & Waters, H. S. (2006) Narrative assessment of attachment representations: Links between secure base scripts and adolescent attachment, *Attachment & Human Development*, 8(3), pp. 221–240. doi: 10.1080/14616730600856099.

Easterbrooks, M. A., Bureau, J. F. & Lyons-Ruth, K. (2012) 'Developmental correlates and predictors of emotional availability in mother–child interaction: A longitudinal study from infancy to middle childhood', *Development and Psychopathology*, 24(1), pp. 65–78. doi: 10.1017/S0954579411000666.

Elkind, D. (1967) 'Egocentrism in adolescence', *Child Development*, 38(4), pp. 1025–1034. doi: 10.2307/1127100.

Emerson, E. and Hatton, C. (2007) *The mental health of children and adolescents with learning disabilities in Britain*. Available at: www.lancaster.ac.uk/staff/emersone/FASSWeb/Emerson_07_FPLD_MentalHealth.pdf (Accessed: 22 January 2018).

Erikson, E. H. (1956). The problem of ego identity. *Journal of the American Psychoanalytic Association*, 4(1), 56–121.

Fagot, B. I. (1997) 'Attachment, parenting, and peer interactions of toddler children', *Developmental Psychology*, 33(3), pp. 489–499. doi: 10.1037/0012-1649.33.3.489.

Fazel, F. & Stein, A. (2002) 'The mental health of refugee children', *Archives of Disease in Childhood*, 87(5), pp. 366–370. doi: 10.1136/adc.87.5.366.

Featherstone, B., White, S. & Morris, K. (2014) *Re-Imagining Child Protection: Towards Humane Social Work with Families*. Bristol: Policy Press.

Felitti, V., Anda., R.,Nordenberg, D.,Williamson, D., Spitz, A., Edwards, V., Koss, M. & Marks J. (1998) 'Relationship of childhood abuse and household dysfunction to many of the leading causes of death in adults: The Adverse Childhood Experiences (ACE) Study', *American Journal of Preventive Medicine*, 14(4), pp. 245–258. doi:10.1016/S0749-3797(98)00017-8.

Felsman, D. E. & Blustein, D. L. (1999) 'The role of peer relatedness in late adolescent career development', *Journal of Vocational Behavior*, 54(2), pp. 279–295. doi: 10.1006/jvbe.1998.1664.

Ferguson, H. (2011) *Child Protection Practice*. Basingstoke: Palgrave Macmillan.

Fish, M. (2004) 'Attachment in infancy and preschool in low socioeconomic status rural Appalachian children: Stability and change and relations to preschool and kindergarten competence', *Development and Psychopathology*, 16(2), pp. 293–312. doi: 10.1017/S0954579404044529.

Fitch, K. (2009) *Teenagers at risk. The safeguarding needs of young people in gangs and violent groups:* NSPCC Inform. Available at: www.nspcc.org.uk/globalassets/documents/research-reports/teenagers-at-risk-report.pdf (Accessed: 22 January 2018).

Flavell, J. H. (1996) 'Piaget's legacy'. *Psychological Science*, 7(4), pp. 200–203.

Foley, P. & Leverett, S. (2008) *Connecting with Children: Developing Working Relationships*. Bristol: Policy Press.

The Fostering Network (2016) *Over 9,000 more fostering households urgently needed during 2016*. Available at: www.thefosteringnetwork.org.uk/media-release-news/2016/over-9000-more-fostering-households-urgently-needed-during-2016 (Accessed: 2 April 2017).

Fraley, R. C. (2002) 'Attachment stability from infancy to adulthood: Meta-analysis and dynamic modeling of developmental mechanisms', *Personality and Social Psychology Review*, 6, pp. 123–151. doi: 10.1207/S15327957PSPR0602_03.

Fraser, A. (2010) 'Growing through gangs: Young people, identity and social change in Glasgow', PhD thesis, Glasgow University, UK. Available at: http://theses.gla.ac.uk/2343/ (Accessed: 22 January 2018).

Freud, A. & Dann, S. (1951) 'An experiment in group upbringing', *Psychoanalytic Study of the Child*, 6, pp. 127–168. doi: 10.1080/00797308.1952.11822909.

Frost, N. & Parton, N. (2009) *Understanding Children's Social Care: Politics, Policy and Practice*. London: Sage.

Fuentes, M., Salas, M., Bernedo, I. & Martin, M. (2015) Impact of the parenting style of foster parents on the behaviour problems of foster children, *Child Care Health Development*, 41(5), pp. 704–711. doi: 10.1111/cch.12215.

Fuhrmann, D., Knoll, L. J. & Blakemore, S. J. (2015) 'Adolescence as a sensitive period of brain development', *Trends in Cognitive Sciences*, 19(10), pp. 558–566. doi: 10.1016/j.tics.2015.07.008.

Gardiner, B. (2012) *Should smacking be banned?* Available at: https://yougov.co.uk/news/2012/02/22/should-smacking-be-banned/ (Accessed: 22 January 2018).

Goldberg, S., Benoit, D., Blokland, K. & Madigan, S. (2003) 'Atypical maternal behavior, maternal representations, and infant disorganized attachment', *Development and Psychopathology*, 15(2), pp. 239–257. doi: 10.1017/S0954579403000130.

Goleman, D. (1995) *Emotional Intelligence*. New York: Bantam.

Goodman, A. & Gregg, P. (eds.) (2010) *Poorer Children's Educational Attainment: How Important are Attitudes and Behaviour?* York: Joseph Rowntree Foundation.

Gough, D. & Stanley, N. (2004) 'Parenting capacity'. *Child Abuse Review*, 13(1), pp. 1–4.

Gove, M. (2012) 'The failure of child protection and the need for a fresh start', Education Secretary speech on child protection on 19 November at the Institute of Public Policy Research. Available at: www.gov.uk/government/speeches/the-failure-of-childprotection-and-the-need-for-a-fresh-start (Accessed: 23 January 2018).

Green, H., McGinnity, Á., Meltzer, H., Ford, T. & Goodman, R. (2005) *Mental health of children and young people in Great Britain*. Available at: http://digital.nhs.uk/catalogue/PUB06116 (Accessed: 22 January 2018).

The Guardian (2017) Young people and mental health: 'Since diagnosis, I have taken massive strides', *The Guardian*, 31 March. Available at: www.theguardian.com/lifeandstyle/2017/mar/31/young-people-and-mental-health-since-diagnosis-i-have-taken-massive-strides (Accessed: 31 March 2017).

Hagell, A., Coleman, J. & Brooks, F. (2013) *Key Data on Adolescence*. London: Public Health England.

Hall, G. S. (1904) *Adolescence: Its Psychology and Its Relation to Physiology, Anthropology, Sociology, Sex, Crime, Religion, and Education* (Vols. 1 & 2). Englewood Cliffs, NJ: Prentice-Hall.

Hamilton, C. E. (2000) Continuity and discontinuity of attachment from infancy through adolescence, *Child development*, 71(3), pp. 690–694. doi: https://doi.org/10.1111/1467-8624.00177.

Hamm, M. P., Newton, A. S., Chisholm, A., Shulhan, J., Milne, A., Sundar, P. & Hartling, L. (2015) 'Prevalence and effect of cyberbullying on children and young people: A scoping review of social media studies', *JAMA Pediatrics*, 169(8), pp. 770–777. doi: 10.1001/jamapediatrics.2015.0944.

Hardie, E. & Tilly, L. (2012) *An Introduction to Supporting People with a Learning Disability*. London: Sage.

Harris, J. (2000) 'Attachment theory underestimates the child', *Behavioral and Brain Sciences*, 3(21), pp. 30, doi: 10.1017/so140525x09000119.

Harris, J. & Unwin, P. (2009) 'Performance management in modernised social work.' In J. Harris & V. White (eds), *Modernising Social Work: Critical Considerations*. Bristol: Policy Press.

Harris, P. L., Johnson, C. N., Hutton, D., Andrews, G. & Cooke, T. (1989) 'Young children's theory of mind and emotion', *Cognition & Emotion*, 3(4), pp. 379–400. doi: 10.1080/02699938908412713.

Hazan, C. & Shaver, P. (1987) 'Romantic love conceptualized as an attachment process', *Journal of Personality and Social Psychology*, 52(3), pp. 511. doi: 10.1037/0022-3514.52.3.511.

HCPC (Health and Care Professions Council). (2017) *Standards of Proficiency: Social Workers in England*. London: HCPC. Available at: www.hcpc-uk.org/publications/standards/index.asp?id=569 (Accessed: 27 June 2018).

Hickman, L. J., Jaycox, L. H. & Aronoff, J. (2004) 'Dating violence among adolescents: Prevalence, gender distribution, and prevention program effectiveness', *Trauma, Violence, & Abuse*, 5(2), pp. 123–142. doi: 10.1177/1524838003262332.

Hird, M. J. (2000) 'An empirical study of adolescent dating aggression in the UK', *Journal of Adolescence*, 23(1), pp. 69–78. doi: 10.1006/jado.1999.0292.

HM Government (2008) *Tackling violence action plan. Saving lives. Reducing harm. protecting the public. An action plan for tackling violence 2008–11*. Available at: http://webarchive.nationalarchives.gov.uk/20100408132733/www.homeoffice.gov.uk/documents/violent-crime-action-plan-08/ (Accessed: August 2017).

HM Government (2011) *Prevent strategy*. Available at: www.gov.uk/government/uploads/system/uploads/attachment_data/file/97976/prevent-strategy-review.pdf (Accessed: 22 January 2018).

HM Government (2012) *Suicide prevention strategy for England*. Available at: www.gov.uk/government/publications/suicide-prevention-strategy-for-england (Accessed: 22 January 2018).

HM Government (2016) *Ending gang violence and exploitation*. Available at: www.gov.uk/government/uploads/system/uploads/attachment_data/file/491699/Ending_gang_violence_and_Exploitation_FINAL.pdf (Accessed: 22 January 2018).

HM Government (2017) *Preventing suicide in England: Third progress report of the cross-government outcomes strategy to save lives*. Available at: http://iapdeathsincustody.independent.gov.uk/wp-Content/uploads/2017/01/Suicide_report_2016_A1.pdf (Accessed: 22 January 2018).

HM Government (2018) *Working Together to Safeguard Children: Statutory Guidance on Inter-Agency Working to Safeguard and Promote the Welfare of Children*. Available at: https://assets.publishing.service.gov.uk/government/uploads/system/uploads/attachment_data/file/729914/Working_Together_to_Safeguard_Children-2018.pdf (Accessed: 16 August 2018).

Howe, D. (2008) *The Emotionally Intelligent Social Worker.* Basingstoke: Palgrave.

Howe, D. (2011) *Attachment across the Lifecourse: A Brief Introduction.* Basing-stoke: Palgrave Macmillan.

Howe, D. & Fearnley, S. (1999) 'Disorders of attachment and attach-ment therapy', *Adoption & Fostering*, 23(2), pp. 19–30. doi: 10.1177/030857599902300205.

Howe, D. & Fearnley, S. (2003) 'Disorders of attachment in adopted and fostered children: Recognition and treatment', *Clinical Child Psychology and Psychiatry*, 8(3), pp. 369–387. doi: 10.1177/1359104503008003007.

Howe, M. L. & Courage, M. L. (1993) 'On resolving the enigma of infantile amnesia', *Psychological Bulletin*, 113(2), pp. 305–326. doi: 10.1037/0033-2909.113.2.305.

Hussain, F. & Raczka, R. (1997) 'Life story work for people with learning disabilities', *British Journal of Learning Disabilities*, 25(2), pp. 73–76. doi: 10.1111/j.1468-3156.1997.tb00014.x.

Independent Inquiry into child Sexual Abuse (2017*) The protection of children outside the United Kingdom: Investigation into child sexual abuse related to child migration. Programmes background statement.* Available at: www.iicsa.org.uk/sites/default/files/Child%20Migration%20Programmes%20case%20study%20-%20Background%20Statement.pdf (Accessed: 4 November 2017).

Jackson, S. M., Cram, F. & Seymour, F. W. (2000) 'Violence and sexual coercion in high school students' dating relationships', *Journal of Family Violence*, 15(1), pp. 23–36. doi: 10.1023/A:1007545302987.

Jacobsen, H., Ivarsson, T., Wentzel-Larsen, T., Smith, L. & Moe, V. (2014) 'Attachment security in young foster children: Continuity from 2 to 3 years of age', *Attachment & Human Development*, 16(1), pp. 42–57. doi: 10.1080/14616734.2013.850102.

Jameson, C. (2010) The 'short step' from love to hypnosis: A reconsideration of the Stockholm syndrome, *Journal for Cultural Research*, 14(4), pp. 337–355. doi: 10.1080/14797581003765309.

Jay, A. (2014) *Independent inquiry into child sexual exploitation in Rotherham (1997–2013).* Available at: www.rotherham.gov.uk/downloads/file/1407/independent_inquiry_cse_in_rotherham (Accessed: July 2017).

Jobe-Shields, L., Swiecicki, C., Fritz, D., Stinnette, J. & Hanson, R. (2016) 'Post-traumatic stress and depression in the non offending caregivers of sexually abused children: Associated with parenting practices', *Journal of Child Sexual Abuse*, 25(1), pp. 110–125. doi:10.108/10538712.20151078867.

Jones, R. (2014) *The Story of Baby P. Setting the Record Straight.* Bristol: Polity.

Johnstone, L. & Boyle, M., Cromby, J., Dillon, J., Harper, D., Kinderman, P., Longden, E., Pilgrim, D. & Read, J. (2018) *The Power Threat Meaning Frame-work: Overview.* Leicester: British Psychological Society.

Kaler, S. R. & Freeman, B. J. (1994) 'Analysis of environmental deprivation: Cognitive and social development in Romanian orphans', *Journal of Child Psychology and Psychiatry*, 35(4), pp. 769–781. doi: 10.1111/j.1469-7610.1994.tb01220.x.

Karaian, L. (2015) Selfies, sexualisation and 'self-exploitation' in law-and-order times. In D. Egan, E. Renold & J. Ringrose (eds.), *Children, Sexuality and 'Sexualisation': Beyond Spectacle and Sensationalism*. London: Praeger. pp. 18–35.

King, K., Kraemer, L., Bernard, A. & Vidourek, R. (2007) 'Foster Parents' Involvement in Authoritative Parenting and Interest in Future Parenting Training', Journal of Child & Family Studies, 16 (5), pp. 606-614. doi: 10.1007/s10826-006-9110-5.

Kinniburgh-White, R., Cartwright, C. & Seymour, F. (2010) 'Young adults' narratives of relational development with stepfathers', *Journal of Social and Personal Relationships*, 27(7), pp. 890–907. doi: 10.1177/0265407510376252.

Klaus, M., Kennell, M.D. & Klaus, P.H. (1996) Bonding. Building the Foundations of Secure Attachment and Independence. New York: Addison-Wesley

Koenig, A. L., Cicchetti, D. & Rogosch, F. A. (2004) 'Moral development: The association between maltreatment and young children's prosocial behaviors and moral transgressions', *Social Development*, 13(1), pp. 87–106. doi:10.1111/j.1467-9507.2004.00258.x.

Lamb, M. E., La Rooy, D. J., Malloy, L. C. & Katz, C. (eds.) (2011) *Children's Testimony: A Handbook of Psychological Research and Forensic Practice*. Chichester: Wiley.

Laming, H. (2003) *The Victoria Climbié Inquiry Report*. London: The Stationery Office. Available at: www.victoria-climbie-inquiry.org.uk (Accessed: January 19, 2018).

Laming, L. (2009) *The Protection of Children in England: A Progress Report. Department for Children, Schools and Families*. London: The Stationery Office. Available at: www.gov.uk/government/publications/the-protection-of-children-in-england-a-progress-report (Accessed January 19, 2018).

Lewinsohn, P., Roberts R., Seeley, J., Rohde, P., Gotlib, I. & Hops, H. (1994) 'Adolescent psychopathology: II. Psychosocial risk factors for depression', *Journal of Abnormal Psychology*, 103(2), pp. 302–315. doi: 10.1037/0021-843X.103.2.302.

Lewis, M., Feiring, C. & Rosenthal, S. (2000) 'Attachment over time'. *Child Development*, 71(3), pp. 707–720. doi: 10.1111/1467-8624.00180.

Lillard, A. S., Lerner, M. D., Hopkins, E. J., Dore, R. A., Smith, E. D. & Palmquist, C. M. (2013) 'The impact of pretend play on children's development: A review of the evidence', *Psychological Bulletin*, 139(1), pp. 1–34. doi: 10.1037/a0029321.

Lindsay, D. S., Hagen, L., Read, J. D., Wade, K. A. & Garry, M. (2004) 'True photographs and false memories', *Psychological Sciences*, 15(3), pp. 149–154. doi: 10.1111/j.0956-7976.2004.01503002.x.

McAlister, A. & Peterson, C. (2007). 'A longitudinal study of siblings and theory of mind development'. *Cognitive Development*, 22, pp. 258–270. doi: 10.1111/cdev. 12043.

McCabe, M. P., McGillivray, J. A. & Newton, D. C. (2006) 'Effectiveness of treatment programmes for depression among adults with mild/moderate intellectual disability', *Journal of Intellectual Disability Research*, 50(4), pp. 239–247. doi: 10.1111/j.1365-2788.2005.00772.x.

McElwain, N. L. & Volling, B. L. (2004) 'Attachment security and parental sensitivity during infancy: Associations with friendship quality and false-belief understanding at age 4', *Journal of Social and Personal Relationships*, 21(5), pp. 639–667. doi: 10.1177/0265407504045892.

McElwain, N. L., Booth-LaForce, C., Lansford, J. E., Wu, X. & Justin Dyer, W. (2008) 'A process model of attachment–friend linkages: Hostile attribution biases, language ability, and mother–child affective mutuality as intervening mechanisms', *Child Development*, 79(6), pp. 1891–1906. doi: 10.1111/j.1467-8624.2008.01232.x.

McGaw, S. & Sturmey, P. (1993) 'Identifying the needs of parents with learning disabilities: A review', *Child Abuse Review*, 2(2), pp. 101–117. doi: 10.1002/car.2380020207.

McKeown, J., Clarke, A. & Repper, J. (2006) 'Life story work in health and social care: Systematic literature review', *Journal of Advanced Nursing*, 55(2), pp. 237–247. doi: 10.1111/j.1365-2648.2006.03897.x.

McLeod, A. (2010) '"A friend and an equal": Do young people in care seek the impossible from their social workers?', *British Journal of Social Work,* 40(3), pp. 772–788. doi: 10.1093/bjsw/bcn143.

McNicoll, A. (2014) *'Rise in mental health act detentions as NHS bed availability drops': Community care*. Available at: www.communitycare.co.uk/2014/10/31/rise-mental-health-act-detentions-nhs-bed-availability-drops/ (Accessed: 22 January 2018).

Maccoby, E. & Martin, J. (1983) Socialization in the context of the family: Parent-child interaction. In P. Mussen (ed.), *Handbook of Child Psychology* (4th edn). New York: Wiley.

Maddern, K. (2012) 'How the poorest school beat the odds'. *TES Magazine*. Available at: www.tes.co.uk/article.aspx?storycode=6297647 (Accessed: 22 January 2018).

Marcia, J. E. (1980) 'Identity in adolescence'. *Handbook of Adolescent Psychology*, 9(11), pp. 159–187. doi: 10.1177/0272431689091004.

Markiewicz, D., Doyle, A. B. & Brendgen, M. (2001) 'The quality of adolescents' friendships: Associations with mothers' interpersonal relationships, attachments to parents and friends, and prosocial behaviors', *Journal of Adolescence*, 24(4), pp. 429–445. doi: 10.1006/jado.2001.0374.

Marmot, M. (2010) *Strategic Review of Health Inequalities in England Post-2010. Marmot Review Final Report*. London: University College.

Marshall, C. (2013) *Current Issues in Developmental Disorders*. Hove: Psychology Press.

Maughan, B., Collishaw, S., Meltzer, H. & Goodman, R. (2008) 'Recent trends in UK child and adolescent mental health', *Social Psychiatry and Psychiatric Epidemiology*, 43(4), pp. 305–310. doi: 10.1007/s00127-008-0310-8.

Maughan, B. & Kim-Cohen, J. (2005) 'Continuities between childhood and adult life', *British Journal of Psychiatry*, 187(4), pp. 301–303. doi: 10.1192/bjp.187.4.301.

Mead, M. (1928) 'The role of the individual in samoan culture', *The Journal of the Royal Anthropological Institute of Great Britain and Ireland,* 58, pp. 481–495. doi: 10.2307/2843632.

Meltzer, H., Gatward, R., Corbin, T., Goodman, R. & Ford, T. (2003) *The mental health of young people looked after by local authorities in England*. National Statistics. London: Office for National Statistics. Available at: http://webarchive. nationalarchives.gov.uk/20121006174025/ www.dh.gov.uk/prod_consum_ dh/groups/dh_digitalassets/@dh/@en/documents/digitalasset/dh_4060689. pdf (Accessed: 22 January 2018).

Meltzer, H., Lader, D., Corbin, T., Goodman, R. & Ford, T. (2003) *The Mental Health of Young People Living in Scotland*. London: Office for National Statistics and Scottish Executive. Available at: http://reescentre.education. ox.ac.uk/wordpress/wp-content/uploads/2013/03/Mental-health-Scotland. pdf (Accessed: 18 January 2018).

Mental Health Taskforce (2016) *The five year forward view for mental health. A report from the independent Mental Health Taskforce to the NHS in England February 2016*. Available at: www.england.nhs.uk/wp-content/uploads/2016/02/ Mental-Health-Taskforce-FYFV-final.pdf (Accessed: 22 January 2018).

Merrell, K. W., Gueldner, B. A., Ross, S. W. & Isava, D. M. (2008) 'How effective are school bullying intervention programs? A meta-analysis of intervention research', *School Psychology Quarterly*, 23(1), pp. 26–42. doi: 10.1037/1045-3830.23.1.26.

Mickel, A. (2009) 'Bridgend suicides: The lessons learnt', *Community care*. Available at: www.communitycare.co.uk/2009/07/17/bridgend-suicides-the-lessons-learnt/ (Accessed: July 2017).

Miller, P. J. (1995) *Personal Storytelling in Everyday Life: Social and Cultural Perspectives. Knowledge and Memory: The Real Story, Advances in Social Cognition*. Hillsdale, NJ: Lawrence Erlbaum Associates, pp. 177–184.

Misca, G. (2009) 'Perspectives on the life course: Childhood and adolescence'. In R. Adams, L. Dominelli & M. Payne (eds.), *Social Work: Themes, Issues and Critical Debates* (3rd edn). Basingstoke: Palgrave, pp. 116–128.

Misca, G. (2014a) The 'Quiet Migration.' In A. Abela & J. Walker (eds.), *Contemporary Issues in Family Studies: Global Perspectives on Partnerships, Parenting and Support in a Changing World*. Oxford: John Wiley & Sons.

Misca, G. (2014b) 'The "Quiet Migration": Is intercountry adoption a successful intervention in the lives of vulnerable children?', *Family Court Review*, 52(1), pp. 60–68. doi: 10.1111/fcre.12070.

Misca, G., & Neamtu, N. (2016) Contemporary challenges in social work practice in multicultural societies. *Revista de Asistenta Sociala*, 1(14), pp. 7–9.

Misca, G. & Smith, J. (2014) 'Mothers, fathers, families and child development'. In Abela, A. & Walker, J. (eds.), *Contemporary Issues in Family Studies: Global Perspectives on Partnerships, Parenting and Support in a Changing World*. Chichester: Wiley-Blackwell, pp. 151–165.

Mooney, A., Oliver, C. & Smith, M. (2009) *Impact of Family Breakdown on Children's Well-being: Evidence Review (Research report DCSF-RR113)*. London: Department for Children, Schools and Families.

Mordoch E. & Hall, W. (2002) 'Children living with a parent who has a mental illness: A critical analysis of the literature and research implications', *Archives of Psychiatric Nursing*, 16(5), pp. 208–216. doi: 10.1053/apnu.2002.36231.

Morris, A., Criss, M., Silk, J. & Houltberg, B. (2017) 'The impact of parenting on emotion regulation during childhood and adolescence', *Child Development Perspectives*, 11(4), pp. 233–238. doi:10.1111/cdep.12238.

Moss, E., Cyr, C., Bureau, J. F., Tarabulsy, G. M. & Dubois-Comtois, K. (2005) 'Stability of attachment during the preschool period', *Developmental Psychology*, 41(5), pp. 773. doi: 10.1037/0012-1649.41.5.773.

Munro, E. (2011) *The Munro Review of Child Protection: Final Report, a Child-Centred System*. CM, 8062. London: The Stationery Office. https://assets.publishing.service.gov.uk/government/uploads/system/uploads/attachment_data/file/175391/Munro-Review.pdf

Murphy, M. & Fonagy, P. (2012) 'Mental health problems in children and young people'. In *Annual Report of the Chief Medical Officer* 2012. London: Department of Health.

NHS England (2015) *Future in mind promoting, protecting and improving our children and young people's mental health and well-being*. Available at: www.gov.uk/government/uploads/system/uploads/attachment_data/file/414024/Childrens_Mental_Health.pdf (Accessed: February 2017).

NICE (National Institute for Clinical Excellence). (2017a) *Eating disorders: Recognition and treatment*, [Clinical Guideline NG69]. Available at: www.nice.org.uk/nicemedia/pdf/CG9FullGuideline.pdf (Accessed: 22 January 2018).

NICE (National Institute for Health and Care Excellence). (2017b) *Antisocial behaviour and conduct disorders in children and young people: Recognition and management*. Clinical guideline [CG158] Available at: www.nice.org.uk/guidance/cg158/chapter/introduction (Accessed: 22 January 2018).

NICE (National Institute for Health and Care Excellence). (2017c) *Child abuse and neglect: Recognising, assessing and responding to abuse and neglect of children and young people Draft for consultation*. Available at: www.nice.org.uk/guidance/GID-SCWAVE0708/documents/draft-guideline (Accessed: December 2017).

NICHD Early Child Care Research Network (2002) 'Early child care and children's development prior to school entry: Results from the NICHD study of early child care', *American Educational Research Journal*, 39(1), pp. 133–164. doi: 10.1037/a0033709.

Nicolson, P. (2014) *A Critical Approach to Human Growth and Development: A Textbook for Social Work Students and Practitioners*. Basingstoke: Palgrave Macmillan.

NSPCC (2015). *Spotlight on preventing child neglect*. London: NSPCC

NSPCC (2018) *National case review repository*. Available at: https://learning.nspcc.org.uk/case-reviews/national-case-review-repository/ (Accessed: September 14 2018)

Nunes, T., Schliemann, A. D. & Carraher, D. W. (1993) *Street Mathematics and School Mathematics*. Cambridge: Cambridge University Press.

Oatley, K., Keltner, D. & Jenkins, J. M. (2013) *Understanding Emotions* (3rd edn). Hoboken, NJ: Wiley.

O'Connor, M. J., Shah, B., Whaley, S., Cronin, P., Gunderson, B. & Graham, J. (2002) 'Psychiatric illness in a clinical sample of children with prenatal alcohol exposure', *The American Journal of Drug and Alcohol Abuse*, 28(4), pp. 743–754. doi: 10.1081/ADA-120015880.

O'Connor, T. G., Rutter, M. & English and Romanian Adoptees Study Team (2000) 'Attachment disorder behavior following early severe deprivation: Extension and longitudinal follow-up', *Journal of the American Academy of Child & Adolescent Psychiatry*, 39(6), pp. 703–712. doi: 10.1097/00004583-200006000-00008.

Oda, A. Y. (2007) 'David Elkind and the crisis of adolescence: Review, critique, and applications', *Journal of Psychology & Christianity*, 26(3), pp. 251–256.

Office of the Children's Commissioner (2017) On measuring the number of vulnerable children. Available at: www.childrenscommissioner.gov.uk/wp-content/uploads/2017/07/CCO-On-vulnerability-Overveiw.pdf (Accessed: 22 January 2018).

O'Higgins, A., Sebba, J. & Luke, N. (2015) *What is the relationship between being in care and the educational outcomes of children? An international systematic review.* Available at: http://reescentre.education.ox.ac.uk/research/publications/what-is-the-relationship-between-being-in-care-and-the-educational-outcomes-of-children/ (Accessed: 22 January 2018).

Olweus, D. (1994) 'Bullying at school: Long-term outcomes for the victims and an effective school-based intervention program'. In L. R. Huesmann (ed.), *Plenum Series in Social/Clinical Psychology. Aggressive Behavior: Current Perspectives.* Kansas, KS: Plenum Press, pp. 97–130.

O'Toole, T., Meer, N., DeHanas, D., Jones, S. & Modood, T. (2016) 'Governing through prevent? Regulation and contested practice in State–Muslim engagement', *Sociology*, 50(1), pp. 160–177. doi: 10.1177%2F0038038514564437.

Pace (2018) Parents against Child Sexual Exploitation website [online]. http://paceuk.info/ (Accessed: 20 January 2018).

Paclawskyj, T. R. & Yoo, J. H. (2004) 'Mood, anxiety, and psychotic disorders in persons with developmental disabilities: Approaches to behavioral treatment'. In J. L. Matson, R. B. Laud, & M. L. Matson (eds.), *Behavior Modification for Persons with Developmental Disabilities: Volume 2.* New York: The NADD Press.

Padmore, J. (2016) *The Mental Health Needs of Children and Young People: Guiding you to Key Issues and Practices in CAMHS.* Milton Keynes: Open University Press.

Pasco- Fearon, R. M. & Belsky, J. (2011) 'Infant–mother attachment and the growth of externalizing problems across the primary-school years', *Journal of Child Psychology and Psychiatry*, 52(7), pp. 782–791. doi: 10.1111/j.1469-7610.2010.02350.x.

Pearce, J. (1995) 'Together we stand'. In NHS Health Advisory Service (ed.) *The Commissioning, Role and Management of CAMHS.* London: HMSO.

Perry, J., Williams, M., Sefton, T. & Haddad, M. (2014) *Emergency Use Only: Understanding and Reducing the Use of Food Banks in the UK.* London: Child Poverty Action Group, Church of England, Oxfam GB & The Trussell Trust.

Phinney, J. S. (1989) 'Stages of ethnic identity development in minority group adolescents', *The Journal of Early Adolescence*, 9(1–2), pp. 34–49. doi: 10.1177/0272431689091004.

Piaget, J. (1964) 'Part I: Cognitive development in children: Piaget development and learning', *Journal of Research in Science Teaching*, 2(3), pp. 176–186. doi: 10.1002/tea.3660020306.

Pritchard, C., Davey, J. & Williams, R. (2013) 'Who kills children? Re-examining the evidence', *British Journal of Social Work*, 43(7), pp. 1403–1438, doi: 10.1093/bjsw/bcs051.

Psychologists for Social Change (2018) *Psychologists against austerity.* Available at: www.psychchange.org/psychologists-against-austerity.html (Accessed: 29 July 2018).

Public Health England (2014) *Local action on health inequalities: Building children and young people's resilience in schools.* Available at: www.gov.uk/government/uploads/system/uploads/attachment_data/file/355770/Briefing2_Resilience_in_schools_health_inequalities.pdf (Accessed: 26 July 2017).

Raby, K. L., Steele, R. D., Carlson, E. A. & Sroufe, L. A. (2015) 'Continuities and changes in infant attachment patterns across two generations', *Attachment & Human Development*, 17(4), pp. 414–428. doi: 10.1080/14616734.2015.1067824.

Radford, J. (2010) *Serious Case Review Under Chapter VIII 'Working Together to Safeguard Children' In respect of the Death of a Child Case Number 14.* Birmingham: Safeguarding Children Board. Available at: www.nspcc.org.uk/preventing-abuse/child-protection-system/case-reviews/national-case-review-repository (Accessed: 27 March 2017).

Ramchandani, P. & Stein A. (2003) 'The impact of parental psychiatric disorder on children: Avoiding stigma, improving care', *British Medical Journal*, 327(7409), pp. 242–243. doi: 10.1136/bmj.327.7409.242.

Rasga, C., Quelhas, A. C. & Byrne, R. M. J. (2017) 'How children with autism reason about other's intentions: False-belief and counterfactual inferences', *Journal of Autism & Developmental Disorders*, 47, pp. 1806–1817. doi: 10.1007/s10803-017-3107-3.

Regan, P., Lakhanpal, S. & Anguiano, C. (2012) 'Relationship outcomes in Indian-American love-based and arranged marriages', *Psychological Reports,* 110(3), pp. 915–924. doi:10.2466/21.02.07.PR0.110.3.915-924.

Richards, M. A., Rothblum, E., Beauchaine, T. & Balsam, K. F. (2017) 'Adult children of same-sex and heterosexual couples: Demographic "Thriving"', *Journal of GLBT Family Studies*, 13(1), pp. 1–15. doi: 10.1080/1550428X.2016.1164648.

Ritchie, C. (2005) Critical commentary. Looked after children: Time for change?, *British Journal of Social Work*, 35(5), pp. 761–767. Available at: https://doi.org/10.1093/bjsw/bch284 (Accessed: 20 January 2018).

Roberts, T. A., Auinger, P. & Klein, J. D. (2005) 'Intimate partner abuse and the reproductive health of sexually active female adolescents', *Journal of Adolescent Health*, 36(5), pp. 380–385. doi: 10.1016/j.jadohealth.2004.06.005.

Robinson, L. (2007) *Cross-Cultural Child Development for Social Workers: An Introduction.* Basingstoke: Palgrave Macmillan.

Rogoff, B. (2003) *The Cultural Nature of Human Development.* New York: Oxford University Press.

Rosnay, M. & Hughes, C. (2006) 'Conversation and theory of mind: Do children talk their way to socio-cognitive understanding?' *British Journal of Developmental Psychology*, 24(1), pp. 7–37. doi: 10.1348/026151005X82901.

Rothbaum, F., Weisz, J., Pott, M., Miyake, K. & Morelli, G. (2000) 'Attachment and culture: Security in the United States and Japan', *American Psychologist*, 55(10), p. 1093. doi: 10.1037/0003-066X.55.10.1093.

Royal College of Nursing (2013) *Meeting the Health Needs of People with Learning Disabilities*. London: RCN.

Royal Commission into Institutional Responses to Child Sexual Abuse (2017) Available at: www.childabuseroyalcommission.gov.au/ (Accessed: 23 May 2017).

Ruch, G. (2010) The contemporary context of relationship-based practice. In G. Ruch, D. Turney & A. Ward (eds.), *Relationship-based Social Work: Getting to the Heart of Practice*. London: Jessica Kingsley Publishers, pp. 13–28.

Rutter, M. (2012) 'Resilience as a dynamic concept', *Development and Psychopathology*, 24(2), pp. 335–344. doi: 10.1017/S0954579412000028.

Rutter, M., Graham, P., Chadwick, O. F. & Yule, W. (1976) 'Adolescent turmoil: Fact or fiction?', Journal *of Child Psychology and Psychiatry*, 17(1), pp. 35–56. doi: 10.1111/j.1469-7610.1976.tb00372.x.

Sagi, A., IJzendoorn, M. H., Aviezer, O., Donnell, F., Koren-Karie, N., Joels, T. & Harl, Y. (1995) 'Attachments in a multiple-caregiver and multiple-infant environment: The case of the Israeli kibbutzim', *Monographs of the Society for Research, Child Development*, 60(2–3), pp. 71–91. doi: 10.1111/j.1540-5834.1995.tb00198.

Saleebey, D. (1996) 'The strengths perspective' in social work practice: Extensions and cautions', *Social Work*, 41(3), pp. 296–305. doi: 10.1093/sw/41.3.296.

Sanson, A., Hemphill, S. A., Yagmurlu, B. and McClowry, S. (2011) 'Temperament and social development'. In E. Speed, J. Moncrieff. & M. Rapley (eds.), *The Wiley-Blackwell Handbook of Childhood Social Development: Second Edition*. Oxford: Wiley-Blackwell, pp. 227–245. doi: 10.1002/9781444390933.ch12.

Sawer, P. (2017) 'Social workers should have spotted mother posed danger to murdered Ayeeshia-Jayne Smith, report finds', *The Telegraph*, 5 September. Available at: www.telegraph.co.uk/news/2017/09/05/social-workers-should-have-spotted-mother-posed-danger-murderedayeeshia/ (Accessed: 5 September 2017).

Schaffer, H. R. & Emerson, P. E. (1964) 'The development of social attachments in infancy', *Monographs of the Society for Research in Child Development*, 29(3), pp. 1–77. doi: 10.2307/1165727.

Schlegel, A. & Barry III, H. (1991) *Adolescence: An Anthropological Inquiry*. New York: Free Press.

Schneider, M., Bijam-Schulte, A., Janssen, C. & Stolk, J. (1996) 'The origins of self-injurious behavior of children with mental retardation', *The British Journal of Developmental Disabilities*, 42(2), pp. 136–148. doi: 10.1179/bjdd.1996.012.

Schwartz, P., Maynard, A. & Uzelac, S. (2008) 'Adolescent egocentrism: A contemporary view', *Adolescence*, 43(171), pp. 441–448.

Sears, H. A., Byers, E. S., Whelan, J. J. & Saint-Pierre, M. (2006) '"If it hurts you, then it is not a joke": Adolescents' ideas about girls' and boys' use and experience of abusive behavior in dating relationships', *Journal of Interpersonal Violence*, 21(9), pp. 1191–1207. doi: 10.1177/0886260506290423.

Shapiro, A. & Krysik, J. (2010) 'Finding fathers in social work research and practice', *Journal of Social Work Values and Ethics*, 7, pp. 1–8.

Shapiro, D. L. & Levendosky, A. A. (1999) 'Adolescent survivors of childhood sexual abuse: The mediating role of attachment style and coping in psychological and interpersonal functioning', *Child Abuse & Neglect*, 23(11), pp. 1175–1191. doi: doi.org/10.1016/S0145-2134(99)00085-X.

Sinclair, I., Baker, C., Wilson, K. & Gibbs, I. (2005) *Foster Children; Where They Go and How They Get on.* London: Jessica Kingsley Publishers.

Smyke, A. T., Zeanah, C. H., Fox, N. A., Nelson, C. A. & Guthrie, D. (2010) 'Placement in foster care enhances quality of attachment among young institutionalized children', *Child Development*, 81(1), pp. 212–223. doi: 10.1111/j.1467-8624.2009.01390.x.

Squeglia, L. M., Tapert, S. F., Sullivan, E. V., Jacobus, J., Meloy, M. J., Rohlfing, T. & Pfefferbaum, A. (2015) 'Brain development in heavy-drinking adolescents'. *American Journal of Psychiatry*, 172(6), pp. 531–542. https://dx.doi.org/10.1176%2Fappi.ajp.2015.14101249.

Sroufe, L. A., Egeland, B., Carlson, E. A. & Collins, W. A. (2005) *The Development of the Person: The Minnesota Study of Risk and Adaptation from Birth to Adulthood.* New York: Guilford Press.

Stanley, T. & Guru, S. (2015) 'Childhood radicalisation risk: An emerging practice issue', *Practice; Social Work in Action,* 27(5), pp. 353–366. doi: 10.1080/09503153.2015.1053858.

Stein, H. (2006) 'Commentary on "Seven institutionalized children and their adaptation in late adulthood: The children of Duplessis": Maltreatment, attachment, and resilience in the orphans of Duplessis', *Psychiatry*, 69(4), pp. 306–313. doi: 10.1521/psyc.2006.69.4.322.

Sterling, S. & Emery, H. (2016) *A whole school framework for emotional well being and mental health. A self-assessment and improvement tool for school leaders Partnership for Well-being and mental health in schools.* Available at: www.ncb.org.uk/sites/default/files/field/attachment/NCB%20School%20Well%20Being%20Framework%20Leaders%20Tool%20FINAL1_0.pdf (Accessed: 5 April 2017).

Steventon, J. (2016) *'Less than human': Does asylum system harm child refugees' mental health?* Available at: www.opendemocracy.net/child-refugee-mental-health-asylum-seeker-crisis (Accessed: 26 April 2017).

Sudbery, J. (2009) *Human Growth and Development: An Introduction for Social Workers.* London: Routledge.

Tait, P. (2014) *Bureaucracy creates a 'blanket of blandness' in education.* Available at: www.telegraph.co.uk/education/educationopinion/10546633/

Bureaucracy-creates-a-blanket-of-blandness-in-education.html (Accessed: 22 April 2017).

Takizawa, R., Maughan, B. & Arseneault, L. (2014) 'Adult health outcomes of childhood bullying victimization: Evidence from a 5-decade longitudinal British birth cohort', *American Journal of Psychiatry*, 171(7), pp. 777–784. doi: 10.1176/appi.ajp.2014.13101401.

Tarleton, B., Ward, L. & Howarth, J. (2006) *Finding the Right Support? A Review of Issues and Positive Practice to Support Parents with Learning Difficulties and Their Children*. London: Baring Foundation. Available at: https://baringfoundation. org.uk/wp-content/uploads/2014/10/Findingrightsupport.pdf (Accessed: 18 August 2018).

Thomas, A. & Chess, S. (1977) *Temperament and Development*. Oxford: Brunner/ Mazel.

Turnell, A. & Edwards, S. (1999) *Signs of Safety: A Solution and Safety Oriented Approach to Child Protection Casework*. New York: Norton.

UNICEF (2006) *Behind closed doors: The impact of domestic violence on children*. Available at: www.unicef.org/media/files/BehindClosedDoors.pdf (Accessed: 26 November 2017).

University of Manchester & Health Care Quality Improvement Partnership (2016) *Suicide by Children and Young People in England: National Confidential Inquiry into Suicide and Homicide by People with Mental Illness (NCISH)*. Manchester: University of Manchester. Available at: http://documents. manchester.ac.uk/display.aspx?DocID=37568 (Accessed: 20 August 2018).

Unwin, P. & Hogg, R. (2012) *Effective Social Work with Children and Families: A Skills Handbook*. London: Sage.

Unwin, P. & Misca, G. (2013) 'The changing face of adoption in England: Opportunities and dilemmas', *Social Work Review/Revista de Asistenta Sociala*, 12(2), pp. 1–9.

Unwin, P. & Stephens-Lewis, D. (2016) *Evaluating the health implications of child sexual exploitation on parents. Report for Parents against Child Sexual Exploitation (PACE)*. Available at: http://paceuk.info/wp-content/ uploads/Health-Implications-of-CSE-on-Parents-2016.pdf (Accessed: 4 December 2017).

The Valuing Children Initiative (2017) *Are you responsible for Australia's children? A synopsis of the valuing children initiative benchmark survey: 2016 Part C– April 2017*. Available at: http://valuingchildreninitiative.com.au/wp-content/ uploads/2017/03/Are-you-responsible-for-Australias-children-_A-Synopsis-of- the-Valuing-Children-Initiative-Benchmark-Survey-Part-C_-April-2017-1.pdf (Accessed: 26 November 2017).

Van Ijzendoorn, M. H. & Kroonenberg, P. M. (1988) 'Cross-cultural patterns of attachment: A meta-analysis of the strange situation', *Child Development*, 59, pp. 147–156. doi: 10.2307/1130396.

Vigil, J. & Long, J. (1990) 'Emic and etic perspectives on gang culture'. In C. R. Huff (ed.), *Gangs in America*. Newbury Park, CA: Sage Publications, pp. 55–70.

Vondra, J. I., Hommerding, K. D. & Shaw, D. S. (1999) 'Stability and change in infant attachment in a low-income sample', *Monographs of the Society for Research in Child Development,* 64(3), pp. 119–144. doi: 10.1111/1540-5834.00036.

Vygotsky, L. (1978) 'Interaction between learning and development' In M. Gouvain & M. Cole (eds.), *Readings on the Development of Children.* New York. Scientific American Books, 23(3), pp. 34–41.

Wang, Q. (2004)'The emergence of cultural self-constructs: Auto-biographical memory and self-description in European American and Chinese children', *Developmental Psychology,* 40(1), p. 3. doi: 10.1037/0012-1649.40.1.3.

Warner, J. (2015) *The Emotional Politics of Social Work and Child Protection.* Bristol: Policy Press.

Waters, E. & Cummings, E. M. (2000) 'A secure base from which to explore close relationships', *Child Development,* 71(1), pp. 164–172. doi: 10.1111/1467-8624.00130.

Weare, K. (2015) *What Works in Promoting Social and Emotional Well-being and Responding to Mental Health Problems in Schools.* London: National Children's Bureau.

Weinfield, N. S., Whaley, G. J. & Egeland, B. (2004) 'Continuity, discontinuity, and coherence in attachment from infancy to late adolescence: Sequelae of organization and disorganization', *Attachment & Human Development,* 6(1), pp. 73–97. doi: 10.1080/14616730310001659566.

Wharton, S., English, S. & Hames, A. (2005) 'Assessing parenting skills when working with parents with learning disabilities, *Learning Disability and Practice,* 8(4), pp. 12–15.

WHO (World Health Organization). (2018) *International Classifications of Diseases* [ICD-11]. Geneva: WHO. Available at: https://icd.who.int/browse11/l-m/en (Accessed: 20 August 2018).

Who Cares Scotland (2016) *Outcomes for care experienced children and young people.* Available at: www.parliament.scot/General20Documents/CEYP_outcomes_06.16.pdf (Accessed: 12 December 2017).

Williams, R. & Richardson, G. (1995) *Together We Stand: The Commissioning Role and Management of Child and Adolescent Mental Health Services, Health Advisory Service.* London: HMSO.

Wilson, K., Ruch, G., Lymbery, M., Cooper A., Becker, S., Brammer, A., Clawson, R., Littlechild, B., Paylor, I. & Smith R. (2011) *Social Work: An Introduction to Contemporary Practice.* Harlow: Pearson Education.

Wimmer, H. & Perner, J. (1983) 'Beliefs about beliefs: Representation and constraining function of wrong beliefs in young children's understanding of deception', *Cognition,* 13(1), pp. 103–128. doi: 10.1016/0010-0277(83)90004-5.

Wood, D. & Middleton, D. (1975) 'A study of assisted problem solving', *British Journal of Psychology,* 66, pp. 181–191. doi: 10.1111/j.2044-8295.1975.tb01454.x.

Wood, D., Wood, H. & Middleton, D. (1978) 'An experimental evaluation of four face-to face teaching strategies', *International Journal of Behavioural Development,* 1, pp. 131–147. doi: 10.1177/016502547800100203.

Wood, K. (2016) '"It's All a Bit Pantomime": An exploratory study of gay and lesbian adopters and foster carers in England and Wales', *British Journal of Social Work*, 46(6), pp. 1708–1723. doi: 10.1093/bjsw/bcv115.

YoungMinds (2016) *About self-esteem*. Available at: www.youngminds.org.uk/for_parents/whats_worrying_you_about_your_child/self-esteem/about_self-esteem (Accessed: 1 December 2018).

YoungMinds (2018) *Looking after yourself*. Available at: https://youngminds.org.uk/find-help/looking-after-yourself/ (Accessed: 1 December 2017).

Zubin, J. & Spring, B. (1977) 'Vulnerability: A new view of schizo-phrenia', *Journal of Abnormal Psychology*, 86, pp. 103–126. doi: 10.1037/0021-843X.86.2.103.

Index

CPI Antony Rowe
Eastbourne, UK
February 15, 2019